D1391240

THE ARCHAEOLOGY OF
MEDIEVAL BRITAIN

Series Editor: Dr Helen Clarke

Contemplation and Action

CONTEMPLATION AND ACTION
The Other Monasticism

—— ROBERTA GILCHRIST ——

LEICESTER UNIVERSITY PRESS
London and New York

LEICESTER UNIVERSITY PRESS
A Cassell imprint
Wellington House, 125 Strand, London WC2R 0BB, England

First published in 1995

© Roberta Gilchrist, 1995

Apart from any fair dealing for the purposes of research or private study, or criticism
or review, as permitted under the Copyright, Designs and Patents Act, 1988, this
publication may not be reproduced, stored or transmitted, in any form or by any
means or process without the prior permission in writing of the copyright holders or
their agents. Except for reproduction in accordance with the terms of licences issued
by the Copyright Licensing Agency, photocopying of whole or part of this publication
without the prior written permission of the copyright holders or their agents in single
or multiple copies whether for gain or not is illegal and expressly forbidden. Please
direct all enquiries concerning copyright to the Publishers at the address above.

Roberta Gilchrist is hereby identified as the author of this work as provided under
Section 77 of the Copyright, Designs and Patents Act 1988.

British Library Cataloguing in Publication Data

A CIP catalogue record for this book is available from the British Library

ISBN 0 7185 1730 X

Library of Congress Cataloging-in-Publication Data

Gilchrist, Roberta
    Contemplation and action : the other monasticism / Roberta Gilchrist.
        p.   cm.
    Includes bibliographical references and index.
    ISBN 0-7185-1730-X
    1. Monasteries—Great Britain—History.   2. Hospitalers—Great
Britain—History.   3. Military religious orders—Great Britain—History.
4. Monasticism and religious orders for women—Great Britain—History–
–Middle Ages, 600–1500.   5. Hermits—Great Britain—History.   6. Excavations
(Archaeology)—Great Britain.   7. Great Britain—Antiquities.   8. Christian
antiquities—Great Britain.   9. Great Britain—Church history.   I. Title.
BX2592.G55   1995
271'. 00941—dc20   95-8209
                                                            CIP

Set in Monotype Sabon by Ewan Smith
48 Shacklewell Lane, London E8 2EY

Printed and bound in Great Britain by
Redwood Books, Trowbridge, Wiltshire

UNIVERSITY
OF SHEFFIELD
LIBRARY

Contents

Foreword

This is the fifth publication in Leicester University Press's series *The Archaeology of Medieval Britain*, initiated in 1990. The aim of the books in the series is to present up-to-date surveys of the archaeological evidence for specific aspects of Britain in the Middle Ages. The core period to be covered in depth is from the Norman Conquest of 1066 to the Reformation, but there are no hard-and-fast chronological boundaries and examples of sites, artefacts and archaeological discoveries are drawn from before and after the period, where appropriate. The books are not not narrowly site- or object-orientated, emphasing rather the social and economic aspects of the subjects in question, and pursuing the the most recent thoughts and research in the field. Although primarily devoted to knowledge gained from archaeological excavation and research they also refer to written, cartographic and pictorial evidence and are of interest to archaeologists and historians alike. Their style of presentation and lavish illustrations also make them attractive to general readers interested in Britain's medieval heritage.

Each topic is covered by experts in that field, whose depth and breadth of knowledge throw new and exciting light on the Middle Ages. Archaeological excavations and surveys in recent decades are used as the basis for wide-ranging conclusions and synthesis, and also for discussions of the current state of the subject and pointers to future research.

The series began in 1990 with John R. Kenyon's work *Medieval Fortifications*, followed in 1992 by J. Patrick Greene's *Medieval Monasteries*, and in 1994 both *Medieval Ships and Shipping* by Gillian Hutchinson and *Medieval Towns* by John Schofield and Alan Vince were published. All have fulfilled the aims of a series designed to stimulate new thoughts and ideas, and the current publication, *Contemplation and Action: the other monasticism* by Roberta Gilchrist is no exception. This book tackles the hitherto little re-searched monastic houses outside the mainstream of conventual life: medieval hospitals, houses of the Military Orders, institutions for religious women, and hermitages. It is complementary to and does not impinge upon Greene's *Medieval Monasteries* which appeared earlier. These two books together cover the whole field of monasticism in Britain in the Middle Ages and are in-dispensable to readers wishing to grasp the complexities and implications of medieval religious life. In addition, the gazetteers of religious houses open to the public will enhance everyone's travels through Britain; how better to break a tedious journey than by visiting a secluded spot in the countryside or a quiet oasis in a town?

Roberta Gilchrist is uniquely qualified to write this book. Her doctoral thesis was devoted to a study of religious women and the remains which they left behind them, and she is co-author of a book on religious women in East Anglia. Her concentration on this much neglected aspect of monasticism led her to cast her net wider, hence the chapters on Military Orders and hermit-ages in this book. Her subtitle, *the other monasticism*, truly reflects what we may have not realized before; monasteries were not only great houses occupied by, generally, the sons of the gentry and aristocracy, they served their communities and are the previously unsung heroes of medieval life. I am delighted to include this work in the series *The Archaeology of Medieval Britain*.

Helen Clarke
April 1995

Preface

Monasteries are perhaps the most frequently studied and visited medieval monuments. Their ruined buildings and surviving earthworks are amongst the most tangible remains of the medieval landscape. It is not surprising, therefore, that the very origins of medieval archaeology may be traced to the antiquarian study of monastic sites during the 18th, 19th and early 20th centuries. In recent years, programmes of rural and urban development have resulted in the partial or complete excavation of hundreds of monastic sites. Such opportunities have led to a revival of interest in monasteries, and in common with other branches of medieval archaeology, this recent work has emphasised landscape contexts and economic functions as settlements. Despite advances in archaeological techniques and the amassment of comparative evidence, such an approach provides only a fragmentary picture of medieval monasticism. Only the most mainstream and orthodox forms of monastery have been explored; we are left unaware of 'the other monasticism', a range of religious vocations and associated monasteries that were integral to medieval life.

This book considers types of monastery previously neglected by historians and archaeologists: the medieval hospital, monasteries of the Military Orders, institutions for religious women and hermitages. Each of these categories of monastery are examined in relation to urban and rural landscapes and for the archaeological character of their buildings and precincts. In addition to considering monastic economies and landscapes, emphasis is placed on symbolism and the changing nature of religious belief. Rather than viewing the monastic movement as a series of deserted settlements, this book aims to reintroduce medieval people to our archaeological enquiry. The meaning of different monastic lifestyles will be explored in relation to religious men and women, their patrons and the laity at large.

Chapter 1 introduces the cast of 'the other monasticism', in relation to active and contemplative vocations, the origins of eremitic and cenobitic monasticism and its place within the later medieval social order. Current approaches to monastic archaeology are reviewed and the major themes of the book are outlined. Recurring issues include the developing nature of spiritual mentalities from the late 11th to the mid-16th centuries, and the extent to which monastic experience and relations with lay society changed. Monastic agency is explored by considering the way in which medieval religious people engaged with the material world around them in order to construct both identity and belief. The apparently marginal or alternative character of 'the other monasticism' is examined, revealing the extent to which it was defined intentionally by liminality, a situation beyond the boundaries of ordinary existence.

Chapters 2 to 5 present the archaeology of hospitals, the Military Orders, religious women and hermits, respectively. Chapter 2 surveys recent evidence for infirmary hospitals, leper hospitals, hospices and almshouses. Chapter 3 considers the archaeology of the Templars and Hospitallers. Chapter 4 is largely concerned with nunneries, and compares their incidence and archaeology with other vocations for religious women, including informal communities and vowesses; specific vocations for religious women are considered also in relation to hospitals (Chapter 2), the Military Orders (Chapter 3), hermits and anchoresses (Chapter 5). Chapter 5 reviews evidence for solitary hermits, communal hermitages, anchorholds, Grandmontine and Carthusian monasteries. In each chapter evidence is considered for patronage, patterns in social and economic functions, the siting and forms of the different types of monastery and evidence for standards of living, including diet, sanitation, disease and treatment of the sick. A summary is provided in Chapter 6, where comparisons are drawn between these monasteries and other categories of medieval settlement, both religious and secular. Patterns in the use of space are examined, in relation to issues such as privacy, social status and gender. The meanings of the various vocations of 'the other monasticism' are explored in terms of the siting of monasteries, the iconography of their architecture and symbols and imagery recurring in their material culture.

In writing this book I have benefited from the ideas of many people, drawn from both published sources and works in progress. I have especially valued collaborative work with the historians Marilyn Oliva (on religious women) and Carole Rawcliffe (on hospitals). While working on post-excavation projects with the Museum of London Archaeology Service (on St Mary Spital, St Mary Clerkenwell and St John Clerkenwell), I have gained a great deal from the collaboration of academic and field archaeology; in this, Barney Sloane and Chris Thomas are owed particular thanks. For many years now my research has been encouraged by others who share an interest in things monastic; foremost among them are Margaret Gray, Richard Morris, Philip Rahtz and Peter Ryder.

In researching and writing over the last three years, generous academic and practical assistance have been provided by my dear friends, Jane Grenville, Jez Reeve and Alex West; all have altered holidays, business trips and weekends to suit my monastic preoccupations. Most constant in this endeavour have been Leo and Tosca, who chewed draft manuscripts, sat on my keyboard and generally caused havoc during a semester of study leave, itself a kind of eremitic experience, reminiscent perhaps of St Antony in the desert with his two lions. This book is especially for Jane and Jez, in thanks for their support.

Acknowledgements

I would like to thank Helen Clarke as series editor for her constructive comments on the text of this book, and for adopting an open mind in the first instance to what constitutes the archaeology of monasticism. The text has also been read by Alex West and Carole Rawcliffe, who is always generous with both her time and her infectious enthusiasm for medieval medicine. This book was completed during a semester of study leave from the University of East Anglia. A grant from the Society for Medieval Archaeology in 1989 assisted with the costs of initial research and fieldwork on the subject of charterhouses.

I have been fortunate enough to receive information from a number of archaeological reports in advance of their publication. The following individuals have been particularly helpful in this respect: John Allan, Peter Cardwell, Philip Mayes, Michael Ponsford, Peter Ryder and Barney Sloane. The following institutions have allowed reproduction of illustrations: Canterbury Archaeological Trust, English Heritage, Exeter Museums Service Field Archaeology Unit, Harrogate Museum and Art Gallery Service, Her Majesty's Stationery Office, the Kent Archaeological Society, the Museum of London Archaeology Service, the Norfolk Museums Service Air Photographic Library, North Yorkshire County Council, the Royal Archaeological Institute, the Society of Antiquaries, the Society for Medieval Archaeology, the West Yorkshire Archive and the York Archaeological Trust.

Maps and ground-plans have been redrawn by Philip Judge. Figure 22 is by Robert Smith, and figures 17, 57, 58, 85 and 92 are by Ted West. Unless otherwise acknowledged, all photographs are by the author.

Figures

Abbreviations

Antiq J	*Antiquaries Journal*
Archaeol J	*The Archaeological Journal*
d	pence
HE	Bede's *Historia Ecclesiastica*
Medieval Archaeol	*Medieval Archaeology*
MoLAS	Museum of London Archaeology Service
NRO/DCN	Norfolk Record Office papers of the Dean and Chapter of Norwich Cathedral
pers com	personal communication
Proc Suffolk Inst Archaeol	*Proceedings of the Suffolk Institute of History and Archaeology*
RCHME	Royal Commission on the Historical Monuments of England
s	shillings
unpub	unpublished manuscript
VCH	Victoria County Histories of England

1 Introduction: contemplation and action

If asked to consider the monastic landscape of medieval Britain, the most vivid images drawn to one's mind might include the vast estates and workings of a rural Cistercian monastery, the luxurious lifestyle of urban Benedictines, or the more humble friars, dedicated to a life of poverty and preaching to the urban poor. These pictures have been shaped by the tone of historical and archaeological scholarship, traditionally directed at the monastic mainstream. Absent from our popular perceptions of monasticism are the sisters tending the sick poor in hospitals, the lepers dwelling on the outskirts of towns, the fighting monks devoted to the recapture of Jerusalem, and the hermit sequestered in his cave, to name but a few. Study of medieval monasticism has tended to concentrate on the major orders of the 11th to 13th centuries: the Benedictines, Cistercians, Augustinians, Dominicans and Franciscans. Yet outside this supposed mainstream there existed a variety of religious lifestyles which were central to everyday life and ordinary people in the middle ages. Study of these monastics has remained on the margins of modern historical and archaeological scholarship. This book is the first to examine the archaeology of a different kind of monasticism, one which was constant and integral to medieval life, and which consisted of a variety of vocations which together might be termed: 'the other monasticism'.

This book aims to redress the imbalance by considering the material culture associated with four broad categories of monastic experience: the medieval hospital, monasteries of the Military Orders, institutions for religious women and hermitages. In concentrating on these apparently more marginal monasteries it is my intention to step outside the prevailing models of monastic archaeology in order to explore the meaning of monasticism to medieval people. Why were religious men and women drawn to a particular vocation? What did the different types of monasticism mean to patrons, and why did they support them? How did attitudes towards monasticism change in the later middle ages? The social and economic roles of the monasteries will be considered, together with their relationships to lay society and the changing nature of religious mentalities. Each of the four categories of monastery will be reviewed according to its place within the medieval rural and urban landscape, the character of its buildings and precincts, its economic functions and symbolic meanings.

All of the categories of religious people to be considered in this study observed a monastic lifestyle. This generally included the taking of sacred vows, following a monastic rule, adopting a habit, or distinctive garb, and pledging to live in the service of God. According to one's calling this service could take different forms. Many were devoted to a life of contemplation, serving God and others through meditation and prayer. Such was the life of enclosed nuns, anchorites, Carthusian and Grandmontine monks (Chapters 4 and 5). Others fulfilled their calling through a life of action: men and women served in hospitals, knight-monks fought or raised revenues to regain Jerusalem, and hermits provided useful works in their maintenance of roads, bridges and lighthouses (Chapters 2, 3, and 5). Whether active or contemplative, these monastics played a central role in medieval society. Many of them interacted daily with secular people, providing practical assistance and spiritual succour, and their monasteries formed an essential part of the physical, economic and symbolic landscape of medieval Britain. Despite their apparent distance from the secular world, they brought hope to lay people through their prayers of intercession, and comfort through their dedication to charity and hospitality.

The monastic life was modelled on the early ascetic tradition which developed in the deserts of 3rd- and 4th-century Egypt, Syria and Palestine (see pp. 157–8). Two distinct forms of monastic life evolved: the eremitic (derived from *eremos*, the Greek for desert), and the cenobitic (from the Greek *koinobion*, meaning communal life). The eremitic calling dominated early monasticism; individuals withdrew from the world to live as solitary religious. Within western monasticism, the cenobitic vocation was more prevalent, in which religious lived as part of an organised monastic community. Most later medieval monastic practices were based on the Benedictine Rule, initiated at Monte Cassino by Benedict of Nursia (*c*480–543); this tempered the ascetic practices of desert monasticism with the communal lifestyle of the monastery. The cenobitic vocation was followed by members of monastic hospitals, nunneries and preceptories (monasteries of the Military Orders), while hermits pursued an eremitic life in emulation of the desert fathers. Certain monastic orders, in particular the Carthusian and Grandmontine, aimed to preserve the integrity of the hermit's solitude while dwelling with others in communal monasteries.

Despite its ancient roots, the contemporary social order was integral to the structure of later medieval monasticism. Monks and nuns were drawn from the aristocracy and gentry, while lay-monastics serving in hospitals, nunneries, Grandmontine and Carthusian monasteries were from the lower social orders. Most hierarchical were the Military Orders, such as the Templars, who were structured according to medieval codes of honour and warfare. Attitudes toward gender influenced the participation of women in the monastic movement. For instance, while their affiliation with the Military Orders and the more eremitic communities was constrained, religious women developed their own more fluid, alternative monasticisms as part of a wider international movement. Patterns of patronage can be discerned which comment on the meaning of monasticism to different social groups. In some cases ethnicity may be linked with interest in a particular form of religiosity: for example, the initial connection between Anglo-Saxons and the vocation of the anchoress (Chapter 5). At times endowment of monasteries took on a more political function; in Wales and Ireland in particular the benefaction of certain monastic groups was associated with the process of Anglo-Norman domination.

The nature of monastic continuity and change forms one theme of this study. The relative popularity of the two forms of monastic life, the eremitic and the cenobitic, fluctuated according to patterns in popular religious belief.

Eremitic monasticism seems to have been valued particularly during times of crisis, such as the period of unrest following in the wake of the Norman Conquest of Britain, and in the years of spiritual reflection and mysticism following the plagues and famines of the second half of the 14th century (Chapter 5). The communal monasticism of the 12th century took on the penitential tone of earlier ascetics. Such withdrawal and austerity can be recognised in the material culture of religious women (Chapter 4), lepers (Chapter 2) and eremitic monasteries (Chapter 5). In western Britain, eremitic monasticism demonstrated a continuity with the Early Christian heritage; hermitages were sited at shrines linked with early British saints. Hospitals, hospices and hermitages were frequently located at shrines, wells and bridges, all foci for popular devotion, and closely linked with medieval pilgrimage.

During the chronological period covered in this book, roughly from the late 11th century to the Dissolution of the Monasteries, the monastic experience underwent profound changes. Shifts in belief and lifestyle tended to occur in relation to wider transformations within society. So, for example, even within communal monasteries a growing emphasis on privacy and personal devotion can be detected. Popular support for the Military Orders came and went with the impetus to regain Jerusalem for Christendom, leaving the survivors of the movement, in particular the Hospitallers, to forge a monastic role more closely linked with charity. The character of charitable relief itself changed in the later middle ages. Those considered to be the worthy poor were targeted at the local level: increasing numbers of hospitals were established in parish churchyards as part of increased guild activity and civic interest in charitable relief.

The importance of charity as a religious expression grew in tandem with the pivotal concept of Purgatory. Increasingly, medieval people were concerned with the period in which the soul passed from death to salvation, when sins committed in life were purged by trials and torments of the soul (see pp. 8–9). This tortuous period could be reduced by the carrying out of charitable acts, such as giving alms to the honest sick, poor or aged, or extending hospitality to the traveller. Time spent in Purgatory was thought to have been reduced also by the prayers of others, who might intercede on behalf of one's soul. Naturally, the intercessory prayers of religious men and women were assumed to have possessed a high value. From as early as the 12th century, founders of religious houses expected to be repaid by the prayers of monastic inmates for their souls and those of their family living before and after them. In the later middle ages additional prayers of intercession were provided by the foundation of chantries: the sponsorship of priests who prayed continuously for the benefit of the founder's soul. The growing chantry movement reflected the significance of intercessory prayers to medieval belief, as shown, for example, by the addition of chantry chapels to parish and monastic churches. The place of monastics in lay sympathies varied according to the perceived potency of their intercessory prayers. In other words, the benefaction shown to the different types of monastery changed according to the respect with which lay people viewed their vocations. Throughout the period, there were fluctuations in the support of the different monastic orders and vocations, whether cenobitic or eremitic, active or contemplative, male or female.

Monastic archaeology

Until the 1970s monastic archaeology concentrated on the study of the development of the church and cloisters, and aimed at recognising a series of plan 'types' typical of the specific orders of monasteries, such as Benedictine, Cistercian, Franciscan, and so on. Following the more widespread emphasis on landscape and environment which developed in the study of medieval rural settlement at this time (see, for example, Taylor 1992), there was a very visible shift towards the study of the inner and outer courts, the service areas contained within the monastic precinct but quite separate from the religious church and cloisters. Research strategies for monastic archaeology have prioritised the following themes: the study of timber phases, whether as precursors to masonry buildings or as outbuildings; the examination of outer court development; and approaches to rural estates, water management, and fishponds in the monastic economy (for example, Baker and Baker 1989; Coppack 1989; Moorhouse 1989; Bond 1989 and 1993). Archaeologists have concentrated on the economic roles of monasteries, together with their landscape contexts. These approaches are highlighted in the recent works of synthesis on monastic archaeology. Mick Aston adopted W. G. Hoskins's landscape archaeology approach, situating his work as 'an attempt to show monasteries as economic institutions coping with the difficulties and op-portunities presented by the landscapes in which they were built' (Aston 1993: 16). Patrick Greene, in his book *Medieval Monasteries*, cited the major topic studied today as 'the operation of the monastic house as an economic unit' (Greene 1992: 41). Similarly, Glyn Coppack outlined within monastic archaeology 'a growing emphasis on the economic aspects of religious life' (Coppack 1990: 30).

Discussion has centered on rural monasteries and their role in economic production; the archetypal monastery is envisaged as having had a large outer court for industry and storage, and agricultural estates for achieving self-sufficiency. Little consideration has been given to the economic role of monasteries as consumers, as catalysts for trade and urban development or their role in shaping urban landscapes. On the whole, prevailing research designs for monastic archaeology have neglected to consider the social and religious roles of monasteries, especially those which fall outside the primary model of the rural monastery. Despite representing literally thousands of medieval monastic sites, the categories of monastery considered in this study seldom find a place in current discussions of monastic archaeology. Hospitals have been considered difficult to classify, preceptories judged closer in character to manorial settlement, and nunneries dismissed as examples of poor, or failed, monasteries. Issues such as charity, belief, and the changing meanings of monasticism have been considered the exclusive preserve of the medieval historian. As increasing numbers of hospitals and urban monasteries become subject to developer-funded archaeology, it will become necessary to re-examine the varied experience of monasticism with reference to material culture.

Approaches to medieval archaeology have tended to compartmentalise our thinking and our classifications of material culture. Despite a more recent emphasis on examining broader landscape contexts, we specialise in categories of medieval settlement such as churches, monasteries, villages, castles, towns, and so on. We still think in terms of a settlement hierarchy, with upper-status sites represented by castles and monasteries and lower-status ones consisting of peasant houses and urban tenements. It seems unlikely that the landscape would have been perceived by medieval people in such a neatly divided fashion. Our current approaches neglect comparison between settlement types and the identification of patterns of similarity and difference, for example in the use of particular forms of building in secular and monastic settings or in categories of settlement considered to be upper or lower status. This special-isation sometimes inhibits more general contributions to our understanding of medieval life. Recently, monastic archaeology has increased our knowledge of medieval industries, such as milling, fisheries and tile production. Modern archaeological excavation at monasteries has much to contribute to our knowledge of medieval standards of living. Studies of human remains, animal bones and plant fossils will be of tremendous importance in responding to documentary studies of demography, diet and health in monasteries, for example, Barbara Harvey's study of living and dying in medieval Westminster (Harvey 1993). Harvey gave a graphic account of the wealthy Benedictine diet, health and treatment of the infirm. But it is only when archaeological and documentary sources are used together that we can appreciate the inbuilt biases of each source. From documents, Harvey proposed that monasteries were rather insanitary places, with filthy drains prone to blocking up – 'wherever one was, it must have been difficult to forget the plumbing' (Harvey 1993: 90). Archaeology often paints a rather different picture. The emphasis on sanitation at hospitals seems to have been particularly marked, while at some nunneries and hermitages the absence of such facilities may have been a deliberate part of penitential living. Archaeological consideration of diet at hospitals and nunneries may amplify our existing knowledge, so often based on documentary or archaeological sources associated with sites of a higher status.

Monastic agency and material culture

Traditionally, archaeologists and art historians have considered the architecture of the monastic church and cloister as it was determined by filiation, the monastic order to which a monastery belonged. All of the orders arranged their church and main domestic buildings around a cloister. Generally, the church formed the north range and the cloister was attached to the south; around it were ordered the essential components of the monastic plan. The chapter-house, where the daily meetings of the community took place, was situated in the east range, over which was the communal dormitory. The refectory was placed in the south range, with the *lavatorium*, a ritual washing place used before meals, set, most often, in the south cloister walk. The west range was used for a variety of functions, such as the guest hall, cellarage (storage) or offices of the monastic officials.

Variations in the monastic plan were sometimes brought about by the structure of the order. For example, the lay-brothers of the Cistercians were accommodated in an extensive west range of the cloister. More subtle differences of plan were characteristic of particular orders. For instance, early Cistercian churches had a distinctive east end: the 'Bernardine' plan consisted of a short, aisleless and square-ended presbytery. This plan is diagnostic when compared with that of the Norman Benedictines, whose chancels terminated either in an apsed east end, with the aisles carried around the apse as an ambulatory, or in three separate apses. Friars' churches of the 13th century developed a characteristically wide nave used for preaching; this was separated from the friars' choir by partitions, with the space between known as the 'walking place'. The Cistercian refectory of *c*1156–80 was also a distinguishing feature: in contrast to those of other orders it was orientated north–south in order to project from the southern arm of the cloister. The orders differed also in the degree of ornamentation and embellishment which they applied to their buildings. The 12th-century Cistercians were character-ised by an initial austerity in the planning and decoration of their buildings; colour was used sparingly and church interiors were whitewashed. In contrast, Anglo-Norman foundations of the Cluniac order (allied to the French mother house at Cluny) chose highly decorated and elaborate structures, often using complex and innovative iconography in their churches, chapter-houses and *lavatoria*.

Other factors commonly examined in relation to the material culture of monasticism include the influence of a particular patron, or the specific iconographic message signalled in a building's form. Absent from such analyses are considerations of the motivations behind material culture: the way in which medieval people engaged with the material world. Patrons used material culture to display their aspirations, and monastic men and women adopted certain characteristic buildings or landscapes in order to demonstrate their religious identities. Members of monastic orders or groups acted accord-ing to their knowledge of the world around them and, through their own agency, created a place within the social order. Beyond the iconographic content of religious architecture there was a vocabulary of buildings and landscapes from which they might signal a monastic identity. The forms chosen for nunneries or preceptories, for example, may have been drawn from contexts particularly appropriate to feminine or masculine institutions. Here the archaeology of hospitals, nunneries, preceptories and hermitages will consider issues broader than patronage and filiation, examining the extent to which the meanings behind monastic lifestyles can be reconstructed.

Material culture was central in defining monastic vocations. Otherness was signalled through the choice of landscapes and the topographic siting of certain monasteries. Many of the categories of religious described here shared a sense of liminality: a situation beyond the boundaries of ordinary existence. Their vocations and religious identities were assisted by maintaining a distance from mainstream life. Anthropologists have proposed that liminality accompanies rites of passage, such as rituals of initiation, during which social conventions are breached and the normal rules are suspended. Within monasticism the rite of passage is a formal profession of the religious life: the adoption of a new identity and a renunciation of the former sense of self. In relation to the wider society, therefore, all monastics may be considered to take on a kind of 'institutionalised liminality' (Turner 1969: 107). Yet, particular groups within monasticism used this sense of otherness to assist in the definition of their roles. The topographical placement of hospitals symbolised the boundaries between the town and countryside, the healthy and the sick, the known and the other. The marginal landscapes of female religious contributed to their austere vocations and assisted in maintaining the strict sexual segregation and enclosure of women that their society expected, a liminality which, like other aspects of their spiritual life, 'was imaged as continuity with, not as reversal of, the women's ordinary experience' (Bynum 1984: 117). This crossing of boundaries was integral especially to hermits, who exemplified a withdrawal to the wilderness. The lives of hermits, anchorites and lepers transcended the usual conventions; they were placed between the living and the dead, this life and the next. Drawing on recent archaeological and historical studies, this book attempts to capture the meanings behind such monastic vocations through a close examination of the material culture of 'the other monasticism'.

2 Houses of mercy: the archaeology of medieval hospitals

Introduction

The medieval hospital was an institution devoted to the care of needy groups within society: the sick, aged, poor and destitute. It did not function as a modern hospital, treating the seriously ill and urgent medical cases, but represented a form of more general charitable relief. Many hospitals were organised according to monastic principles and some were fully monastic hospital-priories, accommodating both a group of professed religious men or women and a population of resident patient-inmates. Frequently, hospitals were ordered around a monastic cloister and their staff and inmates observed at least a semi-monastic lifestyle, following a rule and wearing a common habit. Such similarities place hospitals within the wider corpus of medieval monasteries. Hospitals had their own particular character, however, outside more mainstream monasticism.

This chapter introduces the distinctive social, religious and economic functions of hospitals, and explores the nature of their form according to their buildings, the spatial arrangement of precincts and their topographic relationships to other settlements and the landscape. The social function of hospitals is discussed according to charity given and received; staffing of hospitals is considered with particular reference to the opportunities which they provided religious women; and treatment of the sick, especially lepers, is assessed within the medieval ideological framework which viewed disease as a punishment for sin.

The foundation and support of hospitals by patrons can be considered according to motives of religious piety, demonstration of power, and the carrying out of genuine welfare concerns. Alms-giving was directly linked to the donor's salvation, since at the Day of Doom it was believed that Christ would judge men and women not by their own piety, but by their actions towards the poor and weak (Duffy 1992: 357). Within this system of charitable provision, however, it is necessary to consider the meaning of the poor and other stigmatised groups to their patrons and the wider society. In dispensing charity the rich not only absolved their own consciences, but were relieved of the burden of their own sins. The notion of charity possessed spiritual qualities in that its practice could cleanse the sins of a pious donor, thus reducing the period spent in Purgatory.

Medieval people were taught that Purgatory was a period in which the soul passed from death to salvation: a place where sins were purged by every kind of physical torment, before final redemption (Duffy 1992: 345).

Charitable giving was a kind of intercession which was thought to hasten the soul's passage through the torments of Purgatory. Charitable relief was a form of social welfare, but according to medieval belief the destitute, towards whom charity was directed, were necessary in order to grant spiritual salvation to others. Thus the problems of poverty and illness were addressed by medieval society but never resolved. Their continued existence was crucial to the medieval social order. In the later middle ages the nature of this provision changed, with groups targeted for charity shifting from the general poor to those considered the more 'honest' poor, and with ecclesiastical benefaction giving way to more secular institutions which reflected a growing public concern and civic responsibility for welfare. Charitable works were carried out by the pious in emulation of the Seven Comfortable Acts (or Works of Mercy) enjoined by Christ upon his disciples: feeding the poor, clothing the poor, bringing them drink, housing the wayfarer, visiting prisoners, nursing the sick (Matthew 25: 35–6) and burying the dead (Tobit 1: 16–17).

Within the term 'hospital' a number of charitable institutions of different function and settlement form can be recognised. These can be defined and enumerated with reference to medieval documents (figure 1). We can estimate that a minimum of 800 hospitals was in existence in England and Wales at the time of the Dissolution, and that perhaps a further 300 had previously fallen out of use (Knowles and Hadcock 1971). A further 202 hospitals have been tentatively identified for medieval Ireland (Gwynn and Hadcock 1970); and 149 for medieval Scotland, of which at least 67 survived up to, or beyond, the Reformation (Cowan and Easson 1976).

In contrast to the monasteries to which they are akin, hospitals have been the subject of little archaeological scholarship. Their more modest architecture, and less imposing landscape settings, attracted antiquarian attention only in passing. Many have disappeared without note, or, as one antiquary commented on the destruction of St Peter's Hospital, Bury St Edmunds 'The passing of the little chapel ... appears to have been unwept and unrecorded' (Harris 1919). A similar paucity of architectural study is apparent, with only two volumes on English hospitals having been written (Godfrey 1955; Prescott 1992). These survey works concentrate on describing the nucleus of the hospital, its chapel and infirmary, and the final phases of the house, which are most likely to survive as standing buildings. In recent years several hospitals have been subject to modern excavation in advance of urban development and renewal. Those studied most substantially include St Mary Spital, London (Thomas *et al* 1989; and forthcoming), St Mary, Ospringe (Kent) (Smith 1980) and St Bartholomew, Bristol (Ponsford and Price forthcoming). When the results of these excavations are combined with historical and architectural research, it is possible to define the range of hospital types and forms, and their development over time.

Hospitals can be categorised according to their specialised functions: infirmaries for the sick poor; leper hospitals, or *leprosaria*; hospices for pilgrims and wayfarers; and almshouses, which were religious institutions for the general poor, or targeted groups such as poor priests or mariners. The concept of a specialised hospital, however, is a modern idea. In reality most hospitals performed several functions, including out-door poor relief as a top priority. St Paul's, Norwich, for example, was a monastic hospital which in

Figure 1 Distribution of the major Hospitals in medieval Britain. Based on Knowles and Hadcock (1971), Gwynn and Hadcock (1970) and Cowan and Easson (1976). Additional information on numbers of hospitals in medieval towns from Palliser (1993) and Cullum (1993).

addition had a school, facilities for poor almswomen, beds for the acutely ill, special care for pregnant women, and gave out daily meals and bread to the local poor.

Distinctions between hospitals can be made according to whether they were monastic or non-monastic, or large or small. Other categories of difference must be considered to be more tentative. In their list of religious houses, Knowles and Hadcock classified hospitals in England and Wales according to types: those specifically devoted to the care of the sick made up only 8.4 per cent (112); leper hospitals represented 25.8 per cent (345); hospices accounted for 10.2 per cent (136); and almshouses made up the majority at 55.6 per cent (742). Most examples are assumed to have been mixed communities of male and female inmates; a minimum of 119 are reported as having been for men only and 37 for women (Knowles and Hadcock 1971). In Scotland, only 101 of 149 hospitals can be considered to have served a particular function, of which 8 (7.9 per cent) were for the sick poor, 21 (20.8 per cent) were leper hospitals, 8 (7.9 per cent) were hospices, and 64 (63.4 per cent) almshouses (Cowan and Easson 1976). Functions can be assigned for 78 of 202 possible hospitals in Ireland: 7 (8.9 per cent) for sick poor, 47 (60.3 per cent) leper hospitals, 16 (20.5 per cent) hospices, and 8 (10.3 per cent) almshouses (Gwynn and Hadcock 1970). While the proportions of types are roughly similar for medieval England, Wales and Scotland, the predominance of leper hospitals in Ireland is striking. This disparity may be due in part to the uncertainties of total numbers and functions for Irish hospitals, but also to actual differences in charitable provision. In Ireland the depressed economy seems to have resulted in less attention to charitable relief by lay-patrons. The monastic orders were largely responsible for founding and maintaining hospitals, and, in addition, many founded lay-infirmaries at their own gates. Whereas some hospices and the majority of *leprosaria* were independent of monasteries, almshouses and general infirmaries may have been an integral part of many Irish monastic precincts.

Many more hospitals existed but were not documented as independent institutions, or few references to their existence are extant. Some hospices, for instance, may have been recorded as satellite possessions of religious houses. Additional hospitals are echoed in field or place-names which incorporate *spit*, or *spittal*, and *Maudlin*, derived from Mary Magdalene, who was a favoured patron saint of leper hospitals. Similar undocumented leper houses are suggested in Welsh *ysbyty*, French *laderie* and German *Gutleuthäuser*. The list of medieval hospitals is continuously supplemented through modern historical research on medieval wills, which sometimes contain references to testators who bequeathed sums to hospital communities which are otherwise unknown. Care must be taken, however, to determine whether their proposed hospitals were ever actually instituted.

Certain monastic orders were active in founding hospitals in England, including: St Antoine de Viennoise, St Mary of Bethlehem, St Thomas the Martyr of Acon and St Lazarus of Jerusalem. The last two of these were Military Orders specifically established in order to found and protect hospitals (see pp. 63–9). The order of St Antoine de Viennoise originated in a monastery in the Rhône, where the relics of St Antony attracted pilgrims seeking relief from 'St Antony's Fire': an ergotism caused by rye poisoned by the parasite *Claviceps purpurea*. The disease was rare in Britain but more common in continental Europe. Those who consumed the infected grain suffered from hallucinations and inflammation of the limbs, which would eventually blacken and drop off. A preceptory and hospital of the order was founded in 1243 by Henry III at Threadneedle Street, London, on the site of a former synagogue (Graham 1927: 343, 349). Other hospitaller orders included the Trinitarians (the Order of the Most Holy Trinity for the Redemption of Captives), founded in 1198 for the ransoming of Christian captives taken in the Third Crusade (Gray 1993: 10). Hospital-priories in Britain often included sisters who served in the infirmary. There were ten Trinitarian houses in

England (Knowles and Hadcock 1971: 205), one in Ireland, at Adare (Limerick), and eight in Scotland (Cowan and Easson 1976: 107), these were sometimes known as the Red Friars, although the Trinitarians were never a mendicant order. In Ireland there were 18 houses of the Fratres Cruciferi, hospitallers whose houses included hospitals served by sisters (Gwynn and Hadcock 1970: 209).

Benedictine monasteries normally maintained infirmaries exclusively for their own inmates, but some, such as Reading (Berks), Westminster and Norwich Cathedral Priory, admitted a small number of poor to a hospital or almonry at the gates of the precinct (Harvey 1993: 17; Carole Rawcliffe pers com). The Knights Hospitaller founded a considerable number of hospices and special hospitals for the knights of their order. These will be discussed in the following chapter.

Larger hospitals were autonomous institutions which were ordered along the lines of monasteries (see pp. 14–32). They often followed the rule of St Augustine, the most flexible of the monastic rules and the one most strongly devoted to service towards others, and were staffed by permanent communities of professed brethren and sisters who cared for the inmates. These hospitals provided a religious lifestyle through the observation of monastic routines and the provision of the mass, confession and facilities for burial. Smaller hospitals were not always provided with a chapel and cemetery; for instance, when first established, the *leprosarium* of St James, Dunwich (Suffolk), buried its dead in the mother church at Brandeston (VCH Suffolk II 1907: 137). When first founded, the Domus Dei, at the south gate of Bury St Edmunds, was prohibited from setting up an altar; although private prayer was encouraged, a chapel and cemetery were not provided until the house moved to a larger site (Rowe 1958: 257). In practice, all hospitals were religious institutions, due to the perceived connection between spiritual and physical disease. The monastic hospitals were founded largely between 1100 and 1250. These fulfilled the functions of almshouses, possibly combined with care of the sick poor. At least 220 were founded in 12th-century England, with a further 310 in the 13th century (Rubin 1987: 1).

From the 14th century, smaller hospitals were founded by rich merchants, lay fraternities and guilds. Medieval guilds were often linked to occupations and crafts, and organised work for their members. Guilds sometimes overlapped in both membership and concerns with religious fraternities. Members of fraternities dedicated themselves to the cult of a particular saint or feast, such as the *Corpus Christi*. Among their services were included the performance of plays and the organisation of processions for their special feast day, arrangements for the burial of their members upon death, and charitable works such as the maintenance of bridges and highways and the relief of the poor encompassed in the Seven Comfortable Acts. Thus fraternities and guilds were active in the support of almshouses and *maisons dieu*, sponsoring their foundation in parish churchyards. For example, at the church of All Saints North Street, York, an almshouse was established in the churchyard and a stained glass window depicted a prominent member of the parish, Nicholas Blackburn, carrying out the Seven Comfortable Acts. Hospitals were occasionally superimposed on the guildhall itself, either attached to one end of the hall, such as St Saviour, Wells, or placed in an undercroft, as at the Merchant Adventurers' Hall, York.

A hospital's main income came from grants of property or rents made at the time of foundation, and from subsequent bequests of land or alms. Incomes were subsidised through licences to beg for alms and offerings made towards sacred relics that were sometimes held by hospitals. Hospital-priories such as St Mary Spital, London (and hospitals with parish churches or chapels, such as St Giles, Norwich), attracted additional funds from lay-benefactors through the establishment of chantries and private chapels within the hospital from the 14th century (Thomas *et al* forthcoming). Hospitals which were endowed with rural estates collected revenues from rents, such as St Bartholomew, London, which held lands in Essex (Rawcliffe 1984: 13). From the late 13th to 14th centuries these tenants paid rent in food renders, particularly in grain or stock.

Like monasteries, hospitals were founded in response to a variety of motives. The act of founding such an institution brought benefactors a degree of public recognition, while the prayers of the inmates were viewed as a form of religious intercession on behalf of the founders' souls. Where foundation cartularies survive, it seems that hospitals were linked to the wider chantry movement from an early date. Like chantries, hospitals sometimes functioned, in effect, as prayer factories, with masses and prayers said in the honour of a founder and family in perpetuity. For example, the hospital of Boycodeswade (Norfolk) was founded by Harvey Beleth *c*1181 to support 12 poor persons, with a secular canon or chaplain as warden, 'to serve therein for his own soul and those of his ancestors' (VCH Norfolk II 1906: 439); likewise the leper house at Ickburgh in the same county was granted by William Barentum to Henry Scharping 'for the health of his soul and the souls of his parents' (ibid.). As altruistic gestures, hospitals for the poor, sick and aged met a real urban need: they represented welfare as well as religious provision.

Some hospitals evolved from, or into, other types of religious institution. Particularly close links can be observed between Augustinian priories and hospitals, with several hospitals having developed into fully fledged monasteries: witness the excavated example of St Gregory, Canterbury, where the original 11th-century cruciform church of the hospital was replaced by a 12th-century aisled nave and cloisters for the Augustinian canons (*Canterbury's Archaeology* 1991: 1). Occasionally, the original hospital buildings were retained by newly founded institutions. At Kersey (Suffolk) excavations showed that the original wooden infirmary hall of the 13th century was adapted for the west range of the subsequent priory, which served as the prior's house (*Medieval Archaeol* 3 1959: 306). Others were adapted into hospitals from existing complexes, such as St Mary, York, founded on the site of a Carmelite friary (Richards *et al* 1989), St Anthony, London, established within a confiscated synagogue, and Lewes (Sussex) which grew from a monastic infirmary sited at the gate of the priory. The excavated hospital of St Bartholomew, Bristol, was founded *c*1230 in an existing mercantile house or riverside warehouse belonging to the de la Warre family. The unusual building began as a first-floor hall over an aisled undercroft, some 17m square internally. Conversion to the hospital included strengthening the building by inserting bracing walls, plastering the central area of the undercroft and adding a porch (Ponsford and Price forthcoming).

An additional, less-institutionalised, form of charity was sponsored in houses of pity and *maisons dieu*: small, short-lived foundations established by lay-people. These communities were set up in the founder's house, or in small houses within churchyards, and consequently do not survive, or are difficult to recognise today. However, where excavations have taken place within churchyards, numerous structures have been revealed, for example at Barton-on-Humber and St Helen-on-the-Walls, York (Rodwell and Rodwell 1982; Magilton 1980). *Maisons dieu* are one of several possible functions which such structures may have served, in addition to porters' lodges, mortuary structures and bell-houses.

It is easier to locate the precise situation of the better-documented types of hospital, which may survive as standing buildings and buried archaeological deposits. Some have been subject to antiquarian investigation and more recent archaeological excavation. Through a combination of historical classification, architectural and archaeological evidence, it is possible to consider hospitals according to categories defined by function, date and physical forms.

Infirmaries: 'for sick and impotent persons'

Hospitals which were based around an infirmary embrace two types: those specifically founded to care for the sick poor, and the early almshouses which succoured the needy, poor, aged and homeless. Because these disadvantaged groups were particularly drawn to, or created by, the expanding urban centres of medieval Britain, the distribution of infirmaries was concentrated in towns. For example, of the total minimum number of 90 hospitals in medieval Yorkshire, 72 were in urban, or suburban, situations; likewise of the minimum of 90 hospitals in East Anglia (Norfolk and Suffolk), some 80 per cent were in towns or on their outskirts. Infirmaries were normally placed outside town walls, often marking the gates. But occasionally they were established within town walls, especially if they were unusually early foundations (e.g. St Leonard, York, from the 10th century), or within poorer, marginal, or de-populated parishes (figure 2). Some were sited in Jewish quarters, as an assertion of Christian faith, such as St John the Baptist, Oxford, and St John, Cambridge (Rubin 1987: 108). Entries to ports and harbours were equally appropriate places: national thresholds were similarly marked with hospitals serving the Cinque Ports.

This group of hospitals was organised along monastic principles; in-firmaries were founded as male or mixed houses, with populations of both staff and inmates segregated according to sex. Mixed, or double, hospitals were presided over by a master and staffed by lay-brothers and sisters who cared for male and female inmates. The male and female staff were assisted by servants of both sexes. Mixed hospitals could assume special responsi-bilities not appropriate to male houses, such as the care of pregnant women and orphans, as was the case at St Paul, Norwich. Hospitals were often established for the apostolic number of 12 inmates and a master, warden or prioress. The larger, monastic hospitals, like St Leonard, York, might have had up to 200 inmates, staff and servants, but few were established on this scale. In hospital-priories, such as St Mary Spital, London, religious and caring functions were split between men and women. The canons participated

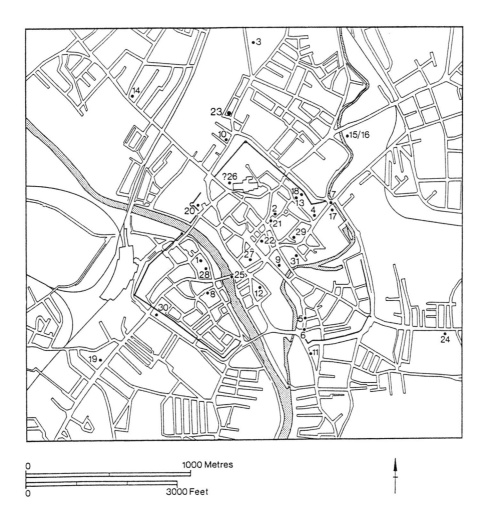

Figure 2 Hospitals and *maisons dieu* in medieval York: 1) Acaster's, North Street, *c*1379, 2) St Andrewgate (pre-1390), 3) St Anthony in the Horsefair (St Anthony of Vienne 1420), 4) St Anthony, Peasholme (1446–50), 5) St Christopher (1436), 6) Cordwainer's (1436), 7) Craven's, Layerthorpe Bridge (1415), 8) Fetter Lane (1552), 9) Trinity, Fossgate (1365), 10) St Giles, Gillygate (1274), 11) St Helen's, Fishergate (1399), 12) Hertergate (1390), 13) Holy Trinity, Aldwark (1439), 14) St Mary Magdalene, Bootham (1361), 15) St Loy (1350), 16) Monk Bridge (1353), 17) Layerthorpe Bridge (1407), 18) St John the Baptist, Merchant Taylor's Hall (1415), 19) St Katherine, extra Micklegate Bar (1333), 20) St Leonard's (1142), 21) Little St Andrewgate (1385), 22) Little Shambles (1470), 23) St Mary in the Horsefair (1318), 24) St Nicholas extra Walmgate Bar (1132–61), 25) Ousebridge (refounded 1302), 26) St Peter's (?936), 27) Peter Lane (pre-1390), 28) Sallay's, North Street (1401), 29) Stonebow Lane (1362), 30) St Thomas extra Micklegate Bar (1389), 31) Whitefriars Lane (1472).

Reproduced with permission of the York Archaeological Trust from J. D. Richards *et al, Union Terrace: Excavations in the Horsefair* (1989), and based on information supplied from Patricia Cullum.

in regular religious observances, while the sisters and lay-sisters cared for the patients and domestic responsibilities of the house. In smaller hospitals, like St John the Baptist, Winchester, the dividing line between the brothers and sisters and their supporting servants was not always clear. However, it seems that the permanently resident brothers and sisters undertook a formal religious vow, in addition to accepting the charity of the house (Keene 1985: 816).

Occasionally, a hospital was made up predominantly of sisters with only a few brothers among the inmates, for instance the Sustren Spital, Winchester (ibid.: 979). In some hospitals there were hierarchies for both sexes which observed differences in religious vocation and social background. In some mixed hospitals, such as St Laurence, Canterbury, a prioress ruled over the female section of the house. At St Paul's, Norwich, the sisters were divided between resident sisters who wore habits and made regular religious observances, and lay-sisters who worked in the hospital, distinguished as 'whole' and 'half' sisters respectively.

Both the larger monastic hospitals and the smaller houses provided an opportunity for women to join a religious community. In contrast to women professed as nuns (see Chapter 4), women in hospitals fulfilled a pastoral role more akin to Martha's active vocation. The large number of hospitals provided places for urban women who could not be accommodated in the smaller number of predominantly rural nunneries. The ideal sexual division of labour in hospitals is demonstrated in a visitation of 1387 to St Thomas the Martyr, Southwark. Here, the brothers were ordered to conform to the Rule of St Augustine, which involved observation of their religious offices, reading, studying the scriptures and attending to the business of the house. The sisters were to supervise the prayers of the sick, visit them personally and manage and feed the servants of the house (Carlin 1989: 32). The brothers were frequently found to maladminister funds at the expense of the sisters. The sisters were deprived of adequate food and clothing at St Mary Spital and St James, Westminster in the 14th century.

During the lifetime of a mixed house, the balance of power and responsibility might change. At St Bartholomew, Bristol, disputes over the rule of the house began in the 1330s, when the brethren were expelled and a new prioress, Eleanor, took charge, leasing out the dormitory where the sisters had dwelled previously, as it was superfluous to the new requirements. The hospital continued as a female house until 1386, when the Bishop of Worcester re-established the right of the founding family of de la Warre to appoint a secular priest as master. The disagreement continued until 1412, and the hospital was refounded in 1445 as a fully male almshouse for 12 poor mariners (Price 1979; Ponsford and Price forthcoming). Similar changes were made elsewhere for unknown reasons. In the late 13th century, St Saviour, Bury St Edmunds, dismissed the poor sisters who had been accommodated in the mixed house, and resolved to maintain old and infirm priests (Burdon 1925: 264). Meanwhile, the reverse had taken place at St Paul's, also known as Norman's Hospital, Norwich, established for 20 poor, aged or sick men and women. By 1385 the hospital had been re-organised to accommodate 14 sisters: seven were permanently resident, referred to as 'whole sisters', who received their board, lodging and clothing; and seven were 'half-sisters' who were not resident (VCH Norfolk II 1906: 447). An obedientary of Norwich Cathedral Priory, acting under monastic direction, continued to manage the revenues of the house, but the day-to-day running was supervised by a sister known as the 'guardyan' or 'gardiane'. The inmates administered an alms-house and hospice until Norman's was granted to the commonality of Norwich in 1565:

> all the chambers, lodgengs, gardyns, and yardes of the hospitall of St Paulle, commonly called the Normans, ... as they were lately in the hands and rule, government and custody of one Mystres Agnes Lyon, now departed, sometyme a syster of the same hows or hospytalle, and hertofore used for the comforte, relief and lodgings of pore straungers, vagrantes, sick and impotent persons ... (NRO/DCN 48/26A/1).

Communities of hospital inmates could comprise either single-sex or mixed groups. The overlap of hospital functions is expressed by the foundation of St James, Westminster, in the 12th century by the citizens of London. In the 13th century this hospital was found to be for 'leprous girls or virgins and no others' (Rosser 1989: 301). This female community was strongly monastic in purpose, made up of celibates and penitents, served by eight Augustinian brothers. The observances of the inmates involved 'daily sixty *Aves* and sixty *Pater Nosters* ... to confess weekly and to communicate four times a year. All were to wear clothes of a single colour, russett or black' (ibid.).

Infirmary hospitals were arranged to accommodate inmates and staff, and to provide all the buildings necessary for a self-contained community. Various forms of infirmary hospital can be identified, but all focused their organisation on the infirmary hall. Thus, the standard hospital plan is characterised by an infirmary hall, with a chapel attached to the east. The resulting arrangement is similar to the chancel and nave of a parish church. Several hospitals of this sort survive today: the classic example is St Mary's Hospital, Chichester (Sussex), where the chapel and an infirmary hall of four bays are contained under one roof (figure 3). English infirmary halls varied in size from four bays up to 16, but cannot compete in scale with the contemporary French hospital halls, such as Notre-Dame des Fontenilles, Tonnerre (Yonne), a massive single-aisled hall with barrel roof. In French hospital-halls the structural distinction between hall and chapel was given less emphasis.

Typically, the hospital hall was divided into three aisles by arcades. The inmates of the hospital would have been given beds in the screened side aisles, with the central space kept clear for the movement of the staff. The infirmary was thus arranged so that inmates could witness the daily celebration of the mass from their beds. In addition to assisting their spritual well-being, the eucharist was considered to have held essential healing qualities (Rubin 1992: 80–82). This motive was clear in the first foundation of St Mary Newarke, Leicester (1331–56), where 20 incurables were housed in an alms-house and 30 temporary inmates were to be accommodated in the nave.

> All the aforesaid poor folk to lodge together in one house where a chapel is to be constructed, and in this chapel masses shall be celebrated for them, one at dawn everyday, and another about 9 o'clock ... 'so that such poor folk, abiding and being in the house, may be able devoutly to behold the elevation of the Body of Christ at the masses to be said in the same chapel' (Thompson 1937: 47).

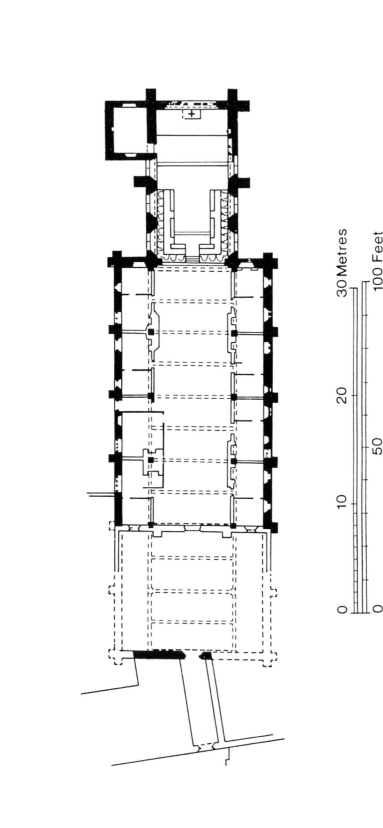

Figure 3 St Mary's Hospital, Chichester (Sussex): the classic infirmary hospital plan, with an infirmary hall of four bays (originally six bays) and chapel to the east. Scale 1:500. Based on *The Archaeological Journal* 92 (1935): 394.

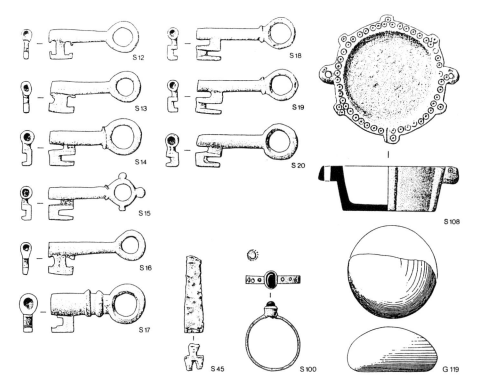

Figure 4 St Mary Spital, London: small finds from Infirmary Hall B1, including a group of copper-alloy keys, possibly for a series of cupboards or lockers. Reproduced with permission of the Museum of London Archaeology Service from Thomas *et al* forthcoming, *Excavations at the Priory and Hospital of St Mary Spital, London*. Scale 1:1.

The infirmary might be further furnished with cupboards by the beds and lamps hung between the beds of the sick 'for their solace', as noted in a visitation of 1303 to St Mary Spital, London (Thomas *et al* forthcoming). Such provision has been recognised through excavations at St Mary Spital, where finds from the 13th-century infirmary hall included a fragment of a Hertfordshire glazed-ware lid, or possibly a lamp for suspension and a large number of small iron- and copper-alloy keys appropriate for a series of cupboards or lockers (figure 4) (Thomas *et al* forthcoming). A similar group of small copper-alloy keys was recovered from St Bartholomew, Bristol (Pons-ford and Price forthcoming), perhaps revealing an emphasis on the security of personal property within medieval hospitals.

Initially, the inmates would have shared the communal space of the aisles. Many hospitals later partitioned this space into cubicles, as excavations have shown at St John, Cirencester (Gloucs), where partitions for the bed-recesses were identified by a slot and posthole (Leech and McWhirr 1982). The lower end of the hall was occasionally screened to provide lodgings for a porter or priest, as indicated at St Anne, Ripon (N Yorks). The upper end of the hall was separated from the chapel by a screen, door or arch. At St Bartholomew,

Figure 5 St John the Baptist, Canterbury (Kent): remains of the infirmary chapel, originally divided by an arcade in order to segregate male and female inmates of the hospital.

Bristol, excavations have suggested that the rebuilding of the first infirmary hall *c*1350–1400 included the construction of a temporary kitchen at the west end of the north aisle, which was later converted to a cell or chamber. This area was screened from the remainder of the hall, which seems to have been converted to serve as a church, including use of the interior for burial (Ponsford and Price forthcoming).

The chapel itself was generally a single cell, although excavations sometimes reveal a second screen which divided a western antechapel from the presbytery, as shown at St Mary, Strood (Kent) (Harrison 1980). Excavations at St Bartholomew, Gloucester, revealed a chapel of two to three bays and a nave of two bays to the east of the seven-bay infirmary hall, measuring some 44m. The hall was partitioned in the 16th century and 19 chambers were made out of the aisles (Hurst 1974). The rebuilding, in the 14th to 15th centuries, of St Giles, later the Great Hospital, Norwich, placed a four-bay infirmary to the west of an aisled nave of three bays and a long chancel for the chantry priests. To the south of the nave was a private chapel and a porch, which provided access to the parochial nave. Many hospitals shared their churches with a parochial congregation, so that a structurally distinct nave was required. Where no such function was required, churches could be built without naves. Some were provided with transepts to the north and south, such as St Bartholomew, Rochester (Kent) and St Giles, Malden (Essex). Surviving inventories show that hospital chapels were equipped with the full range of vestments, copes and altar tapestries, together with incense-boats, censers, cruets and candlesticks, which were all present at St Mary, Dover, in 1535 (Walcott 1868: 296–7).

Arrangements for the infirmary hall and chapel were made more complex in mixed hospitals for men and women. These double, or twin, hospitals were organised to segregate the male and female inmates. Various methods were used to achieve spatial segregation, including a T-shaped plan shown by extant structures at St John, Canterbury, and revealed by excavation at Strood and St Mary Spital, London. At St John, Canterbury, a hall was divided by a central spinal wall, which met a similarly divided chapel at right angles. The male and female inmates would have entered the chapel from their separate halls, and were seated separately for the services (figure 5). To the north of their halls separate latrine blocks served the men's and women's infirmaries (figure 6). One of these still stands, and retains elements of the medieval roof, 11th-century windows with wooden lintels, and parts of the seating for the floor above the original drain. The drain itself retains four round-headed arches; it appears to have been flushed by rainwater from the dormitory roof. Channels from both latrine blocks drained into the River Stour (*Canterbury's Archaeology* 1991: 20). The infirmary hall at St Mary Spital, London, was completely reconstructed following the refoundation of the hospital in 1235 (figure 7). The new hall was an aisled structure, the excavated extent measuring 51 × 16.4m, which met an aisled church at right angles in order to form the T-shaped plan (figure 8) (Thomas *et al* forthcoming).

Alternative methods of segregation included parallel halls for men and women, with a shared chapel, such as St John, Winchester; or fully detached and separate halls and chapels at St Nicholas, Salisbury. A number of infirmary halls were contained within two-storey structures, a pattern replicated across Europe, including the vaulted five-bay infirmary hall at Helligandsklostret in Copenhagen, Denmark (Trabjerg 1993: 118). At least some of these two-storey structures were designed to segregate men and women. At the Newarke Hospital, Leicester, remains of a late-14th-century chapel indicate that it and the adjoining infirmary hall were divided into two storeys, perhaps segregating the 67 men and 27 women recorded in 1525 (Thompson 1937: 181). An excavated example has been suggested at St Mary Spital, London, where a new infirmary hall was built in the late 13th century, to replace the earlier hall, which became the transepts of the priory church. The new building had a central arcade of four piers dividing it into two aisles. The extent of buttressing and the size of the walls and piers led the excavators to suggest a two-storey structure (Thomas *et al* forthcoming).

The two-storey tradition continued to be used in later infirmary halls such as the 16th-century hall of St Bartholomew, Oxford, and the 15th-century foundation of SS John the Baptist and John the Evangelist, Sherborne (Dorset), where the upper hall was occupied by women and the lower by men. Sherborne's chapel communicates with both storeys of the infirmary. Between the chapel and infirmaries there was a screen on the ground floor and a stone arch on the upper (figure 9). Others were constructed with a gallery which ran for three-quarters of the length of the hall, an arrangement which ensured that the inmates on the upper floor could see the high altar: an ideal design for an infirmary hospital which cared for both the body and soul.

Single-sex and double infirmary halls were placed around a quadrangle, close or cloister. At St Giles, Norwich, the extant church and infirmary hall

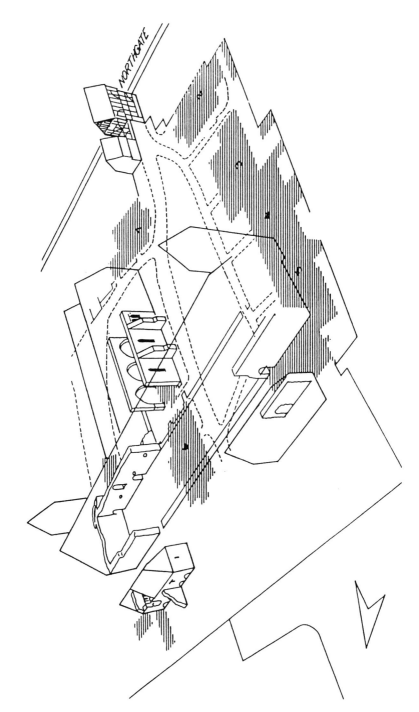

Figure 6 Perspective view of St John the Baptist, Canterbury (Kent): based on evidence of standing buildings and excavations. Reproduced with permission of J.A. Bowen, Canterbury Archaeological Trust.

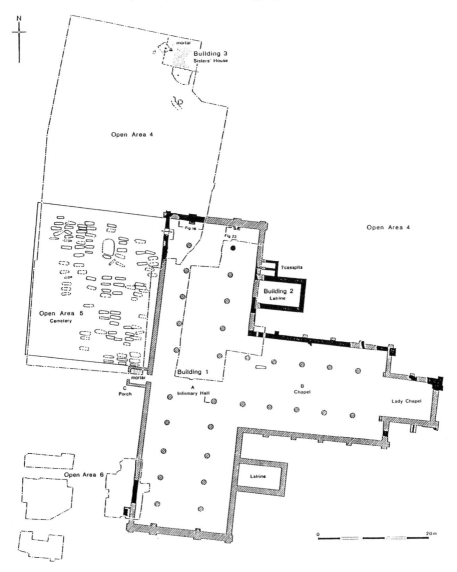

Figure 7 St Mary Spital, London: plan of archaeological features *c*1235–80. Following the refoundation in 1235 an aisled hall was built which joined an aisled church at right angles to form a T-shaped plan. Reproduced with permission of the Museum of London Archaeology Service from Thomas *et al* forthcoming, *Excavations at the Priory and Hospital of St Mary Spital, London.*

form the southern range, abutting a 15th-century cloister to the north (figure 10). The cloister still provides a covered passageway between the buildings, which originally consisted of a refectory to the west and staff lodgings to the north; the eastern range included a chapter-house. Excavations at St Mary, Ospringe (Kent), showed that the main buildings were arranged around a close (figure 11). These included the hall and chapel for inmates, a gatehouse, a two-storey guest hall, and an additional hall, presumably for staff, adjoining

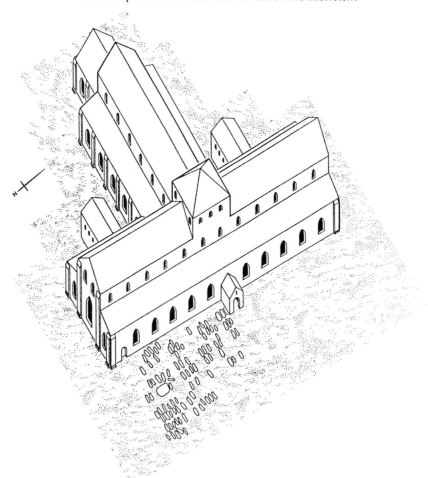

Figure 8   Reconstruction of St Mary Spital, London, *c*1235–80. Reproduced with permission of the Museum of London Archaeology Service from Thomas *et al* forthcoming, *Excavations at the Priory and Hospital of St Mary Spital, London*. Scale 1:200.

a chapel over an undercroft (Smith 1980). To the north of the close was the hospital cemetery, dovecote and millpond. To the west was the service yard, with a penticed walkway leading to buildings which appear to have been the brewhouse and bakehouse. Service buildings have been excavated at other hospitals, including St Saviour, Bury St Edmunds, where a bread oven and timber-lined well have been recorded (*Proc Suffolk Inst Archaeol* 37.2 1990: 159).

Excavations have shown that some sites were reorganised in order to separate the hall and chapel, and to provide a more quadrangular arrangement. For example, St Mary, York, appears to have been provided with a detached chapel, following renewal of the site in the 15th to 16th centuries (Richards *et al* 1989). At St Bartholomew, Bristol, a cloister alley was attached to an existing range to the north of the infirmary hall. A kitchen range to the

Figure 9   SS John the Baptist and John the Evangelist, Sherborne (Dorset): a two-storey hospital of the 15th century. The upper hall was occupied by women and the lower by men.

Figure 10   St Giles, Norwich (Norfolk): 15th-century rebuilding included the addition of a cloister to the north of the church of St Helen and the infirmary hall joined to the west of the church. A tower was built adjacent to the west end of the infirmary. The refectory formed the west range of the cloister.

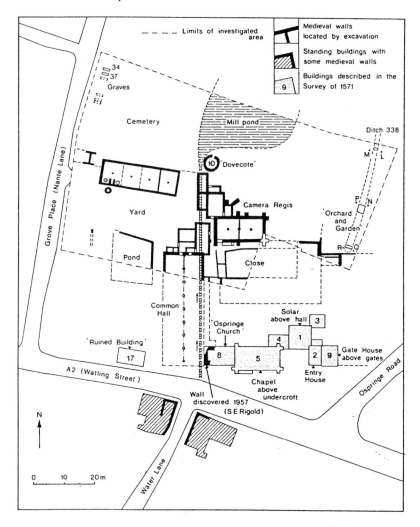

Figure 11 St Mary, Ospringe (Kent): plan of excavated and documented buildings. Reproduced with permission of the Kent Archaeological Society from *Archaeologia Cantiana* 95 (1980).

north-east was rebuilt *c*1350–1400 as two rooms, which, the excavators suggested, may have been divided into hall/pantry and kitchen/larder functions. This phase of building activity included conversion of the original infirmary hall to serve solely as a church. The hall was taken down to ground level, its undercroft filled and human burial commenced throughout its interior. By the 14th century, the south aisle was provided with an upper storey, possibly for the accommodation of staff or inmates (Ponsford and Price forthcoming). Development at St Bartholomew's may be typical of the later phases of hospitals, in which the chapel and hall were separated into discrete buildings and a more regular layout was facilitated through the provision of cloister walks.

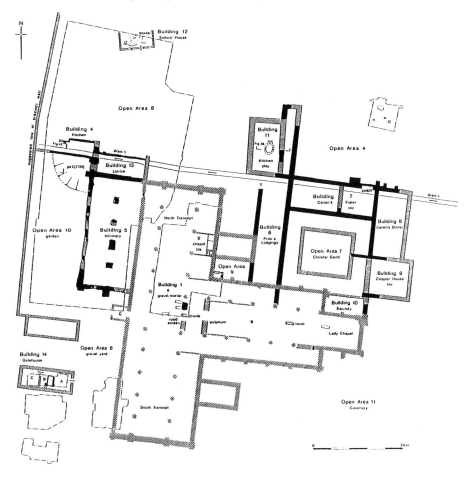

Figure 12 St Mary Spital, London: plan of archaeological features *c*1280–1320. Reproduced with permission of the Museum of London Archaeology Service from Thomas *et al* forthcoming, *Excavations at the Priory and Hospital of St Mary Spital, London.*

The most fully excavated hospital to date must be St Mary Spital, without Bishopsgate, London (Thomas *et al* 1989; forthcoming). It has been proposed that a simple infirmary hall with eastern chapel of *c*1197 preceded the excavated T-shape complex after the refoundation of the site in 1235. Between *c*1280 and 1320, claustral ranges were developed to the north of the church, with the dormitory as the east range, the refectory on the north, and the prior's lodging to the west. A new kitchen was built to the north of the west range, and a second infirmary was built against the west side of the first infirmary. The earlier T-shape arrangement was retained, but the first infirmary was remodelled into a pair of transepts for the church (figure 12). Burial began within the former infirmary, indicating a similar change of function to that proposed for St Bartholomew, Bristol (above). Between *c*1320 and 1350, the infirmary was again extended westward, with a new two-storey structure abutted to the second infirmary.

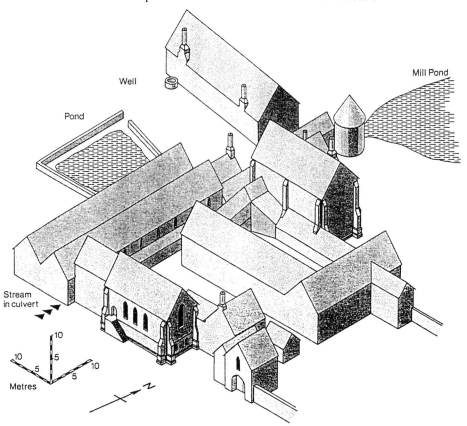

Figure 13 St Mary, Ospringe (Kent): a reconstruction of the major buildings from excavated evidence and the Survey of the Kentish Estates, 1571. Reproduced with permission of the Kent Archaeological Society from *Archaeologia Cantiana* 95 (1980).

Additional groups sometimes resided, or were entertained, within the hospital. Services provided by hospitals often included hospitality to pilgrims and travellers or particular guests who were benefactors of the house. Hospitality for members of the gentry could have dire consequences for the finances of a hospital (Thompson 1937: 143). Ospringe (Kent) enjoyed royal patronage and, in return, held special responsibility for hospitality to the royal household. The guest hall was a four-bayed, buttressed building over an undercroft, situated at the north range of the close (figures 11 and 13). This accommodation may have been reserved as the *camera regis* (Smith 1980: 81). Permanent paying guests were often admitted to hospitals, sponsored by royal or monastic patrons of the house or encouraged by the hospital in order to improve finances. These corrodians, who held a lifetime corrody to reside in the hospital, would have required lodgings separate from those of the staff and inmates. Typical provision may be illustrated by the arrangements agreed in 1392 at St Saviour, Bury St Edmunds, for John Reve of Pakenham. John was to have food and a chamber in the hospital for the remainder of his life, and to receive annually a garment, one pair of stockings and one pair of shoes. In return for the corrody of John Reve, 20 marks (£13 6*s* 8*d*) was paid

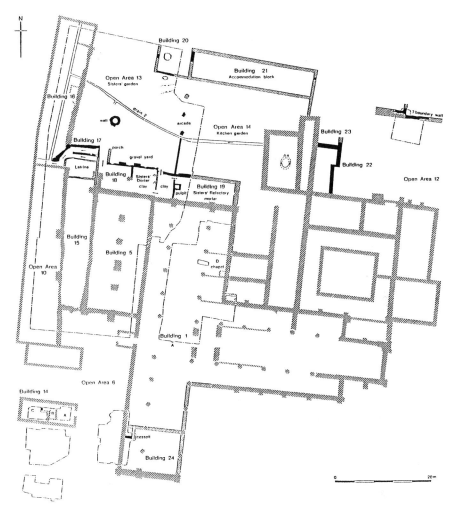

Figure 14 St Mary Spital, London: plan of archaeological features *c*1350–1400. Reproduced with permission of the Museum of London Archaeology Service from Thomas *et al* forthcoming, *Excavations at the Priory and Hospital of St Mary Spital, London.*

towards the new fabric of St Saviour by the sponsor, Robert Ashfield (Burdon 1925: 271).

In hospitals run by secular clergy, such as St Mary, Ospringe, closes were used to order functional areas and social groups within the house. At Ospringe, closes divided religious and non-religious activity areas; elsewhere closes facilitated the segregation of groups with separate social, religious, or gender identities. A separate garden was provided for the sisters of St Giles, Norwich. Excavations at St Mary Spital, London, have identified an area to the north of the infirmary as the garden and dormitory of the sisters (figure 14). Separate stone-built accommodation was provided for the sisters in the 14th century, replacing earlier timber structures. Their range was divided into a refectory to the east, with foundations of a reading pulpit, and a dormitory with porch to the west. The sisters' accommodation was sited adjacent to the kitchen, to which it was later joined by a corridor in order to facilitate greater segregation. The sisters' garden was to the west of the kitchen, separated from it by the kitchen garden and, possibly, an arcade dividing the two gardens (Thomas *et al* forthcoming). This area produced archaeological evidence perhaps indicative of the presence of women, including two bone needles, four thimbles and dress accessories such as buckles, strap ends and pins possibly for fixing a head-dress.

The largest hospitals, like St Leonard, York, were provided with a number of cloisters and chapels, so that groups of staff, servants and inmates could live and worship separately. An extra chapel was sometimes provided at the gate of the hospital just as monasteries had situated a *capella ante portas* for passing travellers. The situation of the excavated chapel at St Saviour, Bury St Edmunds, may suggest a similar function. This chapel, positioned adjacent to an entrance in the precinct wall, may have served some secondary or specialised purpose. The two-chamber chapel was located behind an extant 15th-century western facade. That the eastern section functioned as a chapel was confirmed by the excavation of an altar base and several burials, including one of a priest accompanied by the customary chalice and paten (*Proc Suffolk Instit Archaeol* 37.2 1990: 159).

Additional cloisters and courts could be used as a means of expanding the hospital complex. This principle is best observed in northern European hospitals such as St John, Bruges (modern Belgium), where parallel halls were added to the south of the original 12th-century infirmary until further expansion was prevented by the canal; to the north, four further courts were added. In their latest development, hospitals like St Mary Spital added rows of almshouses to their precinct areas. These tenements, and the presence of secular people resident in the precinct, may have blurred the distinction between the monastery and the urban community outside.

The presence of different social groups within the hospital is reflected most directly by burials excavated from within the hospital precinct. It is possible to recognise founders and patrons, hospital staff and inmates or patients. Benefactors frequently chose to be buried in hospital churches and churchyards, a practice which is well known for all types of monasteries (Clay 1909: 83). Excavations at both St Mary Spital, London, and St Mary, Strood (Kent) showed that, in the 14th century, tombs were constructed at the entrances of hospital chapels, dividing the chapel from the wards or transepts by means of walls or screens (Harrison 1970; Thomas *et al* forthcoming). At St Mary Spital, six burials were excavated in the crossing of the church, three in the chancel and six in the transept chapels; a total of 25 interior burials is known from documents (Thomas *et al* 1989: 91). These interior burials are likely to represent high-ranking patrons or religious personnel of the house. Their high status may be attested by the pathology of their skeletons. This group was found to have the highest level of dental disease, perhaps indicative of a sweet or pulpy diet, and a high incidence of DISH (diffuse idiopathic skeletal hyperostosis), a condition associated with obesity and possibly associated with rich diets, which causes excessive growth of bone tissue and leads eventually to the fusion of large sections of the vertebral column. In

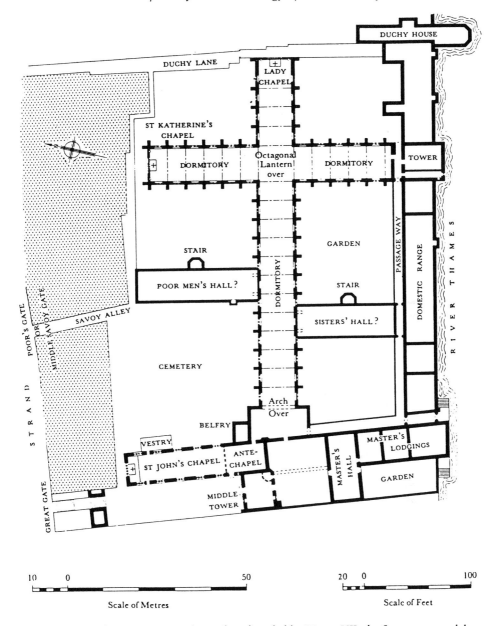

DUCHY HOUSE

DUCHY LANE

LADY CHAPEL

ST KATHERINE'S CHAPEL

DORMITORY   Octagonal Lantern over   DORMITORY   TOWER

STAIR

POOR MEN'S HALL?   GARDEN

DORMITORY   STAIR

SISTERS' HALL?

PASSAGE WAY   DOMESTIC RANGE   RIVER THAMES

SAVOY ALLEY

CEMETERY

POOR'S GATE   MIDDLE SAVOY GATE   PORTER'S GATE

STRAND

Arch Over

BELFRY

VESTRY   ANTE-CHAPEL   MASTER'S LODGINGS

ST JOHN'S CHAPEL   MASTER'S HALL

GARDEN

MIDDLE TOWER

GREAT GATE

10   0   50
Scale of Metres

20   0   100
Scale of Feet

Figure 15   The Savoy Hospital, London: founded by Henry VII, the Savoy was modelled on Santa Maria Nuova, Florence. Reproduced with permission of the Controller of
Her Majesty's Stationery Office, from H. Colvin ed. *A History of the King's Works 3
(1485–1660), Part 1* (1975).

comparison with individuals buried outside the chapel and transepts, this
group was found to be relatively tall, possibly indicating that they had been
better-nourished throughout their lives (Conheeney in Thomas *et al* forthcoming). A small group excavated from the chapel at St Saviour, Bury St
Edmunds, may suggest segregated burial of social groups inside and outside

the chapel. The physical anthropology of the group buried outside the chapel indicates poor oral hygiene, possibly indicative of a lower-status diet, and a number exhibited a lesion of the cranial vault associated with anaemia (Anderson, archive report 1990). From this evidence it seems that a lower-status group, possibly inmates of the hospital, were buried outside the chapel.

Medieval British hospitals were conservative in their development, in contrast to Italian hospitals, which prefigured modern hospital planning through the innovation of a cruciform arrangement of sick wards. Hospitals such as Santa Maria Nuova, Florence (*c*1334), provided single-aisled intersecting wards, each with their own altars. This plan allowed the staff to oversee all rooms simultaneously. Only one English hospital was built to these progressive specifications: Henry VII's Savoy Hospital, London, which was completed in 1517. Descriptions of the Savoy indicate that it was modelled on Santa Maria Nuova: it was a centrally planned, cruciform structure with a lantern over the crossing where wards met (figure 15). Santa Maria Nuova influenced the Savoy in terms of the scale and ground-plan of the hospital, but also in its general aims. The statutes of the Savoy suggest a concern with cleanliness and medical attention for the sick, which included regular attendance by a doctor and surgeon (Park and Henderson 1991: 168). As we shall see, it cannot be assumed that such concern for patient care was standard in earlier hospitals.

A matter of life and death? Medical treatment of the sick poor

Documents suggest that special medical treatment within hospitals for the sick poor was minimal. Treatment of hospital inmates seems to have been limited to bed rest and an adequate diet, administered in a relatively clean, warm environment. There are hardly any references to medieval hospital inmates experiencing surgery, or receiving attention from physicians, and the rare cases that occurred were limited to the late 15th and 16th centuries. Professional medical practitioners instead treated wealthy patients privately, outside institutions. Such care that hospital inmates received may be studied archaeologically through evidence for diet, sanitation and indications of possible medicinal treatment indicated by the presence of specialised implements and medicinal herbs. The health of inmates may be approached through the physical anthropology of excavated skeletons.

The general age and physical well-being of hospital inmates would have varied according to the purpose of the hospital and the types of patient admitted. Two contrasting cases of inmate status are provided by St Bartholomew, Bristol, and St Mary Spital, London, although in neither case can medical treatment of inmates be discerned. Excavations at St Bartholomew recorded 45 burials dated to the mid-14th century and later. The majority of burials represented elderly individuals, indicative of the hospital's function primarily as an almshouse. As a group, the skeletons were characterised by worn teeth, carious lesions and arthritis. Many exhibited degenerative diseases of the joints, and there was one possible example each of senile osteoporosis, a legsore and a bedsore. Seven individuals had indications of healed fractures while two showed signs of chronic anaemia – a childhood condition indicative of poor diet before entry to the hospital (Stroud in Ponsford and Price forthcoming). These people had come to the hospital in order to be cared for in their final years.

The cemeteries at St Mary Spital reflect the changing functions of the hospital over time. In the first phase (*c*1197–1235) a small cemetery of two rows contained an estimated 35 individuals; 13 graves were excavated. Although a small sample, the group was made up predominantly of adult women, and suggests a small, roadside hospital caring for women, possibly in childbirth. In contrast, the cemetery associated with the refoundation (*c*1235–1280) was predominantly male. The population of 101 skeletons is noteworthy for its abnormally low average age at death, with 55.4 per cent estimated at between 10 and 25 years. Most fractures were healed, perhaps indicating some degree of care, and a high incidence of hypoplasia suggested serious childhood illness associated with the poor (Conheeney in Thomas *et al* forthcoming). The age profile of the cemetery suggests that the hospital catered for migrant workers and the young, mobile poor who were attracted to London.

Diet in hospitals is likely to have been adequate by lower-status, medieval standards, and would have consisted of coarse bread, meat or fish, cheese, beer and small quantities of vegetables. Examination of deposits from the sisters' latrine at St John, Canterbury, suggested that some of the cereals consumed were possibly of poor quality, affected by wheat bunt (*Tilletia tritici*), and that inmates of the hospital were infected by the common intestinal worms, round worm and whip worm (Patricia Wiltshire pers com). Accounts from St Giles, later the Great Hospital, Norwich, are complete from the 14th century onwards and give some indications of foodstuffs consumed within the hospital. Particularly useful are entries in the accounts for the hospital gardens which sold surplus from overproduction. From these accounts we may infer that inmates were provided with a diet plentiful in leeks, onions, pears and apples (Carole Rawcliffe pers com). Accounts seldom enumerate incoming food according to different sections of the household. It is likely that the clergy and servants had a far better diet than the poor, who were given pottage, possibly made up of peas, rye or barley, bread and herring.

Hospitals purchased foodstuffs, accepted rents in kind (such as barley) and received gifts of food in alms. For instance, in the 14th century, St John, Cambridge, received grain from its own land, maintained its own fishponds and sheepfold, and regularly purchased butter, eggs, cheese, veal, chickens, fish, and occasionally spices, such as saffron, pepper and cumin (Rubin 1987: 50). Provision made for a corrodian was greater than that afforded an ordinary patient, as shown in a generous corrody granted in 1342 to Sarah, widow of John Balliol, at St Giles, Holborn. Sarah was given a weekly allowance of seven white loaves, four black loaves, 12 pence for ale and an annual kitchen allowance of one bushel of peas, one of oatmeal for porridge, and one of salt (Honeybourne 1963: 23).

Few communities would have achieved self-sufficiency in food production, although stocks of animals were kept by rural and suburban houses, and surplus production is likely to have been limited to the largest hospitals, such as St Giles (later the Great Hospital), Norwich, which was endowed with extensive estates. The Maison Dieu, Dover, was recorded as holding 1600 sheep, 119 cattle and 29 horses, at the time of the Dissolution (Wall 1980: 261). Archaeology has the potential to comment on medieval diet, and our knowledge of the hospital diet is likely to expand as environmental evidence from excavations is reported. For example, the assemblage of animal bones from St Mary, Ospringe, showed equal proportions of the bones of sheep and cattle, with a lower proportion of pig remains. The relative proportion of sheep is high when compared with urban and rural assemblages from other medieval sites, and must reflect the importance of sheep husbandry in Kent in the later medieval period (ibid.). In common with assemblages from monastic sites, a diversity of bird and fish species was found, and in keeping with its responsibility for royal hospitality, the Ospringe assemblage contained evidence of high-status, hunted game, including wild birds and red and fallow deer. Animal bones from St Bartholomew, Bristol, indicated lamb as an important element in the hospital diet before 1300, with growing emphasis on mutton as sheep were increasingly kept for their wool (Ponsford and Price forthcoming). Beef dominated the diet at St Mary Spital until the late 13th century, when it began to decrease in relation to mutton. Diet was made up largely of the main domesticates with a wide variety of fish species (Thomas *et al* forthcoming).

Recently excavated sites have yielded either mineralised or waterlogged plant remains, depending on favourable soil conditions and the detailed sampling and sieving procedures for retrieval. Medieval deposits from St Mary Spital, London, contained copious amounts of fruit remains representing figs, blackberry/raspberry, and apple/pear in late-12th to early-13th-century deposits, and grape, plum, cherry and strawberry in late-13th to early-14th-century deposits (Thomas *et al* forthcoming). This assemblage of soft fruits is fairly common from medieval sites; the absence of vegetable plants such as leek and onion is most likely the result of bias against their survival in the human digestive tract and in buried deposits. The recovery of certain herbs is suggestive of food flavourings and, possibly, plant remedies used for medical purposes.

Hospital staff would have blended and dispensed vegetable drugs of laxative, diuretic, sedative, or stimulant nature. This may not have required the purchase of special medicines, but rather a knowledge of common, local plants and occasional imports such as cloves, cinnamon, ginger and black pepper, the last of these being common in accounts of the hospital of St Leonard, York. Care was required in the collection and storage of herbs, and in the preparation of medicines to the correct strength and consistency. The appropriate knowledge was contained in remedy books which made use of local flora. More specialised herbals, such as *De Simplici Medicina*, were not necessarily for practical use. Medical recipes detailed the preparation and application of compound medicines, such as John Mirfield's *Brevarium Bartholomei* (c1380–95). Mirfield was a clerk at the priory of St Bartholomew, Smithfield, and later at the hospital, whose treatise of therapeutic medicine described over 400 compound medicines, administered by syrup, electuary, pills, powders, waters, oils and salves, although few specialised compounds would have been used in an ordinary English hospital. Syrups were made from a solution of unrefined sugar, or honey and water, and combined with sachets of spices or herbal infusions. Salves incorporated wax, animal fats or oils and were applied heated; they were rubbed into the affected part, or applied as plasters using a piece of linen or a strip of leather (Hunt 1990: 45–6).

Archaeological evidence for herbal medicine at monastic sites has been proposed for Waltham Abbey (Essex), where a pit of *c*1540 contained considerable traces of black henbane (*Hyoscyamus niger L.*) and hemlock (*Conium maculatum L.*), and for Jedburgh Abbey (Roxburgh), where quantities of tormentil (*Potentilla erecta*) indicate use of an astringent (Hunt 1990: 63). Hospital gardens must have included herbs grown for medicinal use. However, some caution must be used in interpreting plant remains, which could have arrived at the site through natural agencies, such as wind and rain, and not as a result of human intervention. Flotation samples from St Giles by Brompton Bridge, Brough (N Yorks), contained plants which possess medicinal properties, such as henbane, a possible anaesthetic. From St Mary Spital there is evidence for the presence of many plants that may, potentially, have had medical uses, equally they may have been used for culinary purposes or simply have grown wild in the area. These include: poppy, mustard, malva, hyoscyamus, hemlock, and in more concentrated occurrence, vervain, hemp, fennel and brassica. More ornamental plants, such as box, suggest the possibility of a formal garden arrangement similar to those excavated at the Augustinian Friary, Hull and the Gilbertine Priory, York (Coppack 1990: 78–80).

One archaeological project was established with the specific task of studying medical practice at a medieval infirmary hospital. A multi-disciplinary team conducted tests at the Scottish medieval hospital of Soutra (Mid Lothian), 35 km south-east of Edinburgh. This hilltop infirmary was established by 1164, and thrived for 300 years with a large community numbering up to 300 (SHARP 1989). Procedures at Soutra included pollen analysis to test for medicinal plants, and microscopic screening and analysis of pit contents for blood residues, the remains of medical preparations (which are expected to leave traces of wine, vinegar, honey or mead), fibres from fabric dressings, human parasites, and pathogens, such as anthrax spores, of which three non-viable examples were reported.

The project at Soutra made optimistic claims for the recognition of medical plants through pollen analysis, particularly flax (*Linum usitatissimum*), hemp (*Cannabis sativa*) and opium poppy (*Papaver somniferum*). All of these may have been processed to be applied externally as plasters or poultices. However, caution must again be exercised, since flax and hemp occur commonly on medieval sites of all types, and are likely to occur within the pollen profile typical of the locality. Botanical specialists would hesitate in isolating these particular species, since opium poppy is not easily separated from other members of the same family. In addition, the results of pollen and residue analysis from Soutra were not adequately linked to archaeological evidence, providing little or no context for the environmental archaeology. Irrefutable archaeological evidence of medical treatment would consist of signs of the preparation of plant mixtures, such as traces of medical compounds as residues in pottery vessels from sealed medieval contexts. Interim reports from Soutra announced remains of cloves and opium poppy adhering to potsherds recovered from excavation. An additional avenue of research may lie in the biochemical analysis of vessels for traces of medical compounds.

Artefacts from hospital excavations sometimes indicate treatment of a medical nature. Excavations at Arundel (Sussex), at a site previously identified as the hospital, and now thought to be the Dominican friary (*Medieval Archaeol* 35 1991: 193), recovered a miniature mortar in Portland Stone, tentatively dated to the 15th century. It was suggested that this find was an apothecary's mortar, because limestone was chosen over the usual sandstone used in larger domestic mortars. This preference in materials may have eliminated the risk of particles of quartz entering mixtures of medical compounds (Dunning 1969). A similarly sized mortar in Purbeck marble was recovered from Ospringe (Smith 1980: 154). Excavations at Soutra have recovered artefacts identified as a glazed 'ointment pot', and a cannula, a surgical implement for unblocking corporeal vessels (*Medieval Archaeol* 33 1989: 235). From St Mary Spital, London, fragments of two glass urinals, or jordans, possibly dating to the 14th century, have been interpreted as being of the piriform type: pear-shaped with sloping sides which run up to a wide rim (Thomas *et al* forthcoming). Such urinals were used in the diagnosis of patients, a painstaking procedure commonly carried out in medieval medical practice in which the colour, clarity and odour of a patient's urine were examined as an aid to diagnosis.

Pottery assemblages occasionally hint at specialised functions, such as the group recovered from St Nicholas's leper hospital (Fife), which is said to have differed from that of contemporary urban assemblages in the locality. Jugs were predominant in the group, in contrast to cooking pots which characterise urban sites. Special forms were identified within the local pottery, a white gritty ware, which may have served some function in the preparation of compounds. These include: a flat-based open bowl, glazed green internally and externally smoke blackened; a small, squat jug; and a glazed tubular spout, which may have formed part of a similar jug (Hall undated rep). Similarly, Ospringe produced a shallow bowl in shell-tempered ware, which was fire-blackened on its exterior (Smith 1980: 174). At St Mary Spital, London, the general absence of tableware implies that inmates used wooden vessels. Eighteen wooden vessels were recovered from the site, some with unusual marks which have been interpreted as indicating personal ownership. Several of the vessels had wide rims which would have helped to avoid spillage and may have been particularly appropriate for feeding the infirm (Egan in Thomas *et al* forthcoming).

Specialised vessels are occasionally detailed within monastic account rolls, such as the mention of 12 earthen dishes for blood-letting, purchased by the Durham infirmarer in 1397–8 (Moorhouse 1993). Regular bleeding was carried out at all monastic infirmaries where, typically, monks were phlebotomised on a six- or seven-week rota in order to maintain good health. Medieval medical recipes and 'leechbooks' indicate the ingredients required for medical compounds, detailing the sequence of preparation and range of implements and vessels used in mixing. Essential apparatus included: *vaissel de areim/ quivre/ estaim/ veirre, morter, pestel, boiste, paele, esquiele, hanap, paellette, pot, picher, galun, sachel, ampulle, sarceyse, pouche, poteau, poke de canevaz, bage de canevaz, basin, possenet, puscette, furn, brasier* and *test* (Hunt 1990: 20). Some recipes required special vessels or practices, such as burial of ingredients in an earthenware pot in the ground for long periods. These

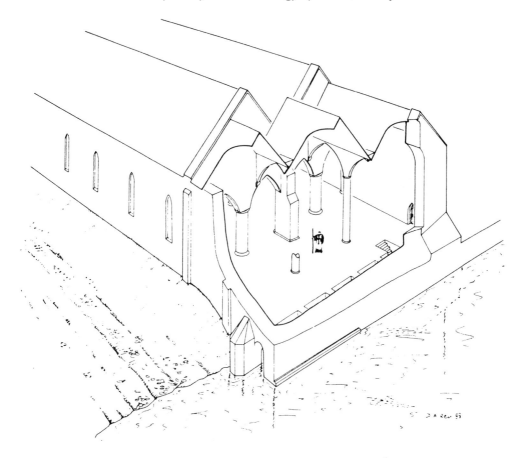

Figure 16   Reconstruction of St John the Baptist, Oxford. Excavations indicated a series of immersion tanks set in the east end of the infirmary chapel, through which the River Cherwell flowed. Reproduced with permission from *Medieval Archaeology* 32 (1988): 270, figure 7.

sources may predict the range of glass, wooden and pottery vessels which we may expect to recover in the excavation of hospitals. In order to recognise their special function, however, archaeologists must consider the context in which vessels are recovered, the possible presence of residues, and their place within the usual range of pottery expected from contemporary domestic sites within the region. Given that hospital inmates experienced the absolute minimum of medical intervention, research intending to focus on medieval medicine would be far better directed towards the infirmary areas of Benedictine and Augustinian monasteries.

In common with monasteries, hospitals emphasised the importance of fresh drinking water and adequate facilities for the disposal of human effluence. Many, including St John and St Mark, Bristol (Bond 1993), piped a supply of freshwater to the hospital precinct. Some, including St Mary, Ospringe, where the watercourse is diverted through a stone-lined channel beneath the latrine, or *reredorter* (figure 11), culverted streams in order to cleanse the latrines. At St Mary Spital, London, excavations revealed a drain to the north of the infirmary, possibly on the site of a latrine block. This drain served other hospital buildings, including the kitchen, before flushing the latrines and finally travelling through a sluice gate into a ditch along the east side of Bishopsgate (Thomas *et al* 1989: 92). The absence of accumulated deposits suggests that the drain was kept 'scrupulously clean'. A pit near the infirmary contained large quantities of straw, possibly from discarded mattresses, indicating that standards of cleanliness in the hospital may have been high (Thomas *et al* forthcoming).

At the infirmary of St John the Baptist, Oxford, a hospital especially for the sick, water may have been used for disinfection, or for a combination of religious and medical purposes. The hospital was subsequently converted to Magdalene College, which retains much of the infirmary hall. On the basis of drawings by the antiquary Buckler (dated to the turn of the 19th century), a series of individual latrine closets was thought to have once existed at the east end of the infirmary. Recent excavations in this area have suggested a more spectacular function. An ashlar-lined culvert was uncovered at the east end of the infirmary, but this was provided with a flight of steps from which access was gained to the interior. This eastern part of the hall appears to have been an annexe divided from the main building, with its own roof (figure 16). It has been suggested that this eastern area was actually a chapel attached to the infirmary hall, and that the River Cherwell was incorporated into the structure in order to serve a specific purpose, perhaps as immersion tanks involved in a healing ritual (*Medieval Archaeol* 32 1988: 270–1; Durham 1991: 69). Such a rite may have been particularly relevant in a hospital dedicated to St John the Baptist, with the undertones of rebirth and repentance through immersion which are associated with this saint. Like the sacrament of the eucharist, baptism was considered to have healing qualities for hospital patients. A dedication to St John the Baptist invoked his intercessory role in healing, which is exemplified by his prominent representation in certain works of art commissioned for hospitals, such as the famous Isenheim altarpiece at the hospital of St Antony of Viennoise (Alsace) (Hayum 1989: 91–3).

Leprosaria: *on the threshold*

Leper hospitals were founded during the centuries in which the disease is believed to have reached epidemic proportions in Britain. The earliest foundations were in the 11th century, at Canterbury, London and Chatham. The majority of *leprosaria* date to the 12th and 13th centuries, corresponding with the growth in urban centres, overseas contact and population density: all factors which encouraged the close human contact in which leprosy thrives. New foundations decreased as leprosy became less prevalent, with a minimum number of only 17 new houses founded in England between the 14th and 16th centuries. Existing leper hospitals changed function as incidence of the disease decreased, often developing into almshouses for other groups stigmatised by society, particularly the mentally ill. In countries more frequently beset by plague, the leper houses became plague hospitals, in particular the

Italian *lazarettos*. It has been argued that leprosy gradually disappeared as townspeople developed another life-threatening disease: tuberculosis. A cross-immunity appears to exist between the two diseases, which is due to their shared bacteria of the same genus. Today, the disease survives in rural areas, clustering within families (Manchester and Roberts 1989: 267). The distribution of late-founded, medieval *leprosaria* may suggest a similar occurrence. As urban foundations in England dwindled or changed function, leper hospitals in Scotland continued to be founded into the 15th and 16th centuries (Ayr, Dumbarton, Dundee, Edinburgh, Haddington, Rulemouth, Stirling, Banff, Forres and Perth). In rural areas, such as Cornwall and Devon, a high density of leper hospitals serviced a disease which survived well into the 17th century (Hart 1989: 261).

Within British medieval society there was no precise medical definition of leprosy, but rather a clear moral definition. From the early 14th century, in urban continental Europe, leprosy was frequently diagnosed by a qualified physician or surgeon, while in contemporary England, diagnosis continued to be carried out by priests. All disease was regarded as both a spiritual and physical affliction, but in the case of leprosy this connection resulted in the belief that the disease was generally brought about by sin, particularly sins of a sexual nature. The leper may have sinned himself, or may have been suffering from the sins of a parent, especially if his mother had been menstruating when he was conceived, or if conception had occurred on a 'banned' day. Leprosy was generally perceived to be punishment for sin, and lepers assumed the role of the religious penitent. The ideology which surrounded medieval leprosy required the sufferer to embrace repentance and poverty, and to wear a distinctive habit.

Biblical attitudes to lepers were superimposed on medieval society, affecting the location of leper hospitals, their dedications and iconography. Attitudes towards the medieval leper derived from Leviticus, when the Israelites were struck with leprosy as divine retribution for worshipping the golden calf.

> And the leper in whom the plague is, his clothes shall be rent, and his head bare, and he shall put a covering upon his upper lip, and shall cry, unclean, unclean. All the days wherein the plague shall be in him he shall be defiled; he is unclean; he shall dwell alone, without the camp shall his habitation be (Leviticus 13: 45–6).

Like the leper of Leviticus, the medieval leper dwelt 'without the camp'. Others, such as St Hugh of Lincoln, viewed lepers as the elect of God, as sufferers given the malady in order to refine their spirituality.

It may be said that *leprosaria* were liminal, placed at the margins of society to act as thresholds. This was an appropriate role for the leper, who was ritually separated from society and symbolically dead. The rites for the separation of lepers represented metaphoric funerals, in which they were formally removed from their communities. According to the rite of Sarum, the priest led the covered leper to the church during the recitation of the seven penitential psalms, followed by the Mass of the Dead in the church, and finally a symbolic burial in the churchyard in which the priest cast earth over the feet of the leper (Clay 1909: 273–6). The ostracism of lepers was due to the medieval understanding of the causes of the disease.

The purpose of *leprosaria* is generally assumed to have been segregation. Their function as isolation hospitals has been used to account for their situation in relation to the topography of medieval towns, pushed to the outer limits of towns and parish boundaries. If isolation was their purpose, was segregation effective, or even aimed for consistently? Skeletons excavated from leper hospitals suggest that not all inmates suffered from the disease, rather that the community was made up of general sick poor and aged (e.g. St Leonard, Newark, Notts; Bishop 1983). Legislation to limit the mobility of lepers began in 1179 with a decree by the Third Lateran Council that lepers should not dwell with healthy men. That this dictat was unsuccessful is shown by the local legislation which repeatedly called for the exclusion of lepers from towns. In London especially, royal and civic ordinances were repeated from the the 13th until the 15th century, when a royal ordinance of 1472 declared that lepers should be removed to hospitals and 'sequestered places prepared specially for them' (Honeybourne 1963: 8). Here, the intention of the municipal authorities was to exclude lepers from urban places, but also, evidently, to remove lepers from the sight of the healthy, more prosperous, town-dwellers.

The disfigurement of leprosy caused discomfort to medieval onlookers, so that the marginal situations of *leprosaria* have been viewed as a response which removed and contained a stigmatised group. Instead, it may be argued that while leper hospitals were placed outside towns, they were located in prominent, highly visible places. *Leprosaria* were founded outside the major gates of walled medieval towns across Europe, like Norwich and Lund (modern Sweden, medieval Denmark), and on the main bridges, roads and thoroughfares leading into major centres of population. Most often, they were situated beyond the walls at the boundary of the city, as at St Mary Magdalene, Bootham, York (figure 2). Such visibility served a variety of individual and collective motives. For the founders of *leprosaria*, charity was displayed for all to see, and the intercessory prayers of the lepers for their founders were assisted by the additional prayers offered by those passing into the town, when these conspicuous sites reminded travellers of the piety of charitable patrons.

More collective concerns were served by the location of leper hospitals at boundaries. Anthropologists have suggested that cultural notions of purity are maintained by symbolic and physical boundaries (Douglas 1970). Spread of infection would have been guarded against by the fear of pollution, which protected boundaries, but in addition the corporate identity of the very town itself was maintained by the marking of boundaries. Towns, including Bury St Edmunds, Beverley and Worcester, were defined spatially by the *leprosaria* outside their gates; those at Holborn, Westminster, Mile End and Southwark defined London's hinterland. Leper hospitals were thresholds which signalled the journeying point at which the town met its surroundings, and at which the traveller or pilgrim passed from one territory into another.

Leper hospitals were dedicated to traditional saints mentioned in the Bible. These saints were sometimes associated with the afflicted or disabled, like St Giles, but were noteworthy for coincidence with pilgrimage, such as James, Catherine and John the Baptist. Above all, the favoured saint was Mary Magdalene, the model of repentance in the face of sexual sin. To medieval

Figure 17 A carved 'leper's head' from Melton Mowbray (Leics) thought to have originated from Burton Lazars. Indications of leprosy include the everted lower eyelid of the right eye, accentuated nasal orifices and withdrawal of the upper lip (Manchester and Marcombe 1990). Drawing by Ted West.

minds this saint represented a conflation of Marys, a composite image which represented, amongst other roles, a sinner who 'had been healed of evil spirits and infirmities' (Luke 8:2), and ministered to Christ in the house of Simon the leper (Mark 14:3), and tended the sick Lazarus (John 11:1) (Haskins 1994: 1–32). Just as St John the Baptist was associated with healing through baptism, Mary Magdalene represented rebirth through repentance and the cleansing of sin. Her association with leprosy was depicted in the iconography expressed in the embellishment of hospitals, for instance the wall-painting which was commissioned at Durham (Clay 1909: 163). An iconography more specifically devoted to leprosy may be apparent in a find associated with St Lazarus, Burton Lazars, where a fragmented sculpture dated *c*1250–1350 appears to depict the head of a leper, possibly that of St Lazarus (figure 17) (Manchester and Marcombe 1990: 88–91).

Leprosy, today's Hansen's disease (*Mycobacterium leprae*), is transmitted through coughing and sneezing. This chronic disease has an incubation period of three to five years. It is characterised by loss of sensation in the limbs, with eventual paralysis, wasting of muscle and development of deformations. Early stages consist of dermatological abnormalities which might be confused with other diseases, such as syphillis, which itself was not common in medieval England. The first stages include raised patches of skin, resembling

UNIVERSITY
OF SHEFFIELD
LIBRARY

The division of the cemetery into three areas and the distribution of the sexes

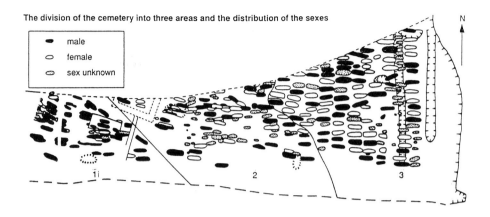

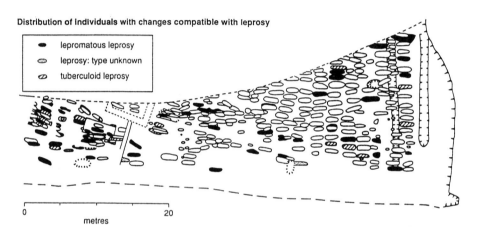

Figure 18   SS James and Mary Magdalene, Chichester (Sussex). Excavated skeletons suggest that low-resistant, lepromatous leprosy corresponded with male burials to the west of the cemetery. Tuberculoid leprosy was associated with mixed burials in the more planned central and eastern sections. Based on F. Lee and J. Magilton, 'The cemetery of the hospital of St James and St Mary Magdalene, Chichester – a case study', *World Archaeology* 21 (1989), figures 3–4.

eczema, and skin ulcers which are reluctant to heal. Advanced leprosy affects the skeleton, particularly the hands, lower legs, feet and skull. These more developed cases can be recognised through the physical anthropology of skeletons excavated from hospital cemeteries.

At SS James and Mary Magdalene, Chichester, a number of individuals had developed facial mutilation (Lee and Magilton 1989); a small group discovered at South Acre (Norfolk) appear to have had sinuses affected by discharging of periodontal abscess cavities (Wells 1967); and at St Margaret, High Wycombe (Bucks), lower extremities attested to the advanced stage of leprosy (Farley and Manchester 1989). Analysis of the cemetery at Chichester provided evidence for the nature of the development of both the disease of leprosy, and the particular hospital (figure 18). Concentrations of more highly degenerated leprous skeletons appear to correspond with the chronological development of the hospital: low-resistant, lepromatous sufferers are co-incident with predominantly male burials towards the west of the cemetery. This would be consistent with the early history of this house which was established for leprous brethren. The more highly planned, central and eastern sections of the cemetery yielded mixed burials of men and women, and a greater incidence of tuberculoid leprosy, a relatively benign form. These areas would be consistent with the later development of Chichester as a mixed almshouse, and with the high-resistant tuberculoid leprosy which is believed to have dominated the later strains of the disease.

It has generally been assumed that *leprosaria* were isolation hospitals, with the aim of segregation taking priority over any form of treatment. Nevertheless, some treatment of skin lesions may have been provided, through applications of herbs such as garlic, honeysuckle, nettle, and scabious. Bleeding and bathing of lepers appears to have been practised at some sites (Manchester and Roberts 1989: 270). Indeed, leper hospitals were sometimes associated with wells thought to possess healing qualities, or with medicinal waters, such as St John the Baptist, Bath. This siting may have been in reference to the case of Naaman the Syrian, the leper who was cured by God after bathing in the River Jordan seven times (Kings 2: 1–27). Leper hospitals sited at wells include Harbledown, Peterborough, Newark, Nantwich, Burton Lazars and Tottenham, the last being associated with St Loy's well.

Leper hospitals do not appear to have been provided with elaborate systems of water supply, disposal or drainage, although excavations at Hulton Low Cross (N Yorks), at the supposed site of a leper house, uncovered a building with a built-in drain (*Medieval Archaeol* 11 1967: 80). The extant chapel at Harbledown (Kent) has a sloping floor for which one antiquary posed an intriguing use: the irrigation of the chapel after the lepers attended mass (Hobson 1926). Water courses appear to have been diverted in order to segregate lepers within an island, such as St Margaret, High Wycombe (Bucks) (Farley and Manchester 1989: 84). At Tours (Indre-et-Loire), La Maladerie Saint-Lazarre was established in a marsh between the rivers Loire and Chev, some 800m south of the medieval town walls (*Archéologie Médiévale* 23 1993: 400). Just as the sick poor at the infirmary of St John the Baptist, Oxford, may have been treated in immersion tanks (above), treatment of lepers was aimed at harnessing the medicinal and spiritual properties of water. Lepers were viewed by medieval society as being in a liminal stage between the living and the dead (below). The association of leper hospitals with water may relate to baptism, with its connotations of cleansing, the crossing of boundaries and the 'symmetry of death and rebirth' (Morris 1991: 18).

Because structural evidence survives for very few leper hospitals, it has previously been assumed that they were seldom substantial, planned settlements. Instead, they are believed to have developed organically, with no predetermined plan, and to have consisted of private dwellings adapted for temporary use, often of wood-and-thatch construction (Clay 1909: 109). Excavations at leper houses have indicated well-defined precinct areas, such as the embanked platform marking the leper hospital at New Romney (Kent) (Rigold 1964), and the boundary walls which enclosed three acres at the

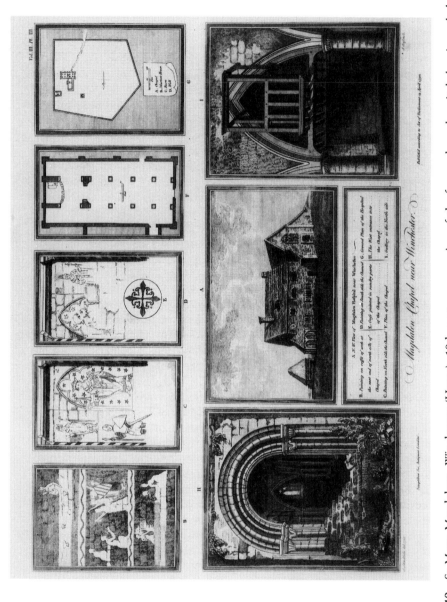

Figure 19 St Mary Magdalene, Winchester (Hants): 18th-century engraving of the former leper hospital showing a lodge set at right angles to the chapel. Reproduced with permission of the Society of Antiquaries from *Vetusta Monumenta* 3 (1796), plate 3.

hospital of St Nicholas, Fife (*Medieval Archaeol* 32 1988: 302). Here, agricultural lands were contained within the precinct and evidence was recovered for clay-lined pits and an oven associated with a structure placed against the boundary wall (Hall, undated interim report). The principal house in England of the order of St Lazarus was on a scale more akin to a monastery. The site of the leper hospital at Burton Lazars (Leics) is marked by an extensive dry moat and a series of fishponds which enclose a rectangular plot of ridge-and-furrow cultivation.

A number of detached chapels survive which indicate that *leprosaria* were not ordered as ranges flanking a cloister. Extant detached chapels include: the Lazar House, Norwich; Harbledown (Kent); St James, Dunwich (Suffolk); and St Mary Magdalene, Stourbridge (Cambs), although documents suggest that this chapel was built after the lepers left the site. A court or close was sometimes formed by the alignment of buildings, particularly where a master or warden's lodge accompanied the chapel, such as the excavated site of SS Stephen and Thomas, New Romney (Kent), where a range nearly abutted the chapel to its north (Rigold 1964: 68). A similar arrangement was recorded in 18th-century drawings of St Mary Magdalene, Winchester, in which a master's lodge is set at right angles to the chapel (*Vetusta Monumenta* 3 1796, plates 1–3) (figure 19). Adjacent to these buildings were a well and an outbuilding identified as a barn. However, accommodation for inmates is notably absent. Originally, individual cells constructed in perishable materials may have been grouped around the chapel, or communal lodging may have been provided in the range labelled 'barn', or in other outlying structures.

It has been suggested that accommodation for leprous inmates would have consisted of cottages or cells grouped around the detached chapel (Clay 1909; Godfrey 1955; Prescott 1992). A contemporary description of Lanfranc's leper hospital at Harbledown (Kent) indicates that lepers were accommodated in small wooden houses set up on the hillside (Clay 1909: 106). The larger houses initially kept communal dormitories, which gave way to individual cells. Where the lodgings of leper hospitals survive, there are indications that communal halls were employed. At St Margaret, Taunton (Somerset), a single-storey hall survives; it was later altered into almshouses. Similarly, at St Mary Magdalene, Glastonbury (Somerset), which seems to have been a leper hospital for poor men, the 13th-century communal hall was not partitioned until the 15th century, when two-room houses were constructed within the shell of the hall (figure 20). Excavations at the leper hospital of St Nicholas, York, revealed a 12th-century aisled structure 20m × 10m. The aisles were created by wooden posts supported on limestone blocks. The central area of the hall contained several pitched tile hearths and the two side aisles were divided into small rooms containing mortar floors and small hearths. This structure was replaced in the 15th century by a narrower hall which was centrally divided (Clarke 1993: 5). A visitation to the hospital at this date confirms that the lepers occupied separate rooms (Clay 1909: 117).

The earliest chapels, such as the 12th-century apsidal example at Dunwich (figure 21), would have lent themselves to the standard arrangements observed for infirmary halls – albeit on a smaller scale. Here a substantial cross-wall divides the chancel, or chapel, from the nave, or hall; a second screen partitioned the presbytery. A similar arrangement has been proposed for the leper

Figure 20   St Mary Magdalene, Glastonbury (Somerset): the 13th-century communal hall was partitioned into two-room houses in the 15th century.

Figure 21   St James, Dunwich (Suffolk): the 12th-century apsidal chapel of the leper hospital. Archaeological deposits have been destroyed by the Victorian burial vault of the Barne family.

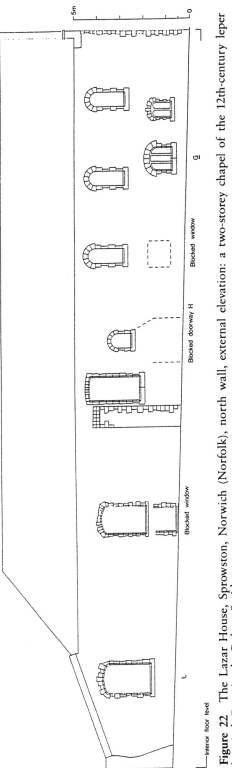

Figure 22 The Lazar House, Sprowston, Norwich (Norfolk), north wall, external elevation: a two-storey chapel of the 12th-century leper hospital. Drawing by Robert Smith.

hospital of St Göran, Visby (Gotland, Sweden), where a possible two-aisled infirmary hall and chancel are structurally integrated (Leistikow 1967: 36). The chapel known as the Lazar House, Norwich, may have provided such an arrangement. It measures approximately 30m in length and retains 12th-century doorways, although these may not be in their original situation. A two-storey arrangement is suggested by upper-storey windows. These appear to be 20th-century renovations, but may shadow medieval windows in the same position (figure 22). Medieval lepers were accommodated in detached cells, partitioned halls and, possibly, western galleries within their chapels.

The siting of leper hospitals, the extent to which they attracted popular support, and the possibility of an iconography of leprosy, all indicate that *leprosaria* fulfilled a variety of practical and spiritual functions more subtle than those of a simple isolation hospital. Indeed, the situation of leper houses was not much different from that of ordinary hospitals. If segregation had been the main aim of English leper hospitals they would have been placed with greater discretion off the main throughfares, and their forms would have been closer to the semi-fortified appearance taken on by some continental houses. For instance, Le Tortoir, Aisne (Laon, France) was built *c*1350 in the form of a square with two-storeyed ranges and imposing corner towers (Leistikow 1967: 34).

Hospices: 'for the comforte of pore straungers'

Certain hospitals were established primarily to provide shelter, hospitality and comfort for strangers. These hospices succoured travelling pilgrims and wayfarers: the mobile rural poor and more affluent travellers. Many were founded privately or by monasteries along the routes to the most popular shrines. These sites had an indirect link with healing, as they were associated with the shrines to which the sick flocked for cure. Shrines were renowned less for sudden miraculous cures than for the gradual improvement experienced by regular pilgrims (Finucane 1977: 76). A network of shrines linked popular medicine and belief with saints approved and venerated by the established church. Hospices along the pilgrims' routes cemented the relationship between popular belief and orthodox worship by providing chapels and accommodation for travellers.

The strong link with pilgrimage is reflected in the distribution and dedications of this category of hospitals. Areas renowned for their shrines, such as Norfolk and Kent, possessed a large number of hospices, many of which were dedicated to saints celebrated by pilgrims. The hospice of Beck (Norfolk), for example, was dedicated to St Thomas of Canterbury. It was established for the reception and entertainment, for a single night, of up to 13 poor travellers or pilgrims on the route to Walsingham, the site of the celebrated shrine to the Virgin. Monasteries established hospices for those travelling to their gates. The abbey of St Benet Hulme (Norfolk) founded two hospices on the causeway leading to the monastery, Hautbois and Horning, in order to serve pilgrims travelling to the shrine of St Theobald at Hautbois. The latter example was established before 1153 by Abbot Daniel, and was administered by the almoner of St Benet's (Knowles and Hadcock 1971: 365).

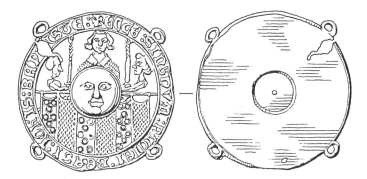

Figure 23 Pilgrim's badge from St Mary Ospringe (Kent): the image shows the face of St John the Baptist, and represents a souvenir of pilgrimage to the relics of St John the Baptist at Amiens Cathedral. Reproduced with permission of the Kent Archaeological Society from *Archaeologia Cantiana* 95 (1980).

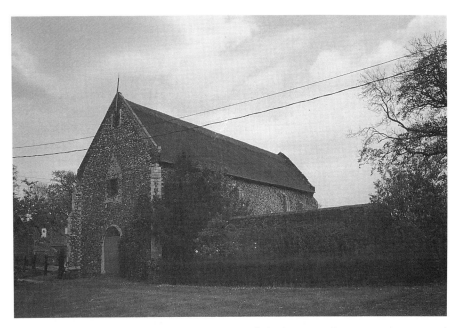

Figure 24 Horning Chapel, Norfolk: chapel of the hospice of St James, maintained by the Abbey of St Benet, Hulme. The 14th-century chapel was detached from any domestic buildings.

The functions fulfilled by hospices were fluid and constantly changing. A hospice might be founded additionally as an almshouse or leper hospital, and their size and complexity varied greatly. Likewise, infirmary hospitals provided hospitality for pilgrims; at Ospringe this function is reflected by the recovery of a leaden pilgrim's badge (figure 23) (Smith 1980: 106). The hospice of St Thomas the Martyr, Canterbury, was founded *c*1175 in order to serve pilgrims. Sited beside a bridge over the River Stour, it survives as a first-floor

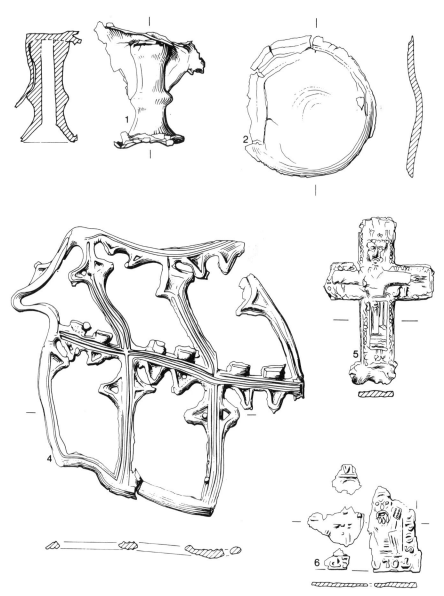

Figure 25   Lead-alloy objects from St Giles by Brompton Bridge, Brough (N Yorks): 1 and 2, chalice and paten from a priest's burial (scale 1:2); 3, lead came from a window; 4, pilgrim's souvenir of the Holy Face, Lucca; 5, pilgrim's badge from SS Peter and Paul, Rome (scale 1:1). Reproduced courtesy of North Yorkshire County Council and Peter Cardwell.

hall over a vaulted undercroft, with adjoining chapel. The two-storey hall and chapel join a vaulted room supported on struts. In contrast, the extant chapel of Horning (Norfolk) was single-storey and detached from any accommodation. The chapel was constructed in knapped flint with ashlar limestone quoins and mouldings (figure 24); the north windows and west door suggest

Figure 26   St Giles by Brompton Bridge, Brough (N Yorks): a reconstruction viewed from the east suggesting the appearance of the hospital in the late 14th century. Reproduced courtesy of North Yorkshire County Council and Peter Cardwell.

a date not earlier than the 14th century. After the Dissolution, its conversion to a farm building involved patching with several phases of rubble and brick and the insertion of an internal upper storey.

   At the hospice of St Giles by Brompton Bridge (Brough, N Yorks), excavations were carried out in advance of river erosion. This hospital was founded before 1181 and sited on the south bank of the River Swale on a medieval route between Swaledale and the Vale of York. St Giles was one of many houses with a dual purpose as hospice and infirmary, in this case also caring for lepers. Its use as a hospice is reflected by pilgrims' souvenirs recovered from the site, including a badge of the Holy Face, from Lucca, and one from SS Peter and Paul, Rome (figure 25). The precinct is defined by the river bank to the north and a steep escarpment to the south. Its layout

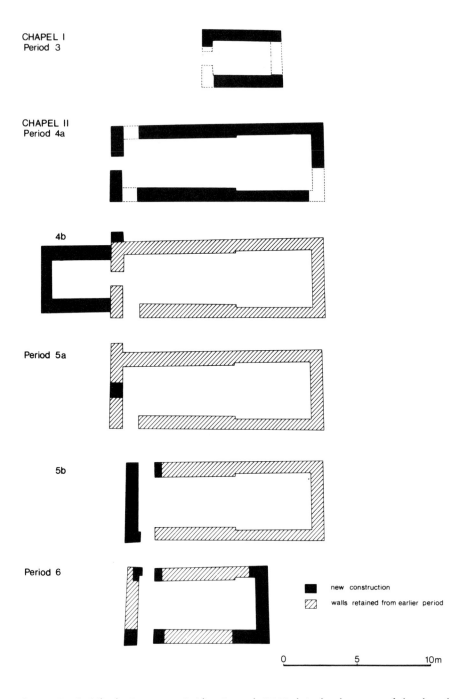

Figure 27 St Giles by Brompton Bridge, Brough (N Yorks): development of the chapel during period 3 (late 12th to mid-13th centuries), period 4 and 5 (mid-13th to late 14th centuries) and period 6 (15th century). Reproduced courtesy of North Yorkshire County Council and Peter Cardwell.

included a detached stone chapel adjacent to the river crossing, with timber buildings to the west. In the 14th century, a guesthouse and dovecote were constructed near the chapel (figure 26). Although originally founded as a male house, St Giles was a mixed community by 1280. The house declined in the 15th century when a new bridge was constructed on another site (Cardwell 1990).

Excavations indicated that the earliest hospital buildings, possibly dating to the 12th century, comprised a timber hall set next to a pebbled yard which was surrounded by stone walls. In the 14th century, a wall was constructed which defined the western limit of the hospital and created an outer yard. A small chapel was built to the east of the site near the river crossing and was separated from the main area of the hospital by a revetted stone bank. This arrangement would have allowed easy access to the chapel for travellers, while protecting the semi-monastic lifestyle of the permanent inmates. This isolated building was a single-cell chapel built in local stone, which was rebuilt and enlarged in the 13th century, according to dated pottery recovered from its foundations (figure 27).

The second chapel was faced in river cobbles and sandstone blocks with internal walls plastered and painted, mainly in red false-jointing which mimicked ashlar. Internal differences in width may have distinguished the nave from the chancel. The floor of the chapel was compacted earth. Post-holes at the west end may have supported a gallery in an arrangement familiar from infirmary chapels. In the 14th century, a west tower was added to the chapel, which itself suffered from structural problems resulting in a change to the positioning of entrances. Eventually, structural problems at the east end of the chapel resulted in the reduction in size of the building, with a new east wall built in mortared stone, used for the first time on the site. A fragment of sculpture recovered from the site represents a portion of a crucifix showing the Virgin Mary at the foot of the cross (figure 28). Although the iconography of the piece is clear, its rough quality makes it difficult to date. The chapel was associated with a cemetery to the south, with 42 burials excavated. A half-timbered guest hall was built to the north of the chapel in the late 14th to early 15th centuries. This structure was equipped with a central hearth and stone-lined garderobe pit; its west end was later partitioned to form a separate chamber (Cardwell 1990).

Brough is likely to be typical of smaller hospitals in terms of the status of its buildings and the materials in which they were built. The early structures were built in timber, to be replaced in stone from local sources in the late 14th century. Only the chapel was built in stone from its earliest inception. However, its earth floor, the late use of mortared stone, and the character of carved stone recovered from the building indicate a fairly low status. Like larger hospitals and monasteries, care was taken at Brough to order space according to functional areas and social groups within the house. The segregation of the chapel from the main complex, and the siting of the half-timbered hall, indicate an arrangement designed to cater for passing pilgrims and travellers.

The fluid and multi-purpose nature of hospices is reflected in their variety of building forms and arrangements. However, these hospitals share associations with major routes of pilgrimage and communication, sited particularly

Figure 28   A Crucifix from St Giles by Brompton Bridge, Brough (N Yorks).

at bridges. According to arrangements at Brough and Horning, detached chapels were provided at hospices in order to facilitate easy access for travellers, and to retain some degree of privacy for permanent inmates of the hospital.

Almshouses: 'for men of good life'

Here, the term 'almshouse' is used to encompass two major categories of hospital distinct from monastic and infirmary hospitals. Earlier examples were founded in order to shelter the aged or infirm; these were often homes for specific groups of elderly (predominantly men), such as mariners or poor priests. Later almshouses founded in the 15th and 16th centuries were residential homes for the poor, often mixed communities and sometimes welcoming married couples. These later foundations were sometimes sponsored by corporate groups, and reflect the growing public and municipal responsibility for welfare provision. At Brentford (Middlesex), for example, the hospital and chapel were administered by the guild of the Nine Orders of Holy Angels. This almshouse was founded at an existing chapel in 1446 in order to serve nine poor men who were weak, impotent, blind, lame or withered (Honeybourne 1963: 56). Some almshouses combined their function with that of a school charity, such as Higham Ferrers (Northants), Ewelme (Oxfords), Tattershall (Lincs) and Heytesbury (Wilts), thus uniting welfare with educational provision.

Earlier almshouses were established for groups of individuals who could no longer care for or support themselves. Almshouses were set up for clergy who had lost their livings as a result of infirmity. At Clyst Gabriel, near

Exeter, accommodation was provided for older priests, curates and chaplains, most commonly suffering from blindness (Orme 1988: 7–8). Here, the retired priests could expect an allowance for food and clothing and accommodation within a walled enclosure which included a chapel, hall, kitchen and dormitory. A similar foundation at Canterbury was established before 1224. At the Poor Priests' Hospital, Canterbury, a hall is arranged at right angles to the chapel (*Medieval Archaeol* 27 1983: 188). Screens separated a service area to the west end from the hall. At the east end was a bench-lined chamber with a fireplace, which seems to have functioned as a warming-room (figure 29).

Almshouses built in the 15th and 16th centuries were based on the collegiate plan, with separate dwellings arranged around a quadrangle. The communal accommodation of earlier almshouses was replaced with individual dwellings which afforded greater privacy. Almshouses built for mixed communities of men and women continued to use two-storey infirmaries in order to facilitate sexual segregation. At Higham Ferrers (Northants) the infirmary of *c*1423 was divided into 13 cubicles, of which those on the upper floor were reserved for the women of the community (Prescott 1992: 69). Perhaps the most celebrated example is Ewelme (Oxfords), built after 1436, in brick. A cloistered courtyard is surrounded by two-storeyed dwellings, each with fireplace, kitchen and garderobe. No special chapel was provided, so that the bedesmen used the south aisle of the parish church. Elsewhere, a special chapel was provided, for example at the Hungerford Almshouses, Corsham (Wilts), where a projecting entrance range contains the chapel and hall; the six two-storeyed dwellings each had separate entrances provided.

Occasionally, almshouses were combined with the foundation of a college. The Maison Dieu, Arundel, was built in 1396 as a hospital and college dedicated to the Holy Trinity. The statutes of the house indicate that it was for '20 poor men, aged or infirm, of good life', and that preference for entry was given to servants or tenants of the patron, the Earl of Arundel (Evans 1969: 66). The brethren of the house wore a common habit: a brown woollen garment with a hood. They were encouraged to occupy themselves with gardening and nursing. Eighteenth-century drawings of the site show that accommodation was ranged around a quadrangle with buildings linked by a pentice walkway. These consisted of a chapel in the north range, a hall as south range, and west and east ranges which contained a master's lodging, brethrens' lodging and a gatehouse. Despite the late date of the Maison Dieu, it seems that communal accommodation was provided in a manner close to that of earlier infirmary hospitals.

Variations on the quadrangular plan include Ford's Hospital, Coventry, which has been described as a 'narrow courtyard plan' (Clay 1909). Ford's was established in 1529, initially for six poor men, and subsequently for five married couples. A narrow court (*c*12 × 3.7m) is surrounded by two ranges of timber-framed dwellings, each designed to communicate with a bed-chamber above (figure 30). The chapel is at one end of the court; the hall at the other. All Saints, or Browne's Hospital, Stamford (Lincs) was completed *c*1490, with a chapel and two-storey hospital under a single roof. The ground-floor living rooms opened into the chapel, with a communal meeting room in the upper storey.

When existing hospitals were renewed, they were remodelled on the

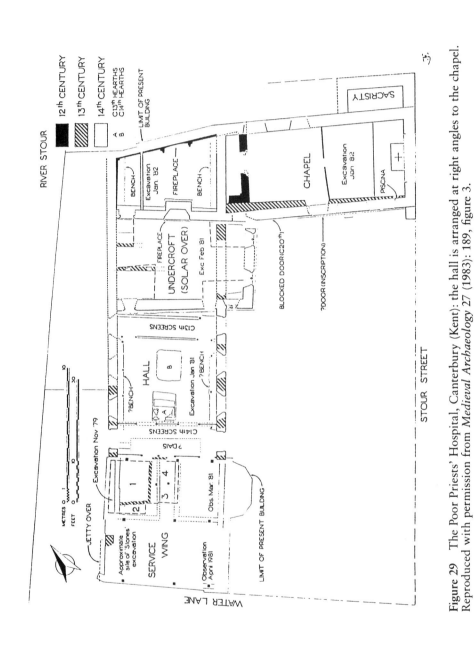

Figure 29 The Poor Priests' Hospital, Canterbury (Kent): the hall is arranged at right angles to the chapel. Reproduced with permission from *Medieval Archaeology* 27 (1983): 189, figure 3.

Figure 30 Ford's Hospital, Coventry (Warwicks): established in 1529 as a narrow courtyard surrounded by two ranges of timber-framed dwellings.

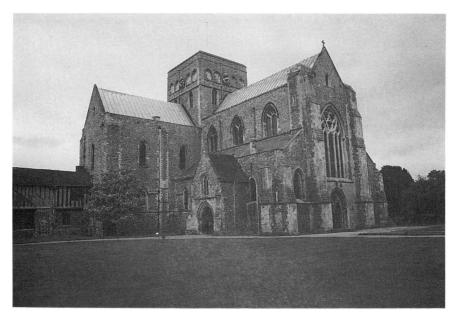

Figure 31   St Cross, Winchester (Hants): the cruciform church, predominantly of the 12th and 13th, century was part of the original foundation by Bishop Henry de Blois.

Figure 32   St Cross, Winchester (Hants): brethrens' houses in the west range of the inner quadrangle of Cardinal Henry Beaufort's 15th-century hospital.

Figure 33 St Cross, Winchester (Hants): interior of the brethrens' hall in the north range of the quadrangle.

collegiate, almshouse arrangement. The hospital of St Cross, Winchester, was first founded in the mid-12th century by Bishop Henry de Blois for the relief of 13 poor men and for the distribution of daily dole to 100 men of good conduct (figure 31). The institution and its buildings were renewed by Bishop William of Wykeham in the 1370s, and expanded further by Cardinal Henry Beaufort shortly defore his death in 1447. Beaufort's hospital provided for two priests, 35 brethren and three sisters, all poor men or women of gentle birth or former members of the Cardinal's household. The new buildings were arranged as an inner quadrangle, entered through a three-storey gatehouse. The brethrens' lodgings were contained in the west and south ranges (the latter now demolished), with their common hall and kitchen in the north range adjacent to the gatehouse (figures 32 and 33).

By the 15th to 16th centuries, new hospitals were built according to plans which allowed a degree of privacy. The piety of later medieval benefactors was channelled into foundations demonstrating a welfare motive which previously seems to have been overshadowed by ecclesiastical functions. These hospitals are testament to an emergent secular movement which acknowledged responsibility for the poor, aged and lonely, and which may have been linked to changing religious beliefs. Late medieval wills suggest that the perceived connection between almsgiving and salvation had been refined somewhat by *c*1500. Works of mercy were considered to be of spiritual note only if they were motivated by genuine charity and dispensed to those in a state of grace (Duffy 1992: 366). These changing attitudes seem to have resulted in an increasing emphasis to target charitable relief towards the honest poor.

Conclusions: the worthy and the 'unclean'

In comparison with larger monastic establishments, hospitals may appear to represent a less-ordered and lower-status type of religious settlement. Measures of economy in building have been suggested by excavations at St Mary Spital, London, and St Bartholomew, Bristol, where in both cases architectural elements were recarved for reuse in programmes of new building. The different functions of hospitals may have resulted in a vocabulary of architectural forms more conservative than that of contemporary mainstream monasticism, more comparable perhaps to parish churches or secular buildings of middling status. Materials used in the construction of hospitals may have varied according to the status of the foundation, with hospices like St Giles by Brompton Bridge, Brough, built exclusively in local materials.

Hospitals were generally arranged around a cloister, courtyard or quadrangle, but like certain categories of monasteries (in particular nunneries, alien priories and preceptories), this arrangement was flexible and loosely ordered. It was not uncommon for cloisters to be placed to the north of churches, contrary to standard monastic ordinances, and for them to be formed simply by pentice walkways placed around the ranges of buildings. In common with monasteries of all types, hospitals adopted closes and courtyards to divide space according to categories of personnel and functional areas within the precinct.

Initially, hospitals of all types, including *leprosaria*, adopted shared accommodation for inmates and patients. As partitioning of common space became usual practice in monasteries, so too did hospitals partition infirmaries. A desire for privacy and the need for private prayer, in addition to a more collegiate purpose, contributed to the widespread adoption of the quandrangular plan which characterises later almshouses. Additional changes included an increased emphasis on sanitation and the provision of fresh water supplies.

Changes in the nature of hospital provision reflect a number of factors, including: fluctuations in urban development and resources, changes in the patterns of disease, developing preferences in the piety of patrons and urban freemen, and the emergence of corporate responsibility for welfare. By the 14th century a growing scarcity of economic resources prompted a more discriminating attitude towards the poor (Rubin 1987: 68–9). Individual patrons and institutions, such as the Benedictine monastery of Westminster, increasingly targeted the worthy, local poor: 'the respectable poor with addresses' (Harvey 1993: 31). In addition to economic factors, the changing meaning attributed to the poor and other stigmatised groups must also be considered . The moral definition of disease is best illustrated by attitudes to leprosy (above), often connected in medieval minds to sin and sexual deviancy. As the threat of leprosy subsided, something of this attitude was transferred to other groups. Later hospital statutes place a stigma similar to that experienced by lepers upon 'lunatics', epileptics and pregnant women who were viewed as being 'dangerously disruptive' (Rawcliffe 1984: 7). In particular, the mentally ill were stigmatised because they were considered to be without reason, and therefore removed from God. The connection of certain diseases with deviancy or demonic possession is demonstrated in an indulgence from Bethlehem Hospital, London, dated 1446 which refers to:

> the multitude of miserable persons of both sexes dwelling there, who are so alienated in mind and so possessed of unclean spirits that they must be restrained with chains and fetters (quoted in Carlin 1989: 34).

More generally, it seems that the poor accommodated in almshouses could occasionally have been viewed as deviant. In addition to the groups of poor priests and others considered worthy of welfare provision, it has been suggested that some almshouses were established with a corrective purpose in mind. In particular, later urban almshouses supervised by town corporations and guilds may have included disciplinary, corrective objectives in their shelter of the poor (Rubin 1987: 127). Some have suggested that charitable provision may have been used more widely as a means of social control, with the foundation of hospitals removing the poor, elderly and sick who may otherwise have constituted a threat to public order (Rosser 1989: 322).

The increasingly secular nature of hospitals resulted both from the development of municipal responsibility and from the mistrust in which monastic hospitals were held. Many hospitals had been accused of financial maladministration (Rawcliffe 1984). Perhaps half of all hospitals were suppressed by 1539, during the Dissolution of the Monasteries; smaller houses survived until the 1547 suppression of chantries. By this time the semi-monastic nature of hospitals had been lost and it was largely the corporately founded, civic hospitals which survived. A handful of others, like the Great Hospital, formerly St Giles, Norwich, survive to the present day after having been transferred to municipal control or private trust.

3 Milites Christi: the archaeology of the Military Orders

Soldiers of Christ

In the 12th century a new form of monasticism emerged from the conflict between East and West in the Holy Land. The Christian military and religious fervour which focused on Jerusalem resulted in an innovative monasticism: Military Orders of knights who were dedicated to fighting for God, but who were at the same time professed monks. Their members displayed the same degree of self-sacrifice which was required to join the more mainstream monastic orders. However, theirs was an active vocation. These *Milites Christi* were prepared to give their own lives to God in defence of the Holy Land.

In order to fund their castles and hospitals in the East, the Military Orders required convents in the West which acted as centres of production and points of collection for dues and voluntary contributions. In Britain, the most populous Military Orders were the Knights Hospitaller and Templar, whose settlements were known respectively as commanderies or preceptories. Here the term preceptory is used to encompass monasteries of all the Military Orders. Although some preceptories observed a fully monastic routine, many were engaged primarily in agricultural production. Consequently, their archaeology has been considered alongside that of manors or granges. Previously, houses of the Military Orders have been omitted from standard works on monastic settlement, prompting G.H. Cook to lament 'Unfortunately nothing is known of the arrangement of the conventual buildings of the English priories of the Knightly Orders' (Cook 1961: 202). Even the most recent works evaluate the remains of preceptories as examples of granges (Coppack 1990: 125–7; Greene 1992: 136–9; Aston 1993: 82), neglecting any discussion of their more monastic aspects.

This chapter considers the archaeology of the Military Orders in Britain, with comparisons drawn from their holdings in Europe and the East. First, the Military Orders are introduced together with their administrative frameworks, patrons and categories of membership. Second, the morphology of monasteries of the Military Orders is presented according to a hierarchy of sites, with consideration of evidence for settlement layout, buildings, agricultural production and iconography. Comparisons are drawn between preceptories and contemporary types of settlement, both secular and religious, in order to address the question: was the preceptory a manor, a grange or a monastery?

The Military Orders were established after the First Crusade and the subsequent occupation of Jerusalem by crusaders from 1099. The Knights of the Temple of Solomon of Jerusalem (the Templars) were established c1120 and confirmed c1127–9, in part of the former al-Aqsa mosque, thought to be the Temple of Solomon. They attended divine offices sung by the canons regular at the church of the Holy Sepulchre. Knights of the Temple took monastic vows of poverty, chastity and obedience; their earliest purpose was to escort pilgrims along the road to Jerusalem (Forey 1992: 6). The Knights of St John of Jerusalem (the Hospitallers) began as a fraternity serving a hospice for poor and sick pilgrims adjacent to the Holy Sepulchre. The Hospitallers were recognised as an order in 1113, and had, from the start, a more charitable role; they maintained hospitals in the Holy Land and ransomed Christian captives. Other orders included those of the Hospital of St Mary of the Teutons in Jerusalem (the Teutonic Knights), the Knights of St Lazarus, and the Knights of St Thomas of Acre (or Acon), originally known as the Military Order of St Thomas the Martyr of Canterbury. The Knights of St Thomas were founded at Acre by the chaplain of Ralph of Diceto, Dean of St Paul's, but the order itself subsequently claimed to have been established by Henry II (Forey 1977: 482). The order of St Lazarus began in the 1130s as a leper hospital outside the walls of Jerusalem; its first military activity was not until La Forbie in 1244 (Nicholson 1993: 5). The primary aim of these orders was the protection of pilgrims journeying to the Holy Land. They assumed an increasingly military role, however, due to the shortage of fighting personnel in the crusader states. Eventually, their central purpose was the defeat of the enemies of Christendom, which included not just the defence of Jerusalem, but, as Military Orders spread across Europe, the defeat of Muslims in 12th-century Spain and the suppression of pagans and heretics in 13th-century central and eastern Europe. Between 1147 and 1505, successive popes sanctioned crusades around the Baltic area against the pagans of the North, mainly involving the Teutonic Knights (Christiansen 1980).

The Military Orders represented a new kind of monasticism. Despite the contradiction which may be perceived between the contemplative nature of monasticism and the violence of warfare, the orders received the support of the most respected churchmen, including St Bernard of Clairvaux, who defended the Hospitallers together with the concept of Christian warfare and the knight-monk: 'Indeed the soldiers of Christ fearlessly fight the battles of their Lord ... for a death either inflicted or suffered for Christ has nothing of sin in it but merits much glory' (*Sancti Bernardi Opera* 3: 217, quoted in Forey 1992: 17). The Military Orders were pledged to follow a monastic rule; those of the Hospitallers, Templars and Knights of St Lazarus followed the basis of the Rule of St Augustine, the shortest and most flexible of the monastic rules. Recruits underwent a period of novitiate, followed by the taking of monastic vows and the donning of a habit. The Hospitallers were identified by a white cross, and the Templars by a red cross. Convents in the West observed the monastic hours of prayer (*horarium*) and employed priests wherever no chaplain of the order was resident. Members of the Military Orders seldom followed an intellectual vocation. They were not expected to sing the offices or spend time in individual reading. Significantly, recent excavations at the British headquarters of St John of Jerusalem at Clerkenwell have not yielded any artefacts associated with literacy, in contrast to all other monasteries excavated in the city. Monastic meditation and contemplation were replaced by military training and administration. In contrast to secular knights, knight-monks were expected to observe a certain modesty in dress and diet. They ate twice a day, during which time they would hear readings, and were allowed meat only three times a week. It seems that one secular pastime was especially difficult to give up: frequent prohibitions were issued to the Military Orders for them to cease hunting and hawking (Forey 1992: 192).

Membership of the Orders was threefold: knights, who were required to be of appropriate descent; sergeants, who were freemen; and non-military sergeants, who acted as administrators. Because priests were not allowed to bear arms, the knights remained untonsured, and required clerics to perform church services. Consequently, there were in addition chaplains of the orders. The Templar Rule demanded of knightly recruits, 'Are you a knight and the son of a knight, or are you descended from knights through your father, in such a way that you should and may be a knight?' (Upton-Ward 1992: 115). At first the Templars observed a strict hierarchy in which only knights were allowed to wear white – symbolic of the purity associated with knighthood – and only they could occupy office within the order. Knights and chaplains were seated first at table, while the sergeants were summoned by a second bell, although both ranks shared the same repast (Forey 1992: 177). Like other monastic orders, the knights began by sharing common dormitories. By the 14th century the larger preceptories possessed individual quarters, and the master was expected to have a separate chamber (Forey 1992: 193). It was expected that preceptories should be governed by knights. In the West, however, it was not uncommon for sergeants to take over this responsibility where knights were not resident. In Britain in 1338, there were 31 knights, 47 sergeants and 78 laymen resident in the 37 Hospitaller preceptories, of which 17 were governed by sergeants and four by chaplains.

The more charitable purpose of the Hospitallers required that their order include sisters and lay-sisters to oversee the running of hospitals. Across Europe there were, in total, 41 houses of sisters of St John of Jerusalem. Occasionally, these were arranged as double houses. At Sigena in Aragon (Spain), for example, there were adjacent communities of knights and sisters, the whole complex being under the authority of the prioress. In England, all sisters of the order lived at Buckland (Somerset) from c1180, when they were gathered together from nine different nunneries of the order. At Buckland the sisters were under the authority of the prior of the adjacent preceptory. According to the inventory of the order taken in 1338, their community numbered 50 sisters, two chaplains of the order and one secular chaplain. The adjacent preceptory of Buckland, in contrast, was occupied by only six brothers and one corrodian (Larking 1857: 19).

Given the more overtly military nature of the Templars, it is not surprising to find that their Rule explicity forbade the acceptance of women to the order. In practice, however, women occasionally attached themselves to Templar houses in the West. Records of the English province from the Inquest of the order in 1185 include a number of widows who payed annual dues *pro fraternitate*. At Cardington (Shrops), in the bailiwick of Warwick, two widows called Matilda and one called Edith paid between one and six pence for their fraternity (Lees 1935: 38–9). The fraternity seems to have been a body of people who affiliated themselves with the Templar or Hospitaller order by paying an annual contribution. More remarkable is the example of Joan Chaldese, who took a vow of chastity and was received as a sister of the Templar order, according to a charter dated c1189–93 associated with Saddlecombe (Sussex) (Lees 1935: 210). Details of annual payments made by the English Templars are recorded in the Close Rolls of Edward II, where they were listed following the confiscation of Templar property. This information includes evidence of the presence of female corrodians at Templar preceptories. The corrodian Agnes received her pension in return for a cash gift of 100 marks, a wood and 80 acres of land (Forey 1992: 106). Some women may have become associated with the Military Orders when their husbands joined as knights. The *Curia Regis Rolls* for 1223–4 suggest that in at least one case the Hospitaller preceptory at Buckland received a husband and wife together, although Alice Fitzmuriel later claimed that she had been placed in the house on the orders of her husband William and against her own will (Forey 1992: 137).

In contrast to other monastic orders, the Military Orders never observed a model of filial organisation. Instead, the Templars divided their holdings into regional units known as provinces; those of the Hospitallers were known as priories. The English Province included Wales, Scotland and Ireland and its holdings were divided into administrative areas known as bailiwicks. The bailiwick could comprise a region, shire or group of villages. The preceptory in charge of the bailiwick administered properties and collected the *confraria*, the contribution which was due for the upkeep of holdings in the East. Traditionally, this contribution consisted of one-third of the annual income of the preceptory. In some areas the bailiwick system was highly developed, particularly in Lincolnshire, whereas in others it was hardly known. In the Templar Inquest of 1185, the following bailiwicks are noted: London, Kent, Warwick, Weston (Herefords), Yorkshire, Ogerston (Hunts and Northants), Lincolnshire, and the Lincolnshire *baillie* of South Witham, Lindsey, Cabourn, Tealby, Goulceby and the Soke of Bolingbroke. Templar preceptories in Essex, Kent, Oxfordshire, Gloucestershire and Hertfordshire consisted of compact manorial holdings, whereas the bailiwicks of the northern counties were structured with a preceptory as the centre of a wide area of outlying semi-independent estates (Lees 1935: xxxvi).

The administrative unit of the Hospitallers was the *titulus*. At first, English properties may have been held by the priory of St Gilles in France until the establishment of the English headquarters of the order at Clerkenwell, London, c1144. Until the 14th century, all English manors were administered by the central house in London (Gervers 1982: liii). Subsequently, bailiwicks were formed centred on the main preceptories of each region. For example, properties in Wales were divided across diocesan boundaries, with Dinmore administering estates in Hereford and Llandaff, Slebech overseeing west Wales, and Halston responsible for properties in north Wales (Rees 1947: 19–20). The head of the order of St Thomas of Acre in London had authority over all holdings in England and Ireland while Burton Lazars (Leics) administered all houses and properties of the Knights of St Lazarus in England.

The central unit was the preceptory and its properties in the surrounding area. The English preceptories were regulated by visitations from the provincial headquarters of the order. For instance, in 1338 the Prior of the English Hospitallers spent 121 days visiting houses of the order, spending up to three days at each one (Forey 1992: 167). Decisions were taken at local chapter meetings on issues such as the admission of postulants, dispensing justice and financial and military matters; regular chapters of the provinces were also held.

The process of founding a preceptory seems to have been somewhat different from that observed for establishing monasteries of other orders. By the 1120s, the Military Orders were actively acquiring land in western Europe. Parcels of land were donated to the orders, but a preceptory was not initiated until a donor provided the means for building the *domus* (Burton 1991: 31). At Temple Newsam (W Yorks), for instance, Templar influence was consolidated through a combination of land grant, sale and exchange (ibid.: 29). The Hospitallers worked actively to obtain properties in areas which suited them. Their vast holdings in Essex were built up from a grant in *c*1125 of 80 acres in north-west Essex, which was subsequently consolidated by large numbers of small grants. From the cartulary of the order it seems that the Hospitallers planned and built up demesnes by courting lesser landholders who could contribute to the gradual accumulation of their concentrated holdings. It was not until 1151 that the first Essex preceptory was made possible by a grant of the parish church of Chaureth and its appurtenant lands by Alfred and Sibyl de Bendaville. In the years that followed, the holdings of Chaureth were supplemented by grants of land in the adjacent parish. By the end of the 12th century, the Hospitallers had accrued a significant landed estate in north central and north-west Essex, administered by Chaureth. In 1225, the church and vill of Little Maplestead was donated by Juliana, daughter of Robert Doisnel, and her husband William, son of Audelin, and Maplestead assumed the role of central preceptory for the Essex Hospitallers (Gervers 1982: xxxvi). Over a period of 100 years the Hospitallers had developed extensive estates from the basis of a single grant of land.

In comparison with monasteries of other orders, the foundation of a preceptory was a gradual process achieved in areas where the Military Orders had made a concerted effort to direct their influence. Patrons tended to be local, as demonstrated by the cartulary of the house of St Lazarus at Burton Lazars (Leics). Ninety per cent of donors came from within five miles of the preceptory (Walker 1990: 171). Preceptories administered estates which had been built up piecemeal from small to middling landowners whose sympathies had been earned. Moreover, these estates were developed in areas which seem to have been targeted by the orders. Although preceptories were eventually established across Britain (figure 34), the Templars seem to have been especially attracted first to Lincolnshire and Yorkshire; the Hospitallers concentrated their earliest attention on Essex and Cambridgeshire. Some monastic orders, particularly the Cistercians, were given waste land in order that they should reclaim it to consolidate their holdings. However, the Hospitallers in Essex accepted only arable land (Gervers 1982: xl). In contrast, the Templars reclaimed tracts of land at Temple Bruer (Lincs) and Temple Newsam (Yorkshire) and assarted woodland at Garway (Herefords). Both orders concentrated their economic base in arable farming, a pattern repeated in Ireland where the Templars grew extensive tracts of wheat and the Hospitallers were overseers of milling and granaries (Falkiner 1907: 291). Like the Cistercians, the Military Orders sometimes depopulated villages in their replanning of the landscape. Earthworks at Shingay (Cambs) represent one such example (Haigh 1988: 79).

What motives lay behind patronage of the Military Orders and its impact on the landscape? Christian kings considered it their obligation to protect God's lands. Stephen and Matilda gave generously to the Temple, and the order of St Lazarus received an annual royal pension from 1184 (Nicholson 1993: 16–17); Henry III contributed financially to the Prussian Crusade led by the Teutonic Knights (Christiansen 1980: 3). In common with the patrons of all monasteries, those of the Military Orders hoped, in return, to receive prayers for their souls and, perhaps, the right to be buried within a preceptory. In addition, however, the crusading cause served as an advertisement for the orders in the West. Grants of land to the Knights Templar in Yorkshire were particularly concentrated in the 1140s and 1150s and again in the 1180s and 1190s after Richard I joined the Third Crusade, suggesting a rough correlation between the Crusades and attention given to the order (Burton 1991: 31). In Essex, grants of land peaked in the mid-13th century during the time that Jerusalem had been regained for Christendom (1229–44) (Gervers 1982: xlvi); this was also a period which saw the rebuilding or extension of preceptories and churches at South Witham (Lincs), Garway (Herefords), and Rothley (Leics), among others. It seems that the patrons of the Military Orders were, in effect, armchair crusaders. They were not themselves active in the Crusade, but they supported the sentiment behind the Orders: the regaining of Jerusalem for Christendom. Indeed, there was little correlation between those who actually went on crusade and those who endowed the Military Orders. Janet Burton has suggested that 'endowment of a preceptory was seen as a suitable method for commuting a crusading vow' (Burton 1991: 31). It has been proposed that the knightly classes may have found the Military Orders more accessible than other religious, since the Templars in particular were portrayed in literature as sharing the interests of secular knights and fighting alongside them (Nicholson 1993: 62).

Occasionally, a lord's crusading efforts resulted in patronage shown to the orders by his tenants, for example in the case of Roger de Mowbray, whose Yorkshire tenants began to grant land to the Templars after his first crusade to the Holy Land (Burton 1991: 34). Donations were made by the families of those entering Military Orders and by landowners who themselves joined, including Robert de Ros II, founder of Ribston (Yorks). Families sometimes showed particular allegiance to an order, such as the Sandford family who founded the Templar preceptory of Sandford (Oxfords), and the de Clares, Earls of Hertford and Pembroke, who founded the Hospitaller preceptory at Carbrooke (Norfolk), and gave other property to the order. Ceramic floor tiles bearing the arms of Clare have been recovered from the outer precinct of the order's headquarters at Clerkenwell.

From the late 12th century all preceptories were entitled to have graveyards, and the Bishop of London formally permitted the burial of outsiders from 1248. In return for their gifts to the order patrons could be buried in the precinct of a religious house. In addition, the Hospitallers sometimes took on responsibility for the burial of hanged criminals who had subscribed to their fraternity of St John the Baptist (Pugh 1981: 567). Others made substantial contributions in return for lifetime corrodies of the order, including Simon of Odewell and his wife Margaret who gave 350 acres to the Essex Hospitallers in 1242 and were granted, in return, lifetime corrodies and the Hospitallers' manor at Coddenham (Suffolk) (Gervers 1982: xliii). Donations to the Military Orders were made from all social levels, from reigning monarchs to smallholders, and, in contrast to other monastic orders, the Military Orders remained attractive beneficiaries well into the 13th century. Estates ceased to grow from 1279, when the Statute of Mortmain prohibited religious houses to receive land without royal licence. Throughout England and France donations of land to the Military Orders began to decline in general after 1200, although in Germany and eastern Europe donations continued throughout the later middle ages (Nicholson 1993: 59, 75).

Criticisms were levied against the Military Orders from the 13th century, after the failure of the Third Crusade and the final loss of Jerusalem in 1244. Many believed that their vast wealth had not been used to best effect for protecting the Holy Land. While the Hospitallers had continued to develop their charitable role, the Templars became adept bankers, specialising in loaning, storing and transporting monies, what C.H. Lawrence called 'a kind of medieval Securicor' (Lawrence 1984: 174). When the crusader states finally collapsed in 1291, after the loss of Acre to the sultan of Egypt, the Templar Order was easily identified as the scapegoat. Having lost the final Christian stronghold in the Holy Land, the Military Orders might have been perceived to have lost their very reason for existence (Nicholson 1993: 125).

From Cyprus the Hospitallers conquered Rhodes in 1306–10, and continued to channel their energies and funds into the island until the 16th century. A different fate was set for the Templars, whose wealth and arrogance had antagonised western monarchs. In 1307–11, the Templars were questioned on charges of heresy at the bidding of Philip IV of France; they were accused of sodomy, excessive secrecy, not believing in the eucharist, not making charitable gifts or practising hospitality (Nicholson 1993: 6). Many of the confessions which were extracted were later recanted, but in 1310, 54 Templars were burnt. Most vulnerable to attack was their admission ceremony, which involved a denial of Christ as a test of obedience. During such ceremonies knights of the order were encouraged to spit on the cross. While the motives behind the suppression of the Templars were more political than religious, rumours of idolatory, heresy, witchcraft and strange rituals have surrounded the order from its dissolution up to the present day.

Pope Clement V dissolved the Templar Order in 1312 and decreed that its lands pass to the Hospitallers. In France, most Templar properties were retained by the Crown; in England they had been seized by Edward II in 1308. He did not surrender them to the Hospitallers until 1314, and even then the acquisition of all properties required the implementation of Parliamentary statutes in 1324 and 1325. Following the fall of the crusader states and the controversial suppression of the Templars, the crusading movement lost favour. The Hospitallers bore the costs of acquiring and maintaining Templar properties, and the fortification of the order's headquarters in Rhodes. Interest in the Military Orders began to wane, and for the Hospitallers neither Jerusalem nor the prosperity of the 12th and 13th centuries were ever regained.

An archaeology of the Military Orders

In England and Wales a total of 70 Templar and 66 Hospitaller preceptories were established in the 12th and 13th centuries (figure 34). Many of these were founded after 1200, when the planting of new monasteries was rare. Thirty-four Templar preceptories were established by 1200, and 36 more afterwards; 34 Hospitaller preceptories (or commanderies) were in place by 1200, and 32 after this date (Knowles and Hadcock 1971). In Scotland there were only three Templar and three Hospitaller preceptories (Cowan and Easson 1976), and in Ireland there were 16 Templar and 21 Hospitaller preceptories (Gwynn and Hadcock 1970). In addition, the Military Orders held extensive lands and an unknown number of *camerae* in each country.

The headquarters of the Knights of St Thomas of Acre was established in London by the late 1220s (Forey 1977: 484), and served as a hospital for the poor and sick staffed by a master and 12 brethren. There were two dependent hospitals in England and two in Ireland. The order of St Thomas of Acre followed the Teutonic Rule up to the mid-14th century, when it ceased to be a Military Order, but retained its hospitaller function.

The Knights of St Lazarus had only one regular preceptory in England at Locko (Derbys), where a preceptory and hospital were attached. This preceptory was an alien priory which owed allegiance to the headquarters of the order in Boigny, near Orleans (VCH Derbys II 1907: 77). Smaller leper hospitals of the order, of which there were 12 in England, were dependent on the head hospital of Burton Lazars (Leics). Responsibility for Burton Lazars was taken over by the Hospitallers in 1414, when houses of St Lazarus, together with the other alien priories, were confiscated by the Crown, as enemy assets, pending a cessation of hostilities between France and England.

Due to their strong links with agriculture, preceptories were located predominantly in the medieval countryside. Where they were associated with towns, preceptories were sited in the more sparsely populated, semi-agricultural suburbs. Suburban sites included the headquarters of the orders in London, the Templar preceptories of Dover, Dunwich and Warwick, and the Hospitaller houses of Beverley and Lincoln. Dover stood in a fairly isolated position, on the cliffs between the town and port. Only a single preceptory, South Witham (Lincs), has been fully excavated, although a number have been subject to partial examination. South Witham was excavated by Philip Mayes in the 1960s (Mayes forthcoming); more piecemeal excavations have been carried out, principally at Clerkenwell (London), Denney (Cambs), Temple Cressing (Essex), Skelton (W Yorks) and Beverley (E Yorks).

A settlement hierarchy can be proposed for preceptories on the basis of their administrative structure and its relationship to the form and function of military monasteries. At the pinnacle of this hierarchy were the mother houses in London, with larger and more elaborately constructed buildings than their dependents. The mother houses were supported by larger and smaller preceptories. The larger houses, often the head of bailiwicks, consisted of a manor with its parish church, tenants and lands. Smaller preceptories were defined by lesser land holdings and were provided with a private chapel. At the base of the hierarchy were the *camerae* which, like the granges of other orders, were farms specialising in arable agriculture, pastoralism, dairying or fish-

Figure 34   Distribution of Templar and Hospitaller Preceptories in medieval Britain: based on Knowles and Hadcock (1971), Gwynn and Hadcock (1970) and Cowan and Easson (1976).

keeping. The administrative term *camera* was used by the orders to refer to smaller preceptories without a resident preceptor; Hospitaller *camerae* therefore paid their *confraria* directly to Clerkenwell. Hence, the religious rank of the settlement could change status according to whether a preceptor was resident. Here the term is used to refer to working farms of the Military Orders, which can be distinguished morphologically from larger and smaller preceptories, and where a continuous conventual life was not observed.

The headquarters of the English Province

The headquarters of the Hospitallers in Clerkenwell was founded on 10 acres of land given by Jordan de Bricet and his wife Muriel de Munten, who also founded the neighbouring nunnery of St Mary Clerkenwell. From *c*1135 the Temple had its headquarters in Holborn but moved to the Temple by 1185. In common with all the major churches of the Military Orders, those of the English headquarters were built with a round nave, a form of iconographic architecture representing the church of the Holy Sepulchre in Jerusalem (see below pp. 94–5). The spatial organisation of the church was affected by the social composition of the Military Orders, which was divided between knights and sergeants who remained untonsured, and the chaplains of the order who performed church services. At first, members of the order were seated in the nave, so that only small presbyteries were required. At Templar Garway (Herefords) and Hospitaller Torphichen (W Lothian), this is reflected in the configuration of the chancel arch, which is ornamented only on its west face, and which would have been viewed by the knights and sergeants in the nave.

At the headquarters in Clerkenwell and Temple the choirs were rebuilt within 50 years of their construction. Both orders replaced the original narrow, apsidal chancels with rectangular, three-aisled structures of four to five bays in length. The Temple church was consecrated in 1185 and survives today, although much rebuilt after bomb damage in the Second World War (figure 35). The central area of the round nave is divided from an encircling aisle by six clustered piers of Purbeck marble that carry a clerestory, providing a lantern effect. The main western entrance was enclosed by a porch in 1195, with three open sides. Inside the church, eight Purbeck marble effigies of knights of the order survive on grave slabs (figure 36). Clerkenwell is reported to have been badly damaged and burnt in the Peasants' Revolt of 1381, although archaeological investigations of the site have revealed no evidence for this. The church was rebuilt with a rectangular aisled nave of six bays, with a massive northwest bell-tower attached. The aisles of the chancel were raised on vaulted crypts. The surviving western part of the Norman crypt of 1144 was built with rounded arches with ribbed vaulting springing from flat pilasters raised on a stone bench against the side walls, and showing traces of chevron decoration.

The claustral buildings of the Hospitallers at Clerkenwell were located to the south of the choir, with additional buildings to the north (Hudson 1902). They seem to have been arranged around a central courtyard or cloister, according to an engraving made by Hollar in 1661 for Sir William Dugdale's *Monasticon Anglicanum*. Excavations have uncovered 12 burials in the area to the north of the nave. Of nine adult skeletons, two were women, one of whom died in childbirth. Four of the individuals may have suffered from rickets, and perhaps represent inmates of the infirmary associated with the site (Conheeney in Sloane and Malcolm in preparation). The cloisters are known to have been rebuilt in 1283–4 (Clapham 1911–15: 37). Recent excavations have revealed a series of stone and timber buildings and cesspits in the area of the outer precinct (Atkinson and Malcolm 1990), including evidence for a stone building over an undercroft. A massive gatehouse was built in 1504 by the Prior Thomas Docwra (figure 37), who remodelled many

Figure 35   The Temple Church, London: the round nave consecrated in 1185.

Figure 36   Effigies of Templar Knights, London Temple: in the foreground, Gilbert Marshall, fourth Earl of Pembroke, d.1241; in the background, an unknown knight.

Figure 37   St John's Clerkenwell, London: gatehouse of the headquarters of the English Hospitallers. The gatehouse was built in 1504 by Prior Thomas Docwra.

of the preceptory's buildings. The gatehouse survives, built in brick with a facing of ragstone, with a ribbed vault bearing two shields of the order, the arms of Docwra and an *Agnus Dei*. A survey of the lead of the priory's roofs made in 1546 gives the dimensions of several of the buildings, which included a dormitory 120 feet long, a refectory 105 feet long, and a 'Yeoman's Dorter', possibly a dormitory for lower-ranking members of the order (Clapham 1911–15: 44). Other buildings included the armoury, parlour, Lord's chamber and counting house. A great barn seems to have been located in the south-western corner of the precinct, and the prior's mansion house was on the east side (Wooldridge 1990). The water supply for the house was drawn from the head at 'Commander's Mantell' in Barnsbury, and two conduit houses are shown on the famous plan of the water supply of the adjacent Charterhouse (Bond 1993). Recent excavations have revealed contrasting areas of land use between the inner, walled precinct and the outer precinct, the latter initially characterised by piecemeal development of timber buildings with evidence for quarrying and industry. After 1300, the outer precinct developed to include structures with chalk foundations associated with cesspits, chalk-lined wells and clay floors. High-quality, innovative architecture is also indicated in the area of the outer precinct during the later middle ages, where fragments of moulded bricks and terracotta mouldings in red and white clay have been recovered from the area of a mansion house (*c*1500–20), which was located close to the extant gatehouse (Sloane and Malcolm in preparation).

Larger preceptories

In common with monasteries of other orders, large and small preceptories were enclosed within precincts. These were most often defined by moats or bank and ditch, which enclosed areas containing halls, a chapel and agricultural and industrial buildings. The majority of sites were enclosed by moats, including even suburban preceptories like Hospitaller Beverley, where excavations have shown that the moat was formed by a massive ditch at least 1.9m in depth. The moat enclosed a rectangular island of *c*83m (east–west) by 121m (north–south), with a resulting precinct of *c*1ha (*Medieval Archaeol* 36 1992: 243). The rectangular moat at Temple Balsall (Warwicks) can be reconstructed from an estate map of 1690 (VCH Warwicks 1969 8: 466); that at Chibburn (Northumb) survives as a series of earthworks 100m across. The moats or banks of most preceptories acted as boundaries, rather than defences, and in the late 12th and 13th centuries moated sites were symbolic of gentry status and synonymous with manorial settlement. For the Military Orders, an additional symbolic impetus towards moat-building may have been inspired by their connections with Jerusalem, the fortifications of which included a moat, main wall and outer wall (Prawer 1985). Larger preceptories were provided with gatehouses controlling ingress to the precinct, such as the 13th-century example at Quenington (Gloucs), with a postern doorway with image niche above. In 1306, Temple Bruer (Lincs) was granted a licence to crenellate a great and strong gate (St John Hope 1908: 181). The defensive capabilities of the Irish preceptories were more tangible, and seem to have assisted in the process of Anglo-Norman domination. At the Hospitaller site

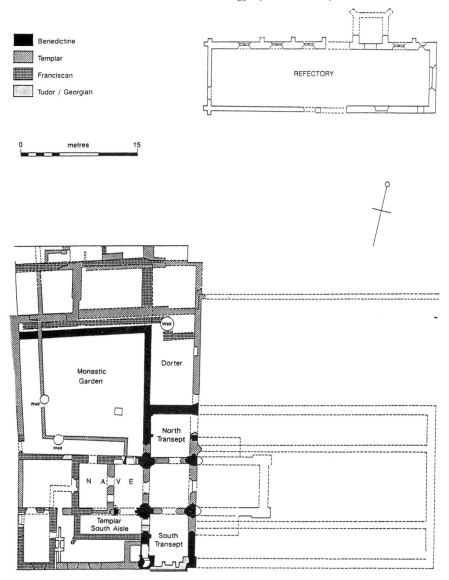

Figure 38 Denney (Cambs): plan of excavated features and standing buildings showing development of the Benedictine monastery, Templar preceptory and Franciscan nunnery. Based on Christie and Coad (1980).

of Kilteel (Kildare, Eire) the preceptory was built on the line of the system of ditch defences protecting the Pale (Manning 1981–2).

Although generally preceptories were not provided with cloisters, their conventual buildings were sometimes grouped around a central space. At Denney (Cambs) this space was a garden (figure 38) (Christie and Coad 1980). At Chibburn (Northumb), and possibly Dinmore (Herefords), ranges provided a formal courtyard; and at South Witham (Lincs) buildings were

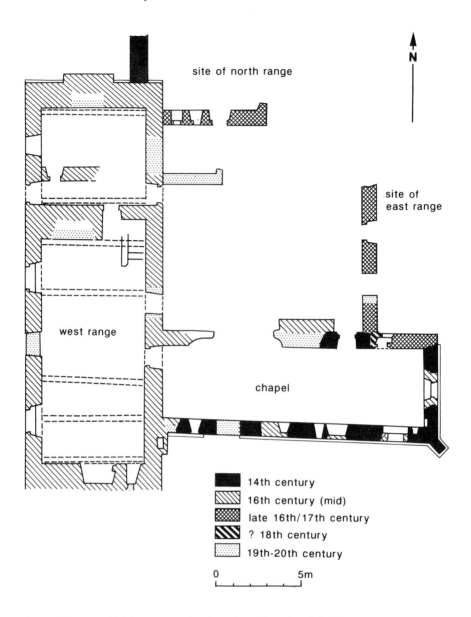

site of north range

N

site of
east range

west range

chapel

■ 14th century

▨ 16th century (mid)

▒ late 16th/17th century

▧ ? 18th century

░ 19th-20th century

0   5m

Figure 39 Low Chibburn (Northumb): plan of medieval buildings. Based on Ryder (1991 unpub).

tucked within the perimeter of the earthwork apparently in order to leave an empty central space (figure 44), although little of the central area was actually excavated. Typical arrangements may be suggested by the remains of the Hospitaller site at Low Chibburn (figure 39), where the dating of the courtyard and its ranges has been subject to many contradictory interpretations. A recent reassessment by Peter Ryder has suggested that only the south-range chapel can be assigned a medieval date; the other ranges represent post-

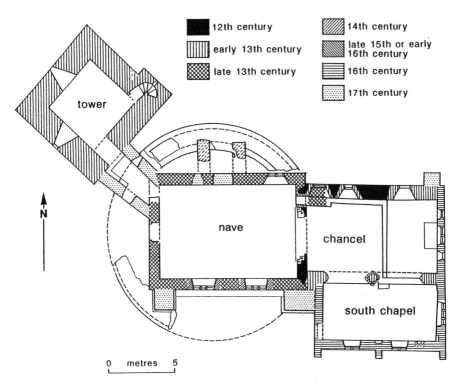

■ 12th century	▨ 14th century	
▥ early 13th century	▧ late 15th or early 16th century	
▨ late 13th century	▤ 16th century	
	▦ 17th century	

Figure 40 Garway (Herefords): the excavated round nave and plan of the 13th-century church and 14th-century detached tower. Based on the RCHME (1931–4).

Dissolution echoes of the former plan (Ryder 1991 unpub). Space within preceptories was ordered centrally, and access between buildings and work areas was provided by roadways, such as the cobbled paths excavated at the *camera* of Etton (E Yorks) (*Medieval Archaeol* 12 1968: 170).

Larger preceptories may have been distinguished from smaller ones not only by their greater land holdings and administrative status, but by the functions served by their chapels. Those of larger houses were shared as the parish church for the preceptory's manorial tenants, and were located near the main hall of the preceptory. At Baddesley (Hants), the church was situated across from the manor house of the preceptory, and at Quenington (Gloucs) the Hospitallers situated their preceptory adjacent to the existing parish church, where excavations revealed very substantial foundations, probably of a hall (*Medieval Archaeol* 16 1972: 173).

Many of the larger preceptories followed the mother houses in adopting a round nave symbolic of the Holy Sepulchre (figure 40). At Garway (Herefords) a detached tower was built to the south of the round nave (figure 41), and at Temple Bruer (Lincs) the apsed east end was replaced by a straight-headed bay flanked by two large square towers. The extant south-eastern tower was recorded by Sir William St John Hope as being 18m high and decorated with ornate corbels, indicating a date of *c*1200. It contains an elaborately arcaded ground storey, which may have served as a chapel or even chapter-house (St

Figure 41   Garway (Herefords): a detached tower was built to the south of the nave.

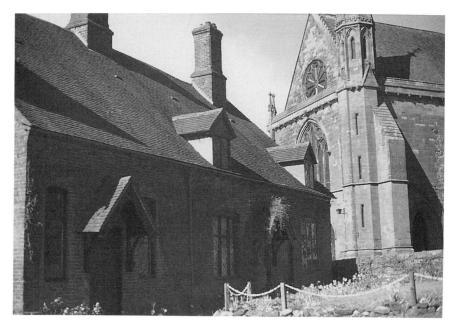

Figure 42   Temple Balsall (Warwicks): a 13th-century hall, formerly with a western cross-wing, survives to the west of the late 13th-century church.

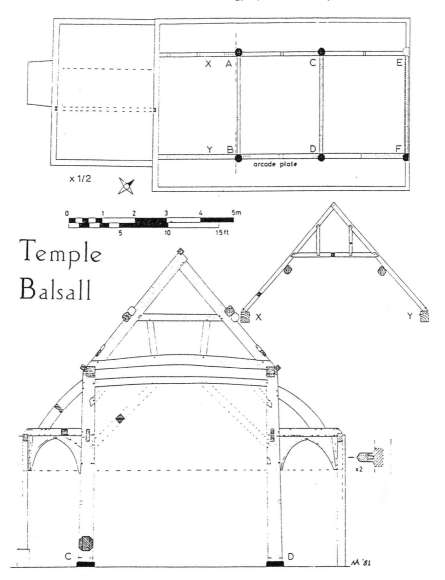

Figure 43   Temple Balsall (Warwicks): outline plan of the hall and section. Reproduced with permission of N. Alcock from *Medieval Archaeology* 26 (1982): 156, figure 5.

John Hope 1908: 192). At Temple Balsall (Warwicks) a capacious chapel of one build was constructed in the 13th century, and at Baddesley a 15th-century chancel was added to the earlier nave. The remains of a large rectangular chapel survive at Hospitaller Any (Limerick, Eire); another rectangular example was excavated at Temple Newsam (W Yorks) early this century, and one at Temple Ewell (Kent) measured 20 × 6.7m and was located at right angles to the hall (*Medieval Archaeol* 12 1968: 167). The excavated chapel at Temple Cressing (Essex) was a single-cell building of flint rubble with greenstone mouldings, constructed on foundations of packed gravel and

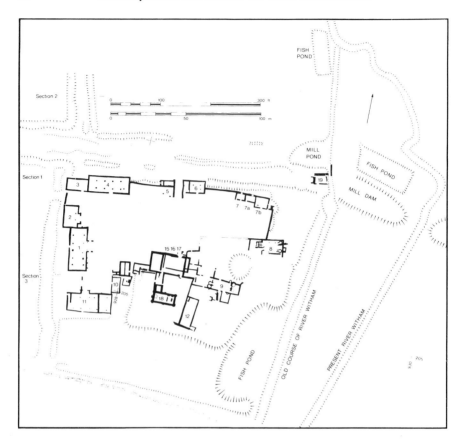

Figure 44 South Witham (Lincs): general site plan of earthworks and structures excavated 1965–7. Reproduced with permission of English Heritage and Philip Mayes.

measuring 12 × 7m internally, with 47 inhumations inside and outside (Hope 1987).

The layout of larger preceptories seems to have consisted of dispersed groups of buildings adjacent to, and detached from, the parish church or chapel. In common with secular manors, this sometimes consisted of a detached ground-floor hall and a two-storey cross-wing or chamber-block. This arrangement can be suggested for Temple Balsall (Warwicks), where an early 13th-century hall, formerly with a western cross-wing, survives to the west of the late-13th-century church (figure 42). The hall is now of three bays, measuring 14.9 × 9.4m internally. It was built before 1250 as an aisled hall (figure 43); the aisle posts have been dated by dendrochronology to 1176–1221 (*Vernacular Architecture* 24 1993: 49).

A two-storey parlour and chamber was added *c*1500 as a cross-wing at the west end of the hall (Alcock 1982: 155). The church formerly had structures attached to the west end. At Templecombe (Somerset), the surviving structure seems to have been a free-standing refectory and kitchen range, complete with a huge fireplace, and located to the south of the site of the chapel. A hall at Sandford (Oxfords) is of two storeys with attic dormers

(Sherwood and Pevsner 1974: 750). Excavations at Temple Cressing (Essex) revealed a masonry hall adjacent to the chapel, with a food oven placed between the two structures, which was packed with 12th-century pottery, oyster shell and pig bones (Hope 1987). Similar spatial relationships are suggested by remains at Garway (Herefords), Quenington (Gloucs), Rothley (Leics), and Yeaveley (Derbys), where conventual buildings were detached from chapels or parish churches but contained within the same complex. Together, these sites indicate that a preceptory's buildings would be ordered around a central space adjacent to a church or incorporating a conventual chapel.

The typical layout of a preceptory may be suggested by South Witham (Lincs) (figure 44), the only preceptory to have been excavated almost fully (Mayes forthcoming). The site was investigated in three seasons between 1965 and 1967, due to threatened destruction from ploughing. Three distinct phases of activity were recognised, the second corresponding with the establishment of a fully developed preceptory in the 13th century in which domestic and agricultural buildings were clearly separated (figure 45).

The Templars acquired land at South Witham between 1137 and 1185. The first phase of Templar occupation focused on an aisled hall (15) with two small ancillary buildings (13, 14). The hall measured at least 15.25 × 8.5m, with the entrance in the north wall. The posts for the building were set out in an irregular manner, possibly indicating that the posts were embedded in a clay wall. Parallel with the east wall, eight internal post holes may have held supports for a bench along the wall. Associated finds included a bone playing piece (or counter) and cooking pots and jugs in Nottingham and Lyveden ware. Two ancillary structures were excavated to the south of the hall, one of which (13) contained four hearths, with evidence of charred grains of wheat. Associated with the buildings were fragments of three stone mortars, of 27 cooking pots and 21 pancheons. The area seems to have been multi-purpose, including cooking, working and storage areas. East of these buildings was a watermill (19), a rectangular building with a large hearth for corn drying against its west wall. Dendrochronology of a timber from the mill race indicated that the tree had been felled c1165.

In the 13th century the preceptory was expanded to include a great and lesser hall, chapel, kitchen and dairy or brewhouse, forming the domestic core of the central court in the south-eastern part of the site. The agricultural buildings were located to the north and west, and fishponds were dug in the south-western corner. The first phase of the great hall (16) consisted of a rectangular building (15.25 × 7.6m) with a western cross-wing (10.36 × 5.79); it was constructed on the site of the earlier Phase 1 hall (figure 46). The hall had an earth floor with a large hearth to the west of the centre of the hall; fragments of lead cames indicate that the windows were glazed. The cross-wing had a stair base in the south wall and a garderobe in the west wall. A passage led from here to the chapel to the south.

The chapel was constructed in Phase 2, indicating elevation of the holding to preceptory status. The rectangular chapel (18) measured 12.8 × 5.0m internally, and was constructed of regular courses of limestone blocks. An altar base was located in the chancel, and footings projecting from the north wall into the chancel have been interpreted as having supported an Easter

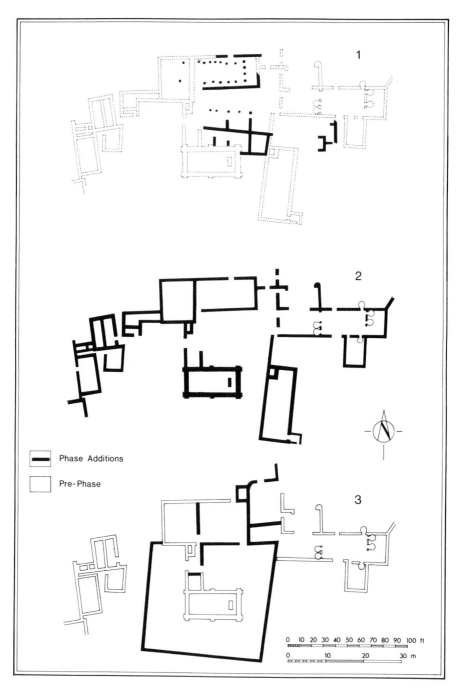

Figure 45   South Witham (Lincs): phased plan of excavated buildings. Reproduced with permission of English Heritage and Philip Mayes.

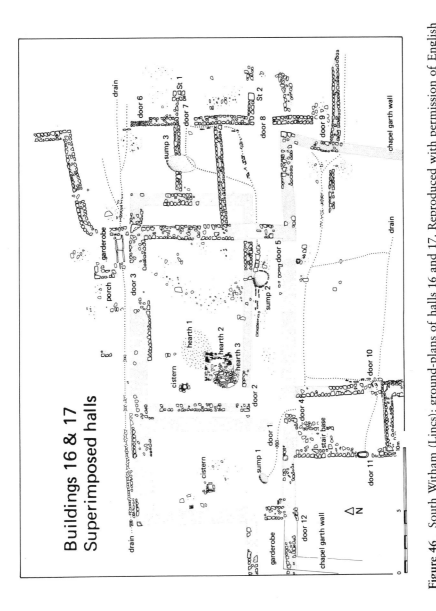

Figure 46 South Witham (Lincs): ground-plans of halls 16 and 17. Reproduced with permission of English Heritage and Philip Mayes.

Figure 47 South Witham (Lincs): reconstruction of the two-storey chapel (building 18). Reproduced with permission of English Heritage and Philip Mayes.

Sepulchre or wall-safe, the latter posssibly for protecting the *confraria*, the funds collected to assist in the crusades. A stair in the north-west angle indicates that the chapel was of two storeys in the nave; a gallery was suggested by the excavator on the basis of a post hole located in the middle of the nave and a post base recorded at the bottom of the blocking wall which divided the chancel from the nave (figure 47). The chapel had painted wall plaster and glazed windows with painted glass quarries. A large, two-storey porch was subsequently added to the north wall.

The kitchen (9) was a long, narrow structure (*c*11.6 × 6.3m) which contained five large ovens, with floors of flagging or ceramic tiles and two hearths. The floor was of compact, clean clay. Associated with the structure were fragments of a large stone mortar, a cresset lamp, a whetstone and pottery, including jugs, pancheons in Nottingham, Lyveden and Stamford wares as well as local sandy wares, cooking pots, six dripping pans and the handle of a pipkin. The brewhouse or dairy (8) measured 13 × 8.1m, and contained a corn-drying kiln, a vat and stone-built hearths. The hearths had bases of 'set pots', metal vessels in permanent stone settings with the hearth below. These were used to heat water for brewing or for scalding dairy equipment.

Gatehouses were built to the north and east. To the south-west of the hall complex a workshop area was constructed, including a forge. Agricultural areas to the north included three aisled barns, two smaller barns and animal houses. The barns had stone walls and thatched roofs. The considerable provision for agricultural storage reflects the function of the preceptory as a reception point for collecting grain from its estates.

In the third phase of occupation the preceptory seems to have been in decline. It became a *camera* run by Temple Bruer (Lincs) until it was abandoned by 1311 as a result of the suppression of the Templars. In Phase 3, the lesser hall was demolished and the watermill went out of use, although documents indicate that a new windmill was constructed. A boundary wall was built around the preceptory and a wall was built to enclose the chapel court. The great hall (17) was rebuilt to a considerable width, 21.8 × 11.4m. It was joined by a passage to the chapel to the south. The hall was roofed in stone with ceramic ridge tiles; it had glazed windows and plastered walls painted red and white (figure 48). Finds from the hall in this period included the base of a bone gaming piece, probably a chess king, a fragment of a zoomorphic aquamanile (an animal-shaped drinking vessel) and a pottery lamp. By 1338, the site was described as a destroyed messuage, and there is no documentary or archaeological evidence to suggest that occupation continued beyond the dissolution of the preceptory.

While in many ways the types of building recognised at South Witham are more typical of a manor than of a monastery, both the domestic and agricultural buildings were built to an exceptional scale, and care was taken to separate monastic and production areas. The width of the aisled halls is noteworthy for the early 13th century and indicates the presence of sophisticated roofs. The two-storey chapel is consistent with many Hospitaller and Templar buildings (below) and suggests that some degree of spatial segregation was expected. The gallery of the nave is likely to have been reserved for the preceptor and brethren, with the ground floor providing for the agricultural labourers and servants of the convent. In the second phase of occupation, two halls were provided in order to ensure separate accommodation for members of the monastery in the great hall, leaving the lesser hall free for servants. There was no evidence for internal partitions in the great hall, or of a screens passage which would normally divide the hall and upper end from the lower service end. In keeping with higher-status halls, services were contained in structures detached from the great hall. The separate cross-wing is likely to have served as the dormitory, with an external staircase to the upper floor and a garderobe provided. The priest may have been given separate accommodation from both groups, perhaps explaining the large porch added to the chapel; its upper chamber could have served such a function. In contrast to many monastic excavations, little evidence was recovered relating to literacy, only the single lead seal-matrix of a 13th-century personal seal. More secular pastimes are suggested by the considerable

Figure 48   South Witham (Lincs): reconstruction of the great hall in Phase 3. Reproduced with permission of English Heritage and Philip Mayes.

number of artefacts of horse furniture, including fragments of 34 iron horse-shoes, an iron stirrup, a copper-alloy harness mount, a possible harness pendant and three spurs. In addition, four iron-socketed and barbed arrow-heads and two with leaf-shaped blades were recorded.

Figure 49 Godsfield (Hants): north side of the stone hall, showing the chapel in the three eastern bays and a separate entrance to the priest's house in the western bay.

Smaller preceptories

Smaller preceptories focused on a hall with integral chapel; often this was a first-floor hall over an undercroft or a chapel over undercroft. One example is Widmere (Bucks), where the rectangular chapel has a 13th-century undercroft of four bays, divided into two aisles by a central row of columns, and roughly domical vaults (Pevsner 1960: 202). Stone halls at Poling (Sussex) and Gods-field (Hants) were divided into two-storey chapels and adjacent residential chambers. At Godsfield the three eastern bays of the hall were occupied by the chapel, with windows dating to the 13th century (figure 49). The western bay was the priest's house, with a chimney stack and separate entrance on the north side. This house was of two storeys, with a single room at each level. From the upper level a squint allowed sight of the high altar; attached to the west side was a garderobe. A 13th-century pyx, a small vessel made to contain the eucharist, was found nearby. Ground-floor chapels adjoined two-storey blocks, possibly priests' chambers, at Swingfield and Sutton-on-Hone (Kent).

The extant stone hall at Temple Strood (Kent), and the now demolished example at the *camera* of Harefield (Middlesex), were partitioned into two chambers in the upper storeys, for accommodation or possibly to form chapels (figures 50 and 51). At both sites ground-floor halls were built next to the older, stone chamber-blocks. Excavations at Strood indicated that a timber ground-floor hall had been added in the 14th century, and a timber-framed cross-wing in the 15th century, after Templar occupation had ceased (figure 52) (Rigold 1965). The arrangements at Harefield and Strood may be seen as

Figure 50   Temple Manor, Strood (Kent): the two-storey stone hall.

Figure 51   Temple Manor, Strood (Kent): the upper-storey chapel with a later-inserted fireplace.

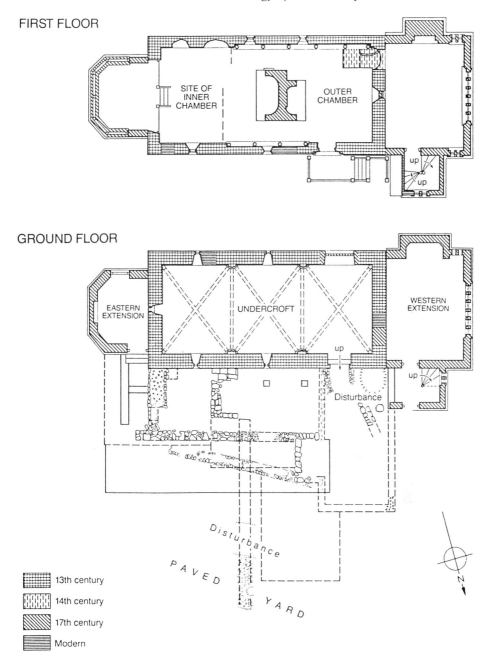

FIRST FLOOR

SITE OF INNER CHAMBER

OUTER CHAMBER

up

up

GROUND FLOOR

EASTERN EXTENSION

UNDERCROFT

WESTERN EXTENSION

up

up

Disturbance

Disturbance

PAVED YARD

13th century

14th century

17th century

Modern

0　5　10　Metres

0　5　10　20　30　Feet

Figure 52　Temple Manor, Strood (Kent): plan of the extant hall and excavated structures. Reproduced with permission of English Heritage from S. Rigold (1962/1990) *Temple Manor, Strood.*

typical of the manorial plan which combined the two-storey chamber-block with the detached ground-floor hall (Blair 1993: 15). At the smaller precep-tories or *camerae*, a solitary chamber-block may have been sufficient to contain all the necessary services of accommodation and a chapel.

Two-storey halls and chapels

Like episcopal and aristocratic residences, preceptories were provided with a combination of stone and timber ground-floor and two-storey halls, in order to meet a variety of functions. A number of two-storey structures survive, with the hall positioned over an undercroft; the 1546 survey of Clerkenwell describes a grand staircase leading to one of the large halls. Two-storey halls, in addition to ground-floor subsidiary halls, were suggested by the excavators of Denney and South Witham. At Denney, the north range was interpreted as a two-storey hall, supported internally on columns and roofed with large Collyweston stone tiles (figure 38). Its 'immaculately clean and unworn sur-face' suggested a specialised function such as a dormitory or infirmary (Christie and Coad 1980: 198); indeed Denney was the official infirmary for knights of the Templar order in England. The purpose of the undercrofts which feature at a number of sites can only be postulated. The lower hall may have been used by lay-members or servants of the house; occasionally, it may have included worship or chapter meetings in a category of monastery which was not specifically provided with a chapter-house. In addition to functional requirements, the two-storey hall may have been a symbol of the social milieu with which the houses identified.

It has been noted elsewhere that throughout northern Europe the Hospital-lers, in particular, preferred two-storey structures (Leistikow 1967). Two-storey halls were the standard accommodation of the headquarters of the order in Rhodes, where the ground floor served as a storeroom entered from the street, and the upper floor formed a residental hall, with a courtyard attached to the building or forming the central focus of a complex of buildings (figure 53) (Kollias 1991: 68). The 15th-century hospital at Rhodes consists of four two-storey ranges grouped around a courtyard. The infirmary was the upper storey of the east range (51 × 12.3m) (figure 54). It is divided centrally by an arcade with capitals bearing the cross and arms of St John. Small chambers in the thickness of the wall are thought to have been isolation rooms; a fireplace was placed in the southern end of the infirmary. The infirmary chapel was formed by placing an altar in an apsed chamber in the east wall.

Perhaps more surprising than two-storey halls are the churches, which are in part two-storey, at Chibburn, Torphichen (W Lothian), Temple Balsall (Warwicks) and, possibly, Coningsby (Hereford), although the last may be the result of a later modification. At Temple Balsall the west end of the nave was of two storeys, as indicated by a staircase in the south-western angle and a blocked doorway above. At a number of German preceptories, including Niederwersel (Hesse) and Wölchingen (Baden-Württemburg), secular rooms were built as the upper storey of a church. At Torphichen, 15th-century alterations included the addition of rooms above the north transept, complete with fireplaces and reached by a stair turret in the north-west corner of the

Figure 53 Street of the Knights, Rhodes: the international headquarters of the Hospitallers. Each country (tongue) had a two-storey hall with storeroom on the ground floor and hall above. A courtyard was attached to the back, or formed the centre of a complex of buildings.

Figure 54 The Hospitaller Infirmary, Rhodes: the infirmary was contained in the upper storey of the east range of a courtyard complex.

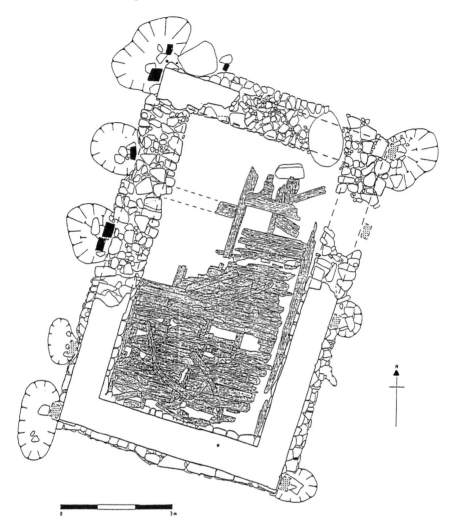

Figure 55 Arundel Square, Waterford (Eire): excavations of a possible hospice owned by the Knights Hospitaller revealed a stone structure with well-preserved wooden floor. Reproduced with permission from *Medieval Archaeology* 35 (1991): 214, figure 5.

crossing. At Chibburn, the medieval chapel seems to have been two-storey at its western end. In this respect, Hospitaller churches may be expected to follow conventions for medieval hospitals, in which an upper storey accommodated additional infirmary space or facilitated sexual segregation (p. 21).

This convention seems to have been used also in hospices of the order, including the two-storey structure which survives at Standon (Hertfords), which was a hospice with dormitory on the first floor, refectory and kitchen on the ground floor, and cellarage beneath. Additional hospices include the remains of a hall at Ansty (Wilts), which contains windows dating to the 15th or 16th centuries. The two-storey convention was followed by military hospices across Europe, including the 15th-century hospice of St Catherine in the burgus at Rhodes (the secular area of the walled city).

Some preceptories established wayside hospitals or hospices nearby. One such candidate is a rectangular stone-built range at Clanfield (Oxfords), known as St Leonard's Chapel (Blair 1985: 209). The hospice at Yspytty Ifan (Clwyd) had its own curtilage and garden west of the present church (Rees 1947: 63). The larger rural preceptories maintained hospices in towns, which provided hospitality for members of the order. A stone hall excavated at Arundel Square in Waterford City (Waterford, Eire) was built on property owned by the Hospitallers and may be an example of an urban hospice. The stone building measured 9.6 × 6m internally and contained a well-preserved wooden floor and wooden uprights placed externally against the walls, possibly to support a cantilevered superstructure (figure 55). Dendrochronological determination of the timbers provided a date of the third quarter of the 12th century (*Medieval Archaeol* 35 1991: 214–15).

Camerae

Like the granges of other monastic orders, the *camerae* of the Templars and Hospitallers were generally farms specialising in arable agriculture, pastoralism, dairying or fish-keeping. The term *camera* was used to refer to holdings without a resident preceptor or which paid their *confraria* directly to the mother house in London. Inventories suggest that, in contrast to granges, some *camerae* were equipped with their own chapels, for example those at Maplebeck (Nottinghams), Cowley and Merton (Oxfords). The chapels of *camerae* must have been fairly modest, insubstantial structures similar to the timber-framed example which survived until recently at Ashley Cum Silverley (Cambs). This was a rectangular building with plaster stud walls, a king-post roof and a small tower at the west end (Haigh 1988: 2).

Excavations at Etton, a *camera* of the preceptory of Faxfleet (E Yorks [Humbs]), revealed a great hall, brewhouse, granaries and cobbled roadways. Its central hall was L-shaped, with a brewhouse at its west end. This was a round building of corbelled construction (*Medieval Archaeol* 12 1968: 170). The granaries were long buildings with flint foundations, internal pillars and external gullies. Building material from the site included a reused stoup (a container for holy water), which was generally placed at the entrance to a church or chapel. The chapels, which most *camerae* possessed, distinguished them from the granges of other monastic orders for which 'the addition of a chapel ... was to remain an exceptional luxury' (Platt 1969: 21). By the 15th century, the Hospitallers, in common with other monastic landowners, leased their *camerae* to secular tenants in return for cash rents. At this time the *camerae* ceased to function as religious settlements, although possession of some chapels was retained.

Excavations at Etton provided evidence for a period of disuse, corresponding with a phase of abandonment following the suppression of the Templars and preceding occupation of the site by the Hospitallers. This period has been estimated as covering ten years, and was recognised by a deposit of earth and building debris which buried the earlier structures.

Military iconography

While the Military Orders may not have been organised along a filial model, such as the Cistercian, convents shared a common purpose in their devotion to Jerusalem. In larger houses this identity was expressed through icono-graphic architecture, particularly that of round-nave churches. In the building of 12th-century churches, a round nave was used to make reference to the nave of the church of the Holy Sepulchre in Jerusalem. The church of the Holy Sepulchre was begun c1114, and was constructed in order to enclose under one roof the Tomb of Christ, the chapels of Calvary and Golgotha, the Place of Anointing and the Prison of Christ (Pringle 1986: 343). Round churches of the Hospitallers included St John's Clerkenwell, Little Maplestead (Essex) and St Giles (Hereford). Templar examples included both the London Temples, Bristol, Dover, Garway (Herefords), Aslackby (Lincs) and Temple Bruer (Lincs). The interior of the naves was actually hexagonal, formed by an arcade which divided the nave from an encircling aisle.

A few round-nave churches, which were not associated with the Military Orders, nevertheless shared the same iconographic archetype. Parish churches were built with round naves in Cambridge (c1130) and Northampton (c1116). Both were dedicated to the Holy Sepulchre, and the former may once have been associated with the Canons of the Holy Sepulchre (Dickinson 1951: 73), a short-lived order which had six houses in England, concentrated in the east Midlands. A proprietary – or private – church was built with a round nave at Orphir (Orkney). The choice of its form has been attributed to Earl Hakon upon his return from pilgrimage to the Holy Land, c1120 (Cruden 1986: 128). When Military churches were later rebuilt, the round nave was replaced by the usual rectangular form. This suggests that the iconographic message of the round nave receded with the loss of Jerusalem and the fading popularity of the Crusades.

Clerkenwell and Temple Bruer were built with crypts beneath the east end, another reference to the original Sepulchre, the Tomb of Christ. The religious topography of Jerusalem was pertinent in additional aspects, such as dedica-tions. For instance, the later London Temple contained a chapel of St Anne over a crypt, perhaps referring to the church over the tomb of St Anne, just north of the Temple precinct in Jerusalem. The topography of Hospitaller Rhodes paid homage to the most popular saints of the order, with gates of the 15th-century walls dedicated to St John, the Virgin, St Catherine, St Antony, St Peter and St George.

Preceptories were often endowed with an existing parish church, so that the form and dedication of the earlier building were retained. In the case of larger preceptories, however, a new building and dedication would be sought more in keeping with the iconography of the order. For example, when the Hospitallers were given the manor and church of Little Maplestead (Essex) in 1225, they took over the existing church of All Saints. By 1245, All Saints had been replaced by a chapel dedicated to St John the Baptist, the patron saint of the order of St John of Jerusalem (the Hospitallers) (Gervers 1982: 70). Moreover, this chapel was built with a round nave – the symbol of the Holy Sepulchre in Jerusalem (figure 56). At Garway (Herefords), in the 12th century, the Templars rebuilt a pre-Conquest church to accommodate a round nave,

Figure 56 St John the Baptist, Maplestead (Essex): the round-nave church built by 1245 on the site of an earlier parish church given to the Hospitallers.

the foundations of which have been partly excavated (*Medieval Archaeol* 29 1985: 184).

Other reminders of the Holy Land may have been integral to the material culture of the preceptory, including, for example, items produced for the convent or artefacts brought back from the East by individual knights. A late-13th-century pottery jug from Etton, a *camera* of Faxfleet (E Yorks [Humbs]), has an insignia under its spout like a cross *pommée* (*Medieval Archaeol* 12 1968: 170), a cross with rounded terminals which was once the armorial ensign of the Crusader Kings of Jerusalem (Pritchard 1967: 98–9). From Phase 1 at South Witham (Lincs), a single fragment was recovered of a jar in Raqqa ware, pottery produced in northern Syria from 1171–1259. The sherd is in a friable, sandy, buff fabric with decoration in black paint under a turquoise glaze; it represents the earliest example of Raqqa ware found in a datable context in north-western Europe.

As patron saint of the order, images of St John the Baptist would have been central to the Hospitallers. The Baptist was linked with healing of the sick poor (see p. 38) and was patron saint of many guilds of barbers and barber surgeons. He was regularly invoked in healing charms, many of which concerned the loss of blood through wounds, a significant consideration for a crusading order. One such image survives from the Hospitaller preceptory at Battisford (Suffolk), where two terracotta plaques were recovered from a late-16th-century timber-framed house. One plaque bears the arms of Sir Giles Russell, Preceptor of Battisford *c*1530, the other is an image of St John the Baptist in a roundel, supported by members of the order. A similar pairing was provided for the gatehouse of the headquarters at Clerkenwell (above), where the arms of Prior Thomas Docwra were accompanied by an image of the *Agnus Dei*, used to signify John the Baptist. From 1190 onwards, the conventual seal of the Priory of England depicted John the Baptist; that of the eleventh prior, Hugh Downay (1216–21), shows the half-figure of John the Baptist resting on water, in his right hand a staff surmounted by a disc, on which is the Paschal lamb, and in his left, a palm-branch (King 1932: 98). The seal used by John Pavley *c*1302 shows the head of the Baptist (Ellis 1986: 24). Few seals of preceptories survive, but those of Godsfield (Hants) and Mayne (Dorset) show the patriarchal cross, while five seals from Torphichen (W Lothian) all illustrate full-length figures of John the Baptist (King 1932: 102). The reverse of the seal of the Master of the Hospitallers, dating to the 12th and 13th centuries, shows a man lying on a mattress or bier, the symbol of the pilgrim hospital in Jerusalem (Nicholson 1993: 108), and one indicative of the charitable functions of the order.

The Templars and the Teutonic Knights of central Europe claimed the Blessed Virgin Mary as their special patron, and dedicated many of their churches to her. The Teutonic Knights chose Marian images suggestive of secular power, in particular the Coronation of the Virgin, to embellish illuminations, effigies and the wall painting in the refectory at Marienburg (Marburg, Poland) (Dygo 1989), a fortress of the order with a formal cloister situated in the centre. The Templars claimed a special connection to the Virgin, having believed that the Annunciation took place in the Temple of Solomon. Both the Templars and the Teutonic Knights concentrated their devotions on female saints in the commissioning of literature and saints' lives and in the acquisition of relics (Nicholson 1993: 111–12, 116–17).

In the Holy Land, the Military Orders commissioned wall paintings for the interior and exterior of their chapels, including those at Crac des Chevaliers and Marqab. Those at the former site included an image of St George, a military saint who may have struck particular resonance with members of the Military Orders (Folda 1982: 195). Occasionally, their iconography favoured certain martyred virgin saints who, like St Catherine, had given their lives in steadfast defence of their Christian beliefs and chastity. St Catherine of Alexandria is portrayed with the wheel, the object of her martyrdom, together with the Crucifixion and St Christopher, amidst 13th-century graffiti in the cave at Royston (Herts), thought to be associated with the Templars. At Hospitaller Rhodes, the chapel of the Grand Master was dedicated to Catherine, its walls decorated with tapestries showing her martyrdom together with scenes of the life of Mary Magdalene (Kollias 1991: 72).

There is no consistent iconography apparent for the architecture of military churches in Britain, and little survives to indicate iconographic textiles, paintings or wooden fittings. Most churches of the orders were shared with parish congregations, and exhibit images typical of parish sympathies, for example the 15th-century wall paintings of St Christopher at Hospitaller Chippenham (Cambs). One surviving panel painting from the parish church of Templecombe (Somerset) has attracted the controversy which still today tracks the Templars. This image of Christ's head was painted on a wooden panel, radiocarbon dated to *c*1280. The figure bears some resemblance to that imprinted on the Turin Shroud (Burman 1986), and it has been used to support the

Figure 57   Garway (Herefords): the chancel arch. Drawing by Ted West.

argument that the Templars brought the shroud to Europe and used it as a focus for their alleged idolatory, accusations of which assisted in their downfall.

Certain Templar churches exhibit oriental influences, and these have been explained through the crusader connection. These include the remarkable chancel arch and graffiti at Garway (Herefords). The semicircular chancel arch may be dated c1180. It is plain on the eastern side, but the western side,

Figure 58 A swastika-pelta graffito from Duxford parish church (Cambs), once held by the Templars. Drawing by Ted West.

which would have been viewed by members of the preceptory, is decorated in three orders: the outer order is made up of chevrons; the middle order is an interlaced chevron pattern; and the inner order has each voussoir moulded across the arch (figure 57). Graffiti inside and outside the church include a Maltese cross on the exterior of the east wall of the chancel, two fish on the west wall and the emblems of the Passion at the west door. Another fish (or a human leg?) is at the west door, and on the piscina in the south chapel is a chalice and wafer, with a fish on one side and a snake on the other. The swastika-pelta graffito is represented in churches of the Templars at Duxford (Cambs) (figure 58) and of the Hospitallers at Chippenham (Cambs). This symbol has late Roman and Early Christian connections, and occurs in mosaics in Antioch and the Church of the Nativity in Bethlehem. In England, the later medieval graffiti are concentrated in churches in Cambridgeshire and Essex, a region where the Military Orders were especially active.

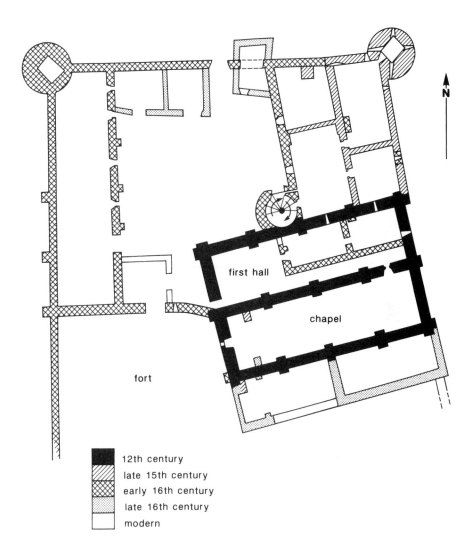

Figure 59   Temple-sur-Lot, Lot-et-Garonne, France: a 12th-century Templar preceptory fortified as a quadrangular castle in the 16th century. Based on *Archéologie Médiévale* 22 (1992): 469.

Swastika-peltae have been noted in a number of churches owned by, or in close proximity to, preceptories, including Whaddon, Swaffham Prior, Teversham and Great Wilbraham (Cambs), Sible Hedingham (Essex) and Rowston (Lincs) (Pritchard 1967: 177–80).

Also unusual is the Geometric window tracery at Temple Balsall (Warwicks). Although largely rebuilt by Sir George Gilbert Scott in 1849, the late-13th-century windows of the nave are authentic. Their strange features include foiled circles, spherical triangles and a proper rose with cusped radiating panels in the top south-western window. Similar features at the London

Temple include the west door with its strange busts and the wheel window over the porch, with heart-shaped openings between the spokes (Gardam 1990: 105). In contrast, the architecture of the Hospitallers appears to exhibit no eastern influence. Indeed, that of the entire walled city of Rhodes drew its inspiration from western Europe, and was completed in Gothic forms reminiscent of French architecture (Kollias 1991).

In the architecture of the Military Orders in the East, the boundary between castle and monastery was indistinct. For example, at Crac des Chevaliers (Syria, the medieval county of Tripoli) the Hospitallers built a concentric castle with central courtyard, fortified with inner and outer curtain walls, protected by towers and a barbican. It has been suggested that the chapels of such Crusader fortresses were decorated with armour, weapons, trophies and other military memorabilia (Deschamps 1973: 157). Such military imagery appeared in mainland Europe: frescoes in the Templar chapel of S. Bevignate, Perugia (Italy), show the knights fighting the Muslims and the devil (Nicholson 1993: 108–9). European preceptories were sometimes more clearly fortified than their British counterparts. For example, at Temple-sur-Lot (Lot-et-Garonne), a 12th-century Templar preceptory consisting of a chapel and hall contained within a rectangular building was substantially fortified by the Hospitallers in the 16th century (figure 59). The chapel, hall and domestic buildings were contained in a fort resembling a quadrangular castle, with defended gateways and *chemin de ronde* on the north wall (*Archéologie Médiévale* 22 1992: 468–70).

In Britain, the military might of the orders was seldom tested, and it is unlikely that military souvenirs embellished the walls of churches. Symbolically, however, preceptories occasionally borrowed from a secular military vocabulary in creating an iconography of fortification. Examples include the embattled church towers at Garway, Temple Bruer and Aslackby (Lincs), and battlements around the upper drum of the nave of the 12th-century Temple church in London (Gardam 1990: 107). Irish preceptories, and those of the Welsh and Scottish borders, drew more realistically from these forms, including the Hospitaller site at Kilteel (Kildare, Eire), which formed part of the defensive network for the Pale. Its remains include a 15th-century tower-house of five stories, and a gatehouse (Manning 1981–2).

Agricultural production

The majority of preceptories were engaged in agricultural production, which is reflected by their predominantly rural distribution and by the impressive agricultural and industrial complexes excavated at South Witham (Lincs), Skelton (W Yorks) and partially extant at Temple Cressing (Essex). Some indication of their output can be made by the returns for each Hospitaller manor made in 1338 (Larking 1857) and by the survey of Templar holdings taken in 1308. Each preceptory or *camera* possessed a house and garden, some of which produced surplus crops for sale, in addition to a dovecote, arable lands, pasture, meadow and rights of pannage. At Quenington (Gloucs), a round dovecote survives with revolving ladder, and at Garway (Herefords), a dovecote to the south of the church can be dated by an in-

Figure 60 Garway (Herefords): the dovecote built in 1326.

scription over the door to 1326: *istud columbarium factum fuit per Ricardum 1326* (this dovecote was made by Richard 1326) (figure 60). Many houses had, in addition, a bakehouse and brewhouse, and some held a windmill. Earthworks at the Hospitaller site of Carbrooke (Norfolk) suggest a series of fishponds to the south of the former preceptory and the extant parish church (figure 61).

In order to fulfill their roles as central places, functioning as agricultural, administrative and financial centres, larger preceptories required storage facilities for grain. At Temple Cressing, two enormous, aisled barns survive, giving some indication of the scale of storage facilities at the preceptory (figure 62). The Wheat Barn has been radio-carbon dated to *c*1255, and the Barley Barn to *c*1200 (Hewitt 1962: 242). More recently, dendrochronological dating has given a range of 1257–80 for the Wheat Barn and 1205–30 for the Barley Barn (*Vernacular Architecture* 24 1993: 50–51). Excavations at Skelton, part of the preceptory of Temple Newsam (W Yorks), uncovered the fragmentary remains of several structures thought to represent agricultural buildings which occupied the northern end of the preceptory enclosure. From evidence of destruction debris, the roofs were covered with sandstone slabs secured by iron nails and had green-glazed, crested ceramic ridge tiles. One structure was a large aisled barn with opposing cart porches, and another was a substantial square structure, possibly a dovecote. A third building was located over a large latrine pit. Other pits south of the barn had been lined with wooden barrels and may have been used in tanning (*Medieval Archaeol* 34 1990: 223–4).

Systems of water management provided site sanitation and mill power for grinding cereals and fulling cloth. The earliest documentary references to

Figure 61 Carbrooke (Norfolk): a series of fishponds to the south of the Hospitaller church. Reproduced with permission of the Norfolk Air Photographs Library of the Norfolk Museums Service and Derek Edwards.

Figure 62 Temple Cressing (Essex): the 13th-century Wheat Barn.

English fulling mills are associated with those at Temple Newsam (W Yorks) and Temple Guiting (Gloucs), which were established by 1185 (Bond 1989: 103). At Temple Balsall, the mill stream and overflow channel bank survive (VCH Warwicks 8 1969: 466), and at Shingay (Cambs), a water meadow survives, divided into narrow strips by ditches which ran into a mill (Haigh 1988: 81). At the *camera* of Washford (Warwicks), a fishpond complex established by the Templars in the 13th century has been excavated. The pond system formed three sides of a rectangular raised area and was fed by a series of channels taken off from the River Arrow. Near the pond three large buildings with stone foundations were detected. To the east, a number of shallow depressions may have represented water meadows (Bond and Aston 1969). A rectangular platform contained evidence of a building with daub walls and an associated fish-breeding tank, which contained pottery dated to the period of Templar ownership of the site (Gray 1969).

Preceptories in context: monastery or manor?

In contrast to other forms of monasticism, the Military Orders were never intended to be either intellectual or ascetic. It is not surprising, therefore, to find few material manifestations of monastic life present in the remains of preceptories. Their limited religious function is reflected by the small size of chapels, and the general absence of a monastic choir where churches of the orders were shared with a parish. British preceptories were not ordered around a cloister, standard to monastic planning, and were not provided with features expected of fully conventual houses, such as a chapter-house. In the case of the English headquarters of the Military Orders, however, buildings may have been arranged around courtyards or cloisters. Hollar's engraving of Clerkenwell, dated 1661, suggests such an arrangement. The headquarters of Military Orders elsewhere adopted formal cloisters, including that of the Teutonic Knights at Marienburg (Marburg, Poland), rebuilt as a massive fortress in brick in the 1270s (Christiansen 1980: 103), and the Spanish Knights of Alcantara. At the international headquarters of the Hospitallers in Rhodes, the accommodation for most of the tongues (languages, or countries) was arranged around a formal courtyard. This convention was adopted by some of the larger preceptories in Britain, such as Chibburn; others grouped their buildings around a central space, including Denney and South Witham. In this respect they may have resembled the larger colleges of secular canons (see Cook 1959) or hospitals (above).

Most British preceptories, however, were ordered as dispersed groups of buildings generally adjacent to, and detached from, the parish church or chapel. This situation was close to that of a secular manor house in having a hall with service apartments at one end and a parlour (with dormitory above) at the other, or, in cases such as Temple Balsall, Strood and Harefield, a stone chamber-block with a timber ground-floor hall. The preceptory shared certain traits with other categories of monastic site, in particular the smaller colleges of canons and alien priories. At the college founded at Thompson (Norfolk), for example, accommodation was provided in a hall some distance from the parish church (Whittingham 1980: 80). Alien priories were established by members of the Norman baronial classes, who granted land to French abbeys, on which daughter foundations could be established. At the alien priory of Cogges (Oxfords) an existing church and manor house were given to the monks of Fécamp in 1103. From the late 12th century a group of domestic buildings occupied the site, and it seems that the monks were moved to a more formal monastic cell (Blair and Steane 1982). Excavations at the alien priory of Fontevrault at Grove (Bedfords) revealed an arrangement not dissimilar to that observed at South Witham. The agricultural function of both sites is reflected by their complexes of substantial agricultural and industrial buildings ordered within the perimeter of an earthwork enclosure (Baker and Baker 1989: 269). Both Cogges and Grove reused existing secular manor houses, gradually replacing timber buildings with more formal stone complexes. The smaller preceptories find their closest analogy with non-conventual houses, such as alien priories and, indeed, the smaller French priories which were non-claustral. This form was fitting for the majority of rural preceptories which were, in effect, alien priories of the Temple and Hospital in Jerusalem.

Many preceptories and alien priories served primarily as centres of agricultural production administered by members of a monastic order. At South Witham and Grove the character of the agricultural buildings was similar to that of a high-status manorial site. The distinction between monastic and secular, however, lay in the size and quality of buildings. Monasteries built agricultural complexes which were frequently renewed, with structures built in stone or timber on a massive scale, such as the barn excavated at Temple Newsam (Skelton, W Yorks) and those surviving at Temple Cressing (Essex). A more telling distinction was the presence of a chapel at preceptories, and even at some *camerae*. Preceptories have been likened to monastic granges, which were farms or subsidiary residences of a monastery. However, chapels were only built at granges if choir monks were expected to be resident (Platt 1969: 40). By extrapolation, the provision of chapels at preceptories implies that some form of regular monastic routine was expected, and the seven services of Divine Office would have been celebrated daily in the chapel. Chapels remained an exceptional luxury at granges, and were not generally constructed until a phase of replanning in the 14th or 15th centuries (ibid.: 25). The standard accommodation of a grange consisted of a hall, chamber and kitchen. By contrast, preceptories were built in the 12th and 13th centuries with a chapel, as opposed to a simple oratory for private worship, or adjacent to a parish church which was absorbed into the monastery.

When compared with secular settlement, preceptories exhibit a number of features which, at least in the 12th century, were more characteristic of aristocratic than manorial settlement. These include provision of a chapel, the tendency for central planning, the grouping together of buildings within defensible enclosures, extensive moats, and two-storey halls and chapels. These features were integral to castles, including Crusader examples in Syria, such as Crac des Chevaliers (Tripoli) and Marqab (principality of Antioch). The dispersed groups of buildings, including a chapel and contained within an enclosure, resemble bishops' palaces (for example, Lincoln and Amberley, Sussex) or aristocratic residences (such as Clarendon, Wilts). The preference for two-storey halls, a trait noted in Hospitaller architecture across Europe (above), draws from prototypes such as the bishop's palace, abbot's lodging or castle, which, in the 12th century, were halls placed over undercrofts. Equally, the two-storey chapel present in many smaller preceptories would have been at home in the castle or episcopal palace.

While many *camerae* of the Military Orders were little more than farms, preceptories seem to have drawn from forms of upper-status planning. Moreover, the models from which the preceptories drew were what the late Maurice Barley once termed 'formal and highly organised masculine institutions': early castles, aristocratic residences and bishops' palaces (Barley 1986: 90). Certainly, the lifestyle enjoyed by the orders can be described as secular and male, an outlook hardly surprising in an order founded for knights. To an even greater extent than other monastics, the Military Orders were subject to frequent prohibitions on hunting, hawking and feasting (Forey 1992: 192). Excavations have yielded no evidence for the material culture of literacy associated with monasteries; indeed, the two gaming pieces, and the assemblage of horse furniture recovered from the great hall at South Witham are finds more typical of castles or the more secular outer courts of monasteries (such as Thornholme, Lincs). Servants of the preceptory were, in addition, almost entirely male, in common with the baronial household. It seems likely that the architecture of preceptories emulated models adopted by secular masculine institutions, in preference to fully monastic archetypes. The choice of such models may have originated from the essentially military nature of the orders, reminiscent of the bonding experienced by men who had trained and fought together in the East.

Was the preceptory manor or monastery? It functioned as both, with predominance of function varying according to its place within the administrative and settlement hierarchy of the Military Orders. Its forms were drawn from secular and monastic planning, particularly from types of settlement with exclusively male military or religious connotations. The preceptory found its archetype and iconography in the East, where the distinction between monastery and castle merged.

4 Sisters of the house: the archaeology of religious women

Brides of Christ

Religious women shared a distinctive vocation within the monastic movement and played a vital role in medieval religious life. Yet, the nature of their lifestyles and contributions to medieval society have been little studied or understood. This chapter introduces the varied archaeology of the religious life for women in the later middle ages, comparing the experience of nuns in Britain with those in other parts of Europe, and with women of different religious vocations.

While Anglo-Saxon monasticism is considered to have been a golden age for female religious, personified by royal abbesses such as Hild, who presided over the double monastery at *Streanaeshalch* (Whitby, N Yorks) (*HE* 3: 24), Norman monasticism is thought to have looked less favourably upon women. Previous scholarship has doubted the value placed on religious women by their contemporaries and has characterised medieval nunneries as having been undisciplined and impoverished institutions (e.g. Power 1922). Lawrence Butler summarised these impressions:

> Prioresses lacked prestige. In a feudal militaristic Anglo-Norman society a Mother Superior was a contradiction in terms ... It was considered that the prayers of women had far less value when offered in intercession to the saints. Nearly all the eighty post-Conquest Benedictine nunneries were small in scale, poorly endowed and lurching from one financial crisis to another, perhaps also beset by scandal (Butler 1989: 3).

This negative image of religious women has resulted partly from the relatively poor survival of documents and material culture associated with them, but also from a prevailing lack of interest in religious lifestyles outside the mainstream of male monasticism. Only now are historians and archaeologists re-evaluating the fragmentary evidence from which to reconstruct a picture of the lives of medieval religious women.

Much of the archaeological evidence pertaining to nunneries was recovered by antiquaries, who were primarily interested in reconstructing the ground-plans of the church and cloister by digging trenches around the walls. Such 'wall-chasing' paid little attention to recording stratigraphic relationships, artefacts, or environmental remains. More recently, a number of nunneries have been excavated, at least in part, although few reports have been fully published. The major excavations include Elstow (Bedfords) (Baker 1971; 1989), St Mary Clerkenwell, London (Sloane in preparation), Polsloe, near

Exeter (*Medieval Archaeol* 23 1979: 250–51) and Denney (Cambs) (Christie and Coad 1980). Others can be studied through standing remains, smaller-scale excavations, earthworks, maps and documents.

The most familiar image of the religious woman is that of the nun, with whom the vast majority of archaeological and documentary evidence is associated. But a great number of other types of religious women are known from across Europe, some of whom lived communally, such as the nuns and hospital sisters, and others who lived a more solitary life as an anchoress or vowess. The nuns and anchoresses sought primarily a contemplative vocation, serving Christ and the community through their prayers. More active vocations were followed by sisters working in hospitals and by women who lived in beguinages, or informal communities of unenclosed religious women (see below pp. 148–51). After considering the archaeology of nunneries a comparison will be made with the evidence for the lives of these women.

Recent work on religious women in medieval England and France has indicated that, contrary to previous stereotyping, they were held in especially high regard by patrons. Nuns in Normandy continued to receive gifts and bequests throughout the medieval period (Johnson 1991: 233), and in East Anglia middle-ranking lay-people continued to leave bequests to nuns right up to the Dissolution, long after they had become disaffected with the wealthier monks and canons (Gilchrist and Oliva 1993: 60–61). These medieval people sought the prayers of religious women for their souls and recognised in them the intercessory role appropriate to women who modelled their lives on the Virgin Mary.

The majority of nunneries founded in Britain after the Conquest were indeed poor in comparison with monasteries founded for men. This disparity seems to have resulted from the different social level at which nunneries were founded: over seventy were established by local lords who held neither title nor high office (Thompson 1991: 163). Of the 64 Irish nunneries founded between the early 12th and 16th centuries, only seven were established by Anglo-Normans; 80 Anglo-Norman houses for men were initiated during the same period, presumably because the latter were considered better allies in a newly acquired land (Margaret Murphy pers com). In contrast, Cistercian nunneries in both Spain and Germany were numerous, powerful and relatively prosperous (Brooke 1974: 169, 173), and the status of founders of nunneries in France seems to have been high (Johnson 1991: 46). British nunneries were established in order to make a more local impact than their wealthier, more political male counterparts. But the religious experience of medieval women was not less authentic, or less valued, than that of religious men. It was different.

In contrast to the Saxon tradition of double houses for religious women and men, founded from the 7th to 9th centuries, nunneries for women only were established from the 10th century onwards. During the early years of Norman monasticism, however, a certain degree of informality allowed the presence of cells of religious women at Benedictine monasteries for men, including Bury St Edmunds, St Albans and Evesham. This flexibility continued elsewhere: in the later middle ages women were accommodated in some Benedictine monasteries for men in France, Germany and Holland. Of the new foundations for women established in England during the 12th century, the heyday of monastic foundation, up to one-quarter originally provided some role for men (Elkins 1988: xvii), whether as canons in double houses or lay-brothers attached to Cistercian nunneries. The majority of Anglo-Norman female houses were, however, for women only, and between 1165 and 1200 the practice of male participation in female houses decreased rapidly (ibid.: 117) as the insistence on strict sexual segregation strengthened. Most nunneries followed the Rule of St Benedict, which stressed the communal nature of monastic life, or that of St Augustine, which was more committed to the service of others. Both rules allowed each house to function independently with regular visitations from the bishop of the diocese.

The filiation of nunneries, or the order to which they were committed, is sometimes difficult to establish with any certainty. Some recorded themselves as Cluniac or Cistercian but were not officially recognised by the order. Indeed, the Cistercians were at first reluctant to accept women, not agreeing until the 13th century. The Premonstratensians, who followed the teachings of Norbert of Xanten, originally admitted women but prohibited them from 1198. In England, only the Cistercian nunneries of Marham (Norfolk) and Tarrant Crawford (Dorset) eventually received recognition by the order. Many small nunneries swapped allegiances between orders, recording themselves alternately as Benedictine, Cistercian, Cluniac and so on. This may have resulted from the nuns following the monastic loyalties of their canon or priest (Thompson 1984: 137). This fluidity, and the degree of uniformity of observances within nunneries, has resulted in historians treating medieval nuns as a single category of religious, with few differences created by filiation. Yet, certain traits specific to monastic orders can be proposed: Franciscan nuns were particularly dedicated to monastic enclosure, in stark contrast to their mendicant brothers, and Dominican sisters were more devoted to learning than the other orders of women. The degree of uniformity is confirmed, however, by the material culture of nunneries. Cluniac nunneries were no more lavishly decorated, nor Cistercian ones more austere than those of other orders.

Greater differences can be perceived in the orders which fostered double houses of nuns and canons. The French order of Fontevrault was based on the teachings of Robert of Abrissel (1115), who believed that Christ had left the apostles under the authority of the Virgin Mary, as his mother. Consequently, the order was established for nuns and canons, to be presided over by an abbess. St Gilbert of Sempringham initiated the only order to have originated in England, after sponsoring the enclosure of seven holy women in a cloister attached to his parish church at Sempringham (Lincs) in 1131. The Gilbertines were a double order for nuns and canons supported by lay-brethren and sisters. The male presence provided canonical support and manual labour to assist the religious women; they in turn were responsible for providing food and clothing (Elkins 1988: 84). Similarly, lay-brothers were at first attached to Cistercian nunneries in Lincolnshire, which had received large grants of pasture land and required assistance with tending sheep (ibid.: 92).

In comparison with their monastic brothers, medieval nuns were expected in practice, as well as theory, to be strictly enclosed within their convents and to minimize their contact with the secular world. It seems that for medieval nuns enclosure became a fourth cardinal vow, as significant to their sprituality

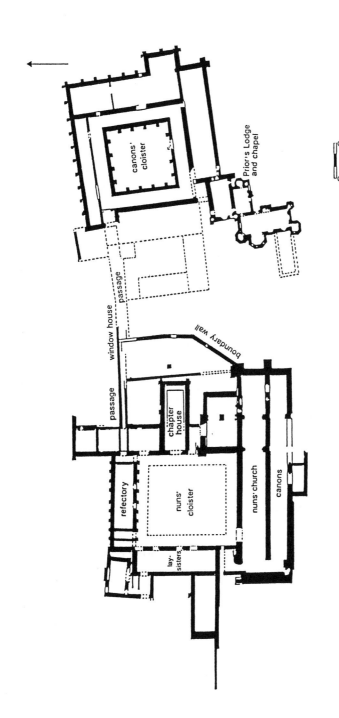

Figure 63 Watton (E Yorks/Humbs): plan of the Gilbertine priory excavated by St John Hope (1901). The nuns' cloister was to the north of the main conventual church, while the smaller canons' cloister and chapel were located separately to the east.

as poverty, chastity and obedience (Power 1922: 342). Central to this tradition was the importance of female virginity and innocence, religious commodities which were defended by physical and psychological barriers. During the early medieval period strict enclosure may have provided protection from marauders for communities of Saxon and Merovingian women vulnerable to attack. By the time the first Cluniac nunnery was founded at Marcigny in 1056, the concept of enclosure was integral to the female monastic identity. Abbot Hugh referred to his foundation of Marcigny as a 'glorious prison' and Peter the Venerable discussed the nun's veil as a symbolic shroud (Schulenburg 1984: 61). The greater enclosure of religious women was justified in the 12th century by the proposed spiritual weakness of the female sex. Theologians, such as Thomas Aquinas, followed patristic writers in stressing the base corporeality of women, who were considered more susceptible to carnality and sexual temptation. Only the physically and spiritually incorrupt virgin could rise above the inheritance of Eve. As Brides of Christ, medieval nuns demonstrated their fidelity through perpetual enclosure. Visits outside the cloister could be allowed only by the bishop with the consent of the abbess.

The spatial segregation of nuns was of paramount importance within double houses. Particularly severe were the observances of Fontevrault, which included 18 rules for women all concerning strict enclosure, in contrast to nine for men which related to obedience. At the mother house in Fontevrault the nuns' cloisters were contained within the walls whereas that of the canons was outside. In the church two separate choirs were provided in order to facilitate segregation (Simmons 1992: 102–3). In Gilbertine houses a similar degree of strictness was observed. Two cloisters and two choirs were provided and food was passed from the nuns' cloister to the canons through a small turning window, approached by a passage from both cloisters (figure 63). During the mass the sacrament was passed through a similar turning window, to a female sacristan (Elkins 1988: 141). The nuns could only speak to their visiting relatives through a narrow aperture.

The insecure filiation of nunneries renders them difficult to quantify according to order. However, approximately 92 English nunneries were, at some time, Benedictine, 34 Cistercian, 23 Augustinian, 11 Gilbertine, 10 St John of Jerusalem (amalgamating into one), 5 Franciscan, 4 Fontevraultine, 4 Cluniac, 4 Premonstratensian, 2 Bridgettine (a Swedish double order) and 1 Dominican. In Wales 3 Cistercian nunneries were founded and one Benedictine (Knowles and Hadcock 1971). In contrast the Scottish nunneries were predominantly Cistercian: 9 Cistercian, 2 Augustinian, 2 Franciscan, 1 Dominican and 1 Benedictine (Cowan and Easson 1976). The Irish houses for women included 50 Augustinian/ Arrouaisian, 5 Cistercian, 4 Franciscan and 3 Benedictine (Gwynn and Hadcock 1970) (figure 64).

It seems that the Norman overtones of the Benedictine and Cluniac orders made them an unpalatable prospect in Wales, Scotland and Ireland. In all cases, the fairly high incidence of nunneries claiming adherence to the Cistercian Rule, if not formal recognition by the order, indicates a commitment to the eremitic movement of the 12th century. Nuns of the Yorkshire Cistercian nunneries expressed their allegiance through the wearing of white habits associated with the order (Elkins 1988: 86). The Irish preference for the Augustinian order is said to have resulted from a visit by St Malachy to

Figure 64 Distribution of nunneries in medieval Britain: based on Knowles and Hadcock (1971), Gwynn and Hadcock (1970) and Cowan and Easson (1976).

Arrouaise in 1139–40, after which he founded nunneries devoted to the order (Gwynn and Hadcock 1970: 307). Some provision for religious women in Ireland may have been provided by the Franciscan Third Order Regular, or the Tertiaries, a 13th-century development of the Franciscans, originally for married men and women. Forty-seven houses of the Tertiaries are known to have been established in medieval Ireland, but few of these ever accommodated women, and there are no records of women of the order in Ireland after 1457 (ibid.: 264). Brethren and sisters of the Third Order may have been accommodated in separate buildings at only four sites: Galway, Carrick-on-Suir (Waterford), Court (Sligo) and Killeenbrenan (Mayo).

In comparing the dates of foundation of monasteries for men with the foundation dates of nunneries, it is apparent that some considerable time elapsed before the initiation of female houses of a newly fashionable religious movement. For example, Benedictine houses for men were established predominantly between 1080 and 1110, whereas nunneries reached their height of foundations *c*1160 (Gilchrist 1994: 41). Patrons were moved to set up nunneries a generation or more after male houses of the same order had been established. This difference in the timing of monastic foundations for women results both from the motivation and social identity of their founders. In England, the first Norman foundations for religious women were established mainly by bishops, such as Malling (Kent), set up by Gundulf, the first Norman bishop of Rochester, *c*1090. In contrast to Benedictine monasteries for men, nunneries were never planned in conjunction with a Norman town or castle as an act of political consolidation. Lay patronage was more important from 1130–65, when most founders of nunneries were the vassals of earls or barons (Elkins 1988: 77).

Aristocratic women established nunneries at Godstow (Oxfords), Elstow (Bedfords), Stixwould (Lincs), Lacock (Wilts), Marham (Norfolk) and Canonsleigh (Devon), often retiring into the convent themselves. Increasingly, nunneries were founded at a middling social level, often jointly by a husband and wife. Such joint foundations have previously masked the active interest shown by women founders. Wives used their own dowries to establish nunneries at Baysdale (N Yorks), Clerkenwell (London), Harrold (Bedfords), Little Marlow (Bucks), Tarrant Crawford (Dorset) and Nun Appleton (W Yorks) (Thompson 1991: 177). In Suffolk alone, three nunneries were founded by women using their own inheritances: at Bungay by Gundreda de Glanville, at Redlingfield by Emma, daughter and heir of the Lord of Redlingfield, and at Flixton by Margery de Creyk. A similar tendency has been recognised in a sample of 26 nunneries in northern France, where 38 per cent were founded by women (Johnson 1991: 34).

The founding family of a monastery could have considerable influence on its affairs in the long term, for example in some cases retaining the right to appoint a prioress. Certain families took a particular interest in establishing nunneries, for instance those founded in the 12th century by two connected families: the de Arches at Nunkeeling (E Yorks) and Nun Monkton (N Yorks) and the de St Quintins at Nun Appleton (W Yorks) and Bullington (Lincs). Such dynasties established nunneries in order to consolidate their own positions in the local community. Women members of the family frequently entered the house as a nun or as the first prioress, as was the case at Nun Monkton, and members of the family regularly requested burial within the convent cemetery. Patronage of prominent families sometimes impacted on the material culture of nunneries, most obviously through the commissioning of heraldic ceramic tiles, such as those of the Uffords at Campsey Ash (Suffolk) and the de Clares at Little Marlow (Bucks). At Campsey, benefaction of the nunnery resulted in the use of the south aisle of the chancel as a private burial area by the family (Sherlock 1970).

At a higher social level, particular orders for religious women found favour within families. The Franciscan nunneries in England were all established by relatives of Blanche, Queen of Navarre, the founder of the first English house at the Minories, Aldgate, London (1293–4). The English houses of Fontevrault can be seen to have resulted from the personal interests of Eleanor of Aquitaine. Following her marriage to Henry II, houses were founded by the king at Westwood (Worcs) and Amesbury (Wilts), and at Nuneaton (Warwicks) by his steward, Robert of Leicester.

Occasionally, female houses were established by collective groups of merchants or townspeople. For example, the people of Torksey (Lincs) seem to have founded the nunnery at Fosse *c*1184, perhaps developing from an anchoress's cell attached to the parish church (Thompson 1991: 28). St Helen Bishopsgate, London, was established *c*1210, and by 1290 the nunnery had received the patronage of the merchant community. The association gathered pace and was reflected in the commissioning of stained glass, such as the roundels to the Grocer's company, which survived until bomb damage to the church (1992–3). Connections with civic groups were cemented through the meeting of guilds at some nunneries. The weavers' guild of Northampton met annually on Easter Monday to offer tapers before the image of Our Lady at the nunnery of Delapré, Northampton; and at Carrow, Norwich, the Saddlers and Spurriers of the City instituted their guild in 1385 in honour of the Blessed Mary and All Saints, meeting before the image of Our Lady at the high altar. Membership of guilds and religious fraternities included participation in special annual masses, feasts and processions, and insured that members would receive prayers and burial upon their death. Through their association with the nunnery, the merchants and guild members were assured the intercessory prayers of the nuns.

Continued patronage of nunneries resulted, no doubt, from the esteem with which the intercessory prayers of nuns were held. But the nuns earned the respect of their local community in other ways, particularly through their charitable acts. Nuns were associated with the running of hospitals and hospices and with giving alms to the poor and needy. Daily alms comprised scraps of food which were left outside a convent's walls; more substantial amounts were given on the anniversaries of deaths, or obits. The nuns of Flixton gave annually 56*s*. 8*d* in alms to the poor on the obit of their founder, Margery de Creyk. Some nunneries offered 'out patient' care, such as phlebotomy, most notoriously in the case of the Prioress of Kirklees, who is reputed to have bled Robin Hood to death. Hospitals in or near the monastic precinct were maintained by the nuns of Castle Hedingham (Essex) and Wilton (Wilts). Others maintained hospitals at a further distance from the convent, including Grace Dieu (Leics), Barking (Essex), Nunkeeling (E Yorks), Wimborne (Dorset), Romsey (Hants), Marrick (N Yorks) and Shaftesbury (Dorset) (Gilchrist 1994: 173). A number of female houses seem to have evolved from hospitals, including St Mary de Pré (Herts) and Thanington (Kent) while others were established for hospitality and care of the poor, such as St Mary Magdalene, Bristol, and Aconbury (Herefords), the latter at first associated with the Knights Hospitaller (Thompson 1991: 39–50). Similarly, in France, strong links existed between enclosed religious women and nursing care, such as the hospital of Saint-Jean founded by the abbey at Ronceray in Angers (Johnson 1991: 51–3). The largesse of the sisters was rewarded with the respect of their local communities.

Further links were encouraged by the schools which many nunneries ran for local children, and by the practice of allowing secular visitors or temporary boarders within the precinct. More permanently resident corrodians included men and women and married couples. In 1414, for example, 15 corrodians were resident in the inner court at Flixton (Suffolk), including four married couples (Gilchrist and Oliva 1993: 65). The presence of schools for female children is implied by episcopal visitations, such as that of 1439 to St Helen Bishopsgate, London, which ordered that visitors to the nunnery after Compline should include only female servants and 'mayde childeryne lerners' (Reddan and Clapham 1924: 9).

In their daily observances the nuns were expected to divide their time between divine services, reading and labour. In the summer months the services began early in the morning (Lauds at 1.00 a.m.) and continued throughout the day (Compline at 7.00 p.m.). Certain nuns fulfilled a liturgical role within their communities as female sacristans or chaplains, as recorded at Romsey (Hants), Campsey Ash and Redlingfield (Suffolk), Elstow (Bedfords) and Barking (Essex) (Power 1922: 64). The others would have participated through their prayers, reading and singing. Attempts were made to increase the resonance of the nuns' singing by placing acoustic jars beneath the choir (see Harrison 1968), as recorded at Farewell (Staffords), St Radegund, Cambridge, and at the western choir of the Swedish nunnery at Bosjökloster. The nuns' labours might include administration, needlework and, very occasionally in poorer houses, light agricultural work.

By the 12th century religious women are thought to have placed less emphasis on the spiritual importance of both manual labour and learning, with French replacing Latin in many nunneries (Power 1922: 301). The significance of needlework is illustrated by finds beneath the floor of the nuns' chapel at Cistercian Wienhausen in Germany, where thimbles, scissors, spindles and small weaving frames were discovered (Moessner 1987: 164–5). The assumed absence of learning in medieval nunneries may have been over-emphasised previously. While few nunneries possessed large communal libraries, the nuns required missals, psalters and antiphons in their daily services, some of which survive and contain the obits of benefactors. In private meditation the nuns used biblical material, female saints' lives and devotional literature, much of which related to the mystical tradition which appealed particularly to women. Some, such as Walter Hilton's *Scale of Perfection*, a late 14th-century guide for anchoresses, were written with women in mind and owned by many small nunneries (Gilchrist and Oliva 1993: 53–4). Books were given to nuns as gifts by their own families or by benefactors. A degree of literacy is suggested by the material culture of nunneries. Excavations at Elcho (Perths), the poorest of the Scottish Cistercian nunneries, recovered fragments of two book clasps and one book-cover catch (Reid and Lye 1988: 70); a bronze lifting tool, used to turn book pages or to apply gold leaf, was recovered from the site of Shouldham (Norfolk), and two styli were excavated from St Mary Clerkenwell, London, one lead and one bone. The funerary monuments of religious women were occasionally graced with the clerical symbol of the book, such as the flat effigy of an abbess *c*1200 at Polesworth (Warwicks). The conventual seals of nunneries, including those of Amesbury, Barking, Denney, Nuneaton, and St Mary, Winchester, sometimes depicted the abbess or prioress holding a book and crozier, her staff of office.

Figure 65 Killone (Clare, Eire): a nunnery founded *c*1189, set in the side of a gently sloping river valley.

Nunneries in the medieval landscape

Some nunneries occupied classic monastic sites: set in the sides of gently sloping river valleys, such as Killone (Clare, Eire) (figure 65) or Marrick (N Yorks). Others like Grace Dieu (Leics) were situated at the foot of a slope, and incorporated rivers or streams in order to bound the precinct. Many were set in less hospitable surroundings such as marsh, fen or moorland. In certain cases the nuns actively sought marginality and isolation, like earlier ascetics who had emulated the desert fathers (below pp. 162–5). In medieval Yorkshire the penitential solitude of the desert was found in the moorlands, and in East Anglia it was sought in the fens and marshlands. The cartulary of Crabhouse tells us that Leva, a hermit, and her followers sought a desert and solitary place (*heremus*) in the fens of west Norfolk (Bateson 1892). When this nunnery was founded the parish was empty of other inhabitants and was not reclaimed from marshland until the 13th-century digging of the old Podike drain. Nunneries at Fosse (Lincs), Higham (Kent), Swine and Nunkeeling (E Yorks) suffered similar environs. The wealthy nunnery of Barking (Essex) was situated on the low-lying alluvium of the River Roding, leading Sir Alfred Clapham to comment that the site's 'desolate nature was probably its chief recommendation' (Clapham 1913: 70).

Topographical isolation contributed to the strict enclosure envisaged for religious women, and was sometimes achieved by placing nunneries on islands. Denney Abbey, which replaced the more frequently flooded site of Waterbeach, occupied a small island or peninsula of raised land near the southern edge of the Cambridgeshire fens (Christie and Coad 1980: 138). Minster-in-Sheppey

(Kent), the site of a Saxon and later medieval nunnery, was placed on the Isle of Sheppey, situated on a steeply rising hill overlooking the estuary of the Medway and surrounding marshes. The nunnery of Bosjökloster (Scania, modern Sweden, medieval Denmark) was situated on an island in the middle of Lake Ringsjön. More typical was Little Marlow (Bucks) perched on a sandy rise in marshy land by the Thames and bounded on all sides by watercourses filled by springs. At the monastic complex of Clonmacnoise (Offaly, Eire) the nuns' church was located approximately 0.5km from the main site, approached by a causeway through the marsh. The church was converted in the mid- to late 12th century from an existing building, and retains a richly ornamented chancel arch and western door with elaborate chevron ornament, incised panels and animal heads (figure 66).

A number of nunneries were established within moated sites, such as Bruisyard, Flixton and Redlingfield (Suffolk). Moat-digging would have assisted in the drainage of marshy sites, such as Waterbeach (Cambs), and would have been consistent with the tendency to delineate the boundaries of female houses by water. It has been suggested that by *c*1200 moat construction was increasingly associated with the gentry (Dyer 1989: 107). Their provision at nunneries and preceptories may reflect the aspirations and social origins of the founders and inmates of these religious institutions. The watery environs of nunneries may have held another significance to medieval people. The medical (humoral) association made between water and the female body was a recurrent theme in the middle ages. According to the Galenic theory of the four humours (based on the writings of the Greek Galen *c*129–200), the dispositions of all people were determined by the composition of the four humours, based on phlegm, blood, yellow bile and black bile. People were categorised according to the resulting humours: phlegmatic, sanguine, choleric or melancholic. Women were seen as phlegmatic and watery by nature (Rawcliffe 1995: 172).

For nunneries associated with medieval towns some degree of isolation was found outside the city walls. Those at Carrow (Norwich), Stamford, Canterbury and Clementhorpe (York) occupied such situations. At Cambridge and Thetford, a greater sense of separation was created by the placing of the nunnery in land contained by rivers, outside the town. Extramural nunneries were sited in the fields beyond the town, such as Godstow (Oxford), Derby Kings Mead, Polsloe (near Exeter), Northampton Delapré, St Mary de Pré (St Albans) and the London houses of the Minories, Haliwell and Clerkenwell. Few were within the heart of towns, excepting the pre-Conquest nunneries which had attracted commerce and urban settlement, including Shaftesbury, Romsey, Wimborne, Wilton and Amesbury, or rare examples of border nunneries placed within the protection of the town. At Chester the nuns were granted a block of land *c*1150 by the fourth Earl of Chester, Ranulf II, within the town walls and the Castle demesne. The site occupied the south-west corner of the city immediately north of the castle (Ward 1990: 3).

Despite the tendency for the founders of many nunneries to crave desolate, insular sites, many established by middle-ranking patrons were set up in association with an existing parish church and manor. In such cases the spatial and social relationship between nunnery and village must have been close. One such example is that of Redlingfield (Suffolk) where Emma de

Figure 66   Clonmacnoise (Offaly, Eire): the nuns' church, located approximately 0.5km from the main monastic complex, retains fine 12th-century carving on its western door and chancel arch.

Redlingfield initiated a nunnery through the donation of the local parish church and manor. Some northern nunneries were planned in conjunction with villages, possibly to provide a community of labourers for the religious women. At Stainfield (Lincs) earthworks testify that a village street and tofts were set out to the south of the precinct, and at Orford (Lincs) a single-sided village stretches to the east of the nunnery (Everson 1989). Nun Monkton village (N Yorks) lay with the apex of the green at the gate of the nunnery precinct, and at Nunkeeling (E Yorks) the nunnery was established immediately to the south of an existing village (Gilchrist 1994: 69). The area of land enclosed within the precinct varied from 18 acres at Lacock (Wilts) to 3 acres at Kington St Michael (Wilts). Even wealthy nunneries like Barking (Essex) commanded precincts of only 11 acres, with 2.5 acres of the total taken up by the parish churchyard (Clapham 1913: 77). The suburban nunnery at Haliwell, London, was set in a precinct of 8 acres.

By monastic standards the endowments of nunneries were meagre. It has been estimated that French nunneries commanded only 15 per cent of the resources enjoyed by their monastic brothers (Johnson 1991: 219), and in East Anglia initial endowments were characterised by small manors, local parish churches and plots of rather unproductive land, as was the case at Blackborough, Crabhouse, Bungay and Marham. Neither Redlingfield nor Flixton were endowed with lands outside their parish boundaries (Gilchrist and Oliva 1993: 24). Many nunneries had centralised estates, which resulted in the working of home farms as the most substantial holdings. The Yorkshire nunneries were most commonly granted pasture land, resulting in over-specialisation in wool. Even the wealthier houses, such as Stixwould (Lincs) and Denney (Cambs) received their grants of land within one or two generations after the foundation of the nunneries and failed to develop an active programme of acquisition and management (Gilchrist 1994: 71–3). In contrast to the standard tenet of monasticism, it seems that very few nunneries would have been able to achieve a level of economic self-sufficiency.

The archaeology of nunneries

The material culture of nunneries followed patterns linked to the social origins of particular houses. While the majority of post-Conquest foundations for women can be characterised by a unified tradition of building materials, forms and iconography, the wealthier communities were built more in keeping with the standards of male monasticism. They form a distinct group in this respect, including the richer nunneries initiated before the Conquest – Amesbury, Barking, Chatteris, Polesworth, Romsey, Shaftesbury, Wherwell, Wilton and Winchester – and certain post-Conquest foundations with royal connections, such as Nuneaton, Carrow and Elstow. These nunneries were built with cloisters on a scale more akin to male houses and tended to have larger, cruciform churches more typical of monasteries. Carrow (Norwich), for example, was a small community of nuns who lived a fairly modest lifestyle. Yet, the relative grandeur of their monastic cloister reflects the status of their royal founder, King Stephen. The fully aisled cruciform church was larger than any other parish or monastic church in Norwich, with the

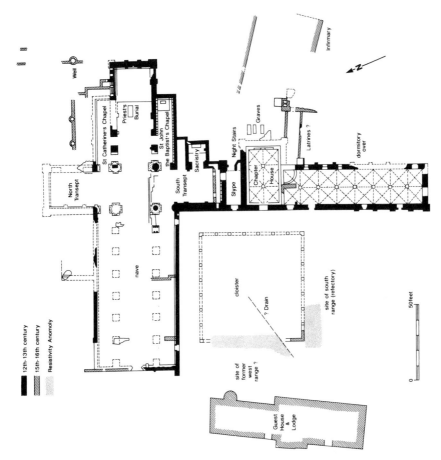

Figure 67   Carrow, Norwich (Norfolk): a small Benedictine community of nuns was founded by King Stephen and provided with a large, aisled cruciform church.

exception of the Cathedral Priory (figure 67). Even these houses, however, were seen to fossilise early in their development. The Norman refoundation of the Saxon Nunnaminster, Winchester, was signalled by complete reconstruction of both the church and domestic buildings. But from the late 12th century until the Dissolution few changes or structural alterations were implemented (Qualman 1986).

Nunneries followed the standard monastic layout in which a central complex of buildings was grouped around a cloister. The church was expected to form the northern range with the cloister formed by three ranges of buildings which together formed a U-shape abutting the church to its south. Given that some nunneries were established at existing parish churches, the cloister sometimes extended to the south of the nuns' choir, leaving the nave open to access from either direction for the parish. In some cases such origins may have resulted in a detached cloister or building complex some distance away from the parish church. It is not clear whether small nunneries such as Redlingfield (Suffolk) or Ickleton (Cambs) ever possessed fully developed

Figure 68 Redlingfield (Suffolk): a medieval building, possibly belonging to the monastic inner court, survives some 30m to the south of the present parish church.

cloisters. At Redlingfield, a single medieval building of masonry construction survives some 30m south of the largely rebuilt parish church (figure 68). At Ickleton, some disagreement exists over whether the buildings of the priory were located to the north of the surviving parish church (Radford 1967: 228) or form part of a house located 1.5km from the church (Haigh 1988: 44). The Cistercian nunnery at Heynings (Lincs) has traditionally been located at the parish church of Knaith (Pevsner and Harris 1964: 290). However, field survey by the RCHME has established the situation of the nunnery at an earthwork site some 3km distant from Knaith (Everson 1989: 145). It remains unclear whether such houses were provided with the usual monastic cloister or whether accommodation was set up nearby, more comparable perhaps to a manor house with private chapel.

Recent excavations have indicated that at nunneries, in common with other monasteries, stone cloisters were preceded by temporary or reused timber lodgings, for example at Polsloe, Exeter. Excavations at St Mary Clerkenwell, London, revealed a range of substantial timber buildings probably dating to the foundation of the nunnery in 1144, one of which may have been converted to serve as temporary accommodation after completion of the later stone ranges (Sloane 1992 unpub). Where parish churches were expanded to accommodate female religious communities, it was customary to begin with the rebuilding of the chancel as a monastic choir. At St Helen Bishopsgate, London, founded c1210, this phase is indicated by the piercing of the north wall of the existing parish church with 13th-century lancet windows. Elsewhere, the claustral plan developed slowly. At Polsloe (Exeter), the nunnery, initiated c1160, only acquired a cloister and walkways c1300. At Elstow excavations suggested a significant interval between the construction of the church and the earliest cloister ranges, the walks of which were probably in timber (Baker 1971).

The cloister and its ranges might be built in stone, rubble, cob or timber, with the exception of the church, which was invariably stone-built. The surveys of the Yorkshire nunneries made at the Dissolution suggest that small houses, such as Wilberfoss, had claustral buildings entirely of timber construction (Brown 1886). Excavations at Waterbeach (Cambs) identified mortared, rubble-wall foundations and traces of wall plaster suggesting that a timber-framed and plastered building had occupied part of the site (Cra'aster 1966). At Cook Hill (Worcs) a range adjoining the ruined chapel is timber-framed and cased with brick. Nunneries which were particularly poor, or in regions with little stone, are more likely to have been built in cob, or earth. Excavations by the late Maurice Barley at the nunnery of Fosse (Lincs) revealed buildings with mud walls, consisting of clay with small fragments of lias limestone (Barley 1964: 174). A survey at the site of Crabhouse (Norfolk) made in 1557 describes walls of earth and brick, noting that only the steeple of the demolished church had 'walls of stone' (Dashwood 1859). Even stone-built cloisters could be of rudimentary construction, such as that surviving at Molough (Tipperary, Eire), where the plainness of the church was relieved only by simple lancets, the pairing in the east end being typical of 13th-century work in Ireland. Excavations supervised by Sir Charles Peers at Little Marlow (Bucks) revealed details of a poor nunnery built in flint and chalk, with no ashlar, and with no evidence for vaulting or embellishment (Peers 1902).

At many nunneries a cloister was formed simply through the creation of lean-to roofs against the main ranges. At Brewood (Shrops) the north wall of the nave retains a string-course which served as weathering for such a pentice roof; hooked corbels below held the roof-plate in place. At Marham (Norfolk), corbels on the south wall of the ruined nave indicate a similar arrangement, and at Campsey Ash (Suffolk) a line of stone moulding surviving on the west range is witness to a pentice roof. Cloister alleys were sometimes created by extending the upper storey of the monastic ranges over a space for the corridor or walkway. Such 'overshot' cloisters were cheaply constructed and typical of the architecture of friaries. Examples of this technique having been used at nunneries include Grace Dieu (Leics) (*Archaeol J* 90 1933: 392) and the trapezoidal cloister at Killone (Clare, Eire). Wealthier nunneries were provided with free-standing cloisters, such as Malling Abbey (Kent) and Lacock (Wilts), both with essentially 13th-century cloisters of continuous open arcades made up of twin columns carrying trefoil-headed arches. The cloister alleys at Lacock are about 3m wide with wooden pentice roofs and contain continuous stone seats.

The north range of the nunnery was usually the church, which was commonly shared with a parochial congregation. This tradition prevailed even at Cistercian Marham (Norfolk), contrary to the practices of the order, and despite the existence of a parish church at the eastern boundary of the precinct. Such an arrangement required particular attention to be paid to the segregation of the nuns from laity. The majority of nunnery churches were unaisled rectangles or parallelograms. Nuns never required the additional altars for the celebration of private masses that were commonplace in the aisles, transepts and chapels of monasteries for men. The nuns' choir was positioned in the eastern end of the church and separated by the *pulpitum* screen. A second screen was placed further west which divided the nuns' church from that of the parish. At Nun Monkton (N Yorks), the junction of the nave and choir can still be discerned by the position of a corbel in the form of a female head, flanked by two birds (Gilchrist 1994: 103). The central nave altar was generally placed against the screen, with doorways to its left and right leading to an antechapel in the space formed by the two screens. A doorway in the antechapel provided an entrance for the nuns from their cloister to the choir without passing through the nave. An additional 'night stair' gave them access to the choir directly from their dormitory over the east range for evening services such as Midnight Matins and Lauds. At Burnham (Berks), a blocked doorway in the extant east range suggests that a gallery over the antechapel may have been entered from the nuns' dormitory.

Alternative means of segregating the nuns from the parish included a 'parallel aisle' arrangement. At St Helen Bishopsgate, London, the nuns occupied a northern aisle adjoining their cloister, and the parishioners were accommodated in the southern aisle. An arcade separated the two aisles, the existing one built *c*1470–75 (figure 69). The nuns reached the choir from their dormitory via the night stairs contained in the thickness of the wall. The nuns' stalls were placed to the west of these stairs. Doorways from their church led to the sacristy and the cloister, providing eastern and western processional routes. Further openings, or squints, retain traces of mortices for iron grilles. Their church contained chapels to St Catherine and St Margaret and an image of St Helen located to the north of the nuns' choir (Reddan and Clapham 1924: 35). Parallel aisle churches were adopted mainly in south-eastern England and include Haliwell (Shoreditch, London), Minster-in-Sheppey (Kent), Higham (Kent), Easebourne (Sussex), Ickleton (Cambs) and Chatteris (Cambs), and in the Midlands, Wroxall (Warwicks).

The necessity of sexual segregration in double houses resulted in a variety of arrangements. In Gilbertine houses the church was attached to the nuns' cloister and possessed parallel choirs for the nuns and canons, as at Watton (E Yorks) (figure 63). In houses of the Swedish double order of St Bridget, buildings of the nuns and canons were placed on opposite sides of a shared conventual church. Arrangements in the English monasteries of Fontevrault are less clear. The cruciform church at Nuneaton (Warwicks) acccommodated the nuns in the western part and the monks in their choir east of the crossing. The surviving cruciform church at Fontevraultine Amesbury (Wilts) is *c*300m south of the presumed site of the priory, where excavations in 1859–60 recorded a possible chapter-house: a rectangular room surrounded by stone benches and containing a richly tiled floor. The extant church seems to have been that of the parish and the brethren, the crossing and chancel of which was rebuilt in the 13th century by the priory in order to accommodate the canons. The dimensions of the choir and transepts appear to have been copied from the priory church which was described in a survey of 1540 (RCHME 1987: 234–5).

Cruciform churches at nunneries most often located the nuns' choir in the crossing or to the east of it. Occasionally, the choir was placed in the eastern bay of the nave, as at Shaftesbury (Dorset) until the 14th century (RCHME

Figure 69   St Helen Bishopsgate, London: the church was arranged as two 'parallel aisles', with the nuns' church to the north divided from that of the parish by an arcade which would originally have held screens.

Figure 70   Killone (Clare, Eire): the church was built on sloping ground, enabling the construction beneath the eastern end of a crypt with a corbelled vault.

Dorset 4 1972: 59). The return stalls backed against the *pulpitum*, which crossed the nave between the first pair of piers. The position of the nuns' choir was sometimes in the west of the church and the parochial nave in the east, contrary to the usual monastic observances. Such an arrangement is recorded for Marrick (N Yorks) and Haliwell, Shoreditch, as well as having been suggested for Davington (Kent), Nunkeeling and Swine (E Yorks). This practice may have stemmed from the western gallery choirs typical of nunneries in Germany, Italy and Scandinavia, such as Roskilde and Asmild, Viborg (Denmark), and Bosjökloster (modern Sweden, medieval Denmark), and the Venetian nunneries of St Maria Dei Miracoli and St Alvise. The tradition may have originated in the earlier Italian and Byzantine tradition of the women's gallery, or *matreum* (Gilchrist 1994: 109). In monastic use, the western gallery would have assisted in increasing the audibility of the nuns' singing by elevating their voices in order to project them through the church.

Nunnery churches were rarely planned with the same degree of ornamentation or complexity as the churches of their male counterparts. Larger churches, such as Carrow (Norwich), appear to have operated only at ground-storey level, with no evidence for access to upper-level galleries or wall-passages. Exceptions are Iona (Argyll), where the windows of the clerestory are sited over the piers, rather than over the arches, and Romsey (Hants) where, in the nave, the main arcade and triforium are combined, providing upper levels. The east end consists of a square-ended choir with ambulatory carried round it, with chapels projecting eastward. An unusual arrangement at Killone (Clare, Eire) provided a passage in the eastern wall of the church which led behind the high altar and up to the wall-walk. The passage passed behind a pair of round-topped lights with chevron-moulded arches with wall-

Figure 71 Burnham (Berks): the east range of this Augustinian nunnery contained the sacristy and chapter-house on the ground floor, with a common dormitory for the nuns above.

shafts beneath the moulded impost, *c*1225. The church (39.3m long) was provided with an eastern crypt of corbelled vault construction, which was entered from an exterior door in the east end and also from a passage to the south which opened from the cellarage of the east range, possibly providing some kind of private chapel (figure 70).

Some impression of the fittings of a small nunnery church can be gained from the dissolution inventory of Minster-in-Sheppey (Kent) (Walcott 1868: 290–93). Over the high altar in the nuns' choir was 'a cross of sylver and gylt with the Crucyfyx, Mary and John'; upon the high altar were altar clothes, a painted cloth of the Resurrection to hang before the rood over the high altar, 'a Lenten Clothe of lynyn', and 'in the nether part of the quire images of our Ladye in alabaster and a cloth painted with her image'. Also prized were 'a lyttyle shryne of timber gylt full of olde relyks, a box of bone with like relyks'. The sacristy contained further altar clothes of red, yellow and blue, a surplice and vestments, 'a clothe to bare over the sacrament', a pair of laten (brass) censors and several books and parchments. A Lady chapel contained further vestments of red damask embroidered with gold, and others of green satin and black velvet. In the absence of libraries in nunneries, the sacristy would have served as a secure store for books owned communally by the house.

The east range of the nunnery contained in its ground floor the sacristy, chapter-house, warming-room and parlour; above was the dormitory of the nuns (figure 71). The sacristy was used to store sacred vessels and vestments and was positioned to enable access for the priest without ingress to the

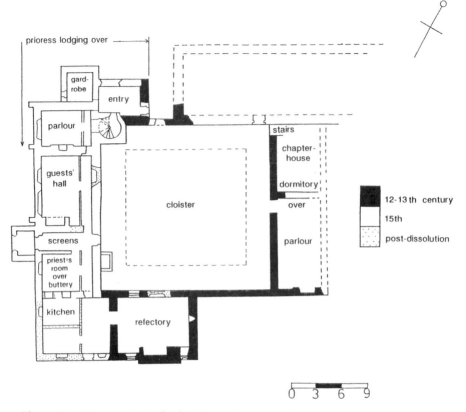

Figure 72   Kington St Michael (Wilts): the extant 15th-century west range and excavated east and south ranges. Based on Brakspear (1922).

nuns' cloister. It was generally placed between the church and chapterhouse, with a doorway in its east wall for the priest, as at Burnham (Berks). The chapter-house was where daily chapter was held: a place of official meeting for the community and an area of burial for heads of the house and revered patrons. Its significance to the community is reflected in the degree of ornamentation given to the entrance: at Lacock (Wilts) and St Radegund, Cambridge (now Jesus College), the entrance is marked by three arches consisting of a central entrance and one large window on each side. At Cambridge the shafts of *c*1230 are topped by stiff-leaf capitals, and at Lacock, the central arch was decorated with colour. At Higham (Kent), in contrast, the chapter-house seems to have been separated from the rest of the range by a simple timber partition (Tester 1967: 146). Sir Harold Brakspear's excavations at Kington St Michael (Wilts) identified the foundations of the east range, the ground floor of which was divided into two rooms with the southernmost distinguished by a large fireplace (figure 72). Brakspear identified this room as the warming-house, the one chamber of the priory which was heated and in which the community met informally. He suggested that the warming-houses of small nunneries became regularly used as parlours, the single room of the monastery in which speaking was permitted (Brakspear

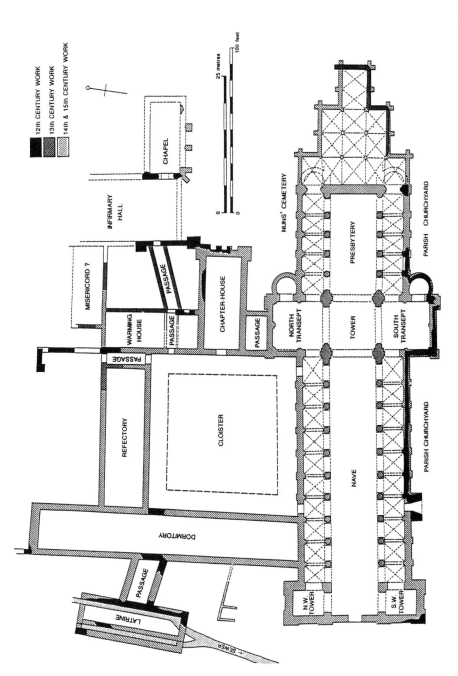

Figure 73 Barking (Essex): the excavated structures and ruins include the extensive church and cloister, infirmary area and latrines flushed by flowing water. Based on Clapham (1913).

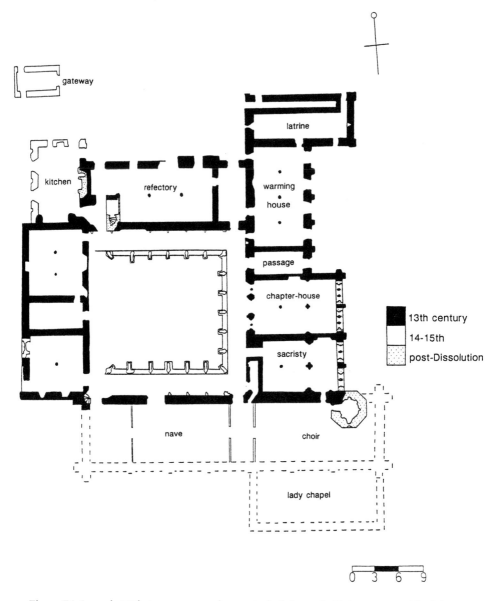

Figure 74 Lacock (Wilts): a nunnery plan typical of the early 13th century, with cloister to the north of the former church. Based on Brakspear (1900).

1922: 249). Only in wealthier houses did the east range project beyond the line of the cloister, such as Elstow, Barking (figure 73) and Nuneaton.

The upper floor of the east range contained the dormitory; at Lacock, approached by a flight of steps contained in the west walls of the sacristy, emerging from a lobby. In the late 14th century it was lengthened beyond the east range over the adjoining latrine block (figure 74). The original latrine was two-storeys and was entered directly from the dormitory. It consisted of

Figure 75   Denney (Cambs): the nuns' refectory formed the northern range of an open court cloister, and was later converted to a farm building.

garderobes placed over a main drain below (Brakspear 1900: 148). Small nunneries, such as Higham (Kent), were provided with latrines more like secular garderobes, emptying into a pit below rather than being flushed by flowing water or drains. Excavation at the site revealed a privy which met the dormitory at first-floor level; the ground floor was paved with flagstones and joined with a drain but was not flushed by flowing water (Tester 1967: 149). Rare examples, like Barking, were provided with more elaborate sanitation, where a great culvert was split into two channels beneath the latrine block, which was joined to the dormitory to its east by a passage (Clapham 1913: 84).

At their inception, nunneries were provided with a common dormitory, but like their counterparts in other types of monasteries, they increasingly divided their dormitories into individual cells. At Littlemore (Oxfords), the east range was rebuilt in the latter half of the 15th century. The new building survives as a range measuring *c*23 by 6.3m and seems to have accommodated twelve cells, six on both sides of a central passage and each measuring *c*3 by 2.4m. Each cell was lit by a single window (Pantin 1970). The growing sense of individual privacy was accompanied by a relaxation of the rules prohibiting private property. An inventory taken at the dissolution of the nunnery of Minster-in-Sheppey (Kent) describes the contents of the chambers of eight nuns. The richest, that of Dame Agnes Browne, included 'stuff given her by her friends', perhaps left in the form of testamentary bequests, and consisting of a featherbed, a bolster, pillows, blankets, coarse coverlets, good and bad (worn) sheets, a carved box, cupboards, chests, silver and gilt goblets, candlesticks, a fire pan and tongues, pewter dishes, a porrenger, basin, skillet, brass

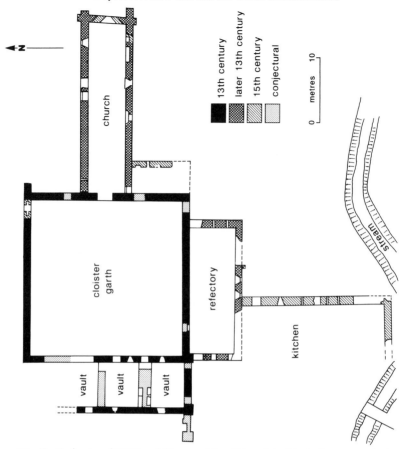

Figure 76   St Catherine d'O'Conyl Shanagolden (Limerick, Eire): the unusual plan of this nunnery features a church projecting at right angles from the east range.

pot, cauldron and drinking pot (Walcott 1868: 296). The more devout Dame Anne Clifford possessed 'a table with a crucyfyx of wod payntyd, and an image of our Lady, payntyd' (ibid.: 297).

The range opposite the church contained the nuns' refectory, most commonly arranged as an upper storey over cellarage. Occasionally, this was accommodated in a self-contained two-storey block, as at Kington St Michael (Wilts) rather than as the usual continuous range of buildings (figure 72) (Brakspear 1922: 250). At the entrance to the refectory a *lavatorium*, or ritual washing place, was situated in the cloister alley. At Lacock (Wilts) this consisted of two recessed compartments with wall-paintings above a cornice. These included St Augustine giving benediction to a kneeling female figure; an abbess with crozier; and a garden (Brakspear 1900: 139–40), an iconographic representation for virginity. Often, the refectory itself was contained on the upper storey above a vaulted cellarage. At Easebourne (Sussex), food was brought to the refectory from a detached kitchen through a slanting hatch located in the west bay of the cellarage. This bay would have served as the pantry and buttery with stairs leading up to the refectory.

At Denney (Cambs), the single-storey nuns' refectory survives almost intact,

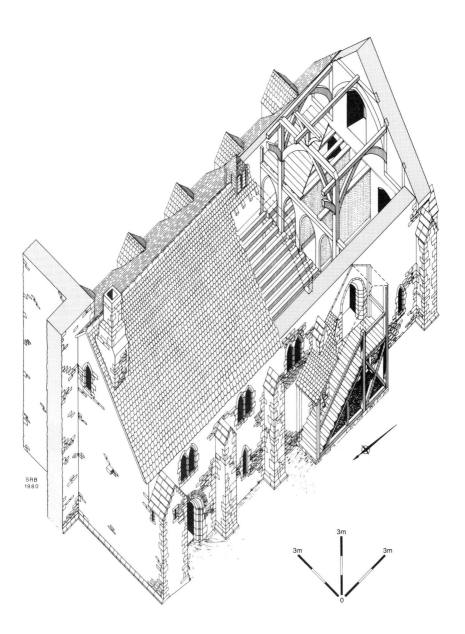

Figure 77 Polsloe (Devon): the west range contained the prioress's lodgings in the northern end of the upper storey, adjacent to the west end of the church, and a guest hall in the central area screened from services in the eastern end. The guest hall had an external entrance from outside the cloister to the south. Reproduced courtesy of Exeter Museums Archaeological Field Unit.

having been converted for use as a barn (figure 75). It measures *c*28 by 6.8m with evidence of external rendering and interior wall-paintings, including representations of birds and ivy in red and black ogee lozenges. Excavations revealed glazed tiles *in situ*, mainly a chequer pattern of dark green, or black and yellow glazes, and the footings for fixed benches around the walls (Poster and Sherlock 1987). A raised dais at the eastern end would have accommodated the upper table of the prioress and senior sisters. A blocked opening above a small northern doorway represents the position of the pulpit, from which the sisters would take turns to read during the meals. Corbels on the south exterior indicate that a pentice walkway provided shelter for the nuns between the ranges. Indications of similar pulpits exist at Elstow, Lacock and Kington St Michael.

The west range of the nunnery commonly accommodated the guest-house, private lodgings for the prioress, storage, and sometimes, offices for the obedientiaries. Like the refectory, one end of the range was often partitioned to serve as a buttery, such as Cambridge, where a rotating hatch passed food from a kitchen located to the west. At Lacock the west range abutted the church, indicating that it was built later. Its ground floor consisted of three chambers, some of which were divided further by wooden partitions. The southernmost chamber was divided into apartments with fireplaces, providing accommodation, possibly for guests or corrodians (figure 74). Evidence of similar provision survives in the west range at St Catherine d'O'Conyl, or 'Manisternagalliaghduff' (Shanagolden, Limerick, Eire), which is divided into three vaulted chambers containing aumbries at ground-floor level and, in the case of the southernmost chamber, a fireplace above (figure 76). Guests were prohibited from entering the nuns' choir, yet long-staying visitors would have expected to observe services. Compromise was found by constructing viewing galleries for seculars at the west end of the church, as at Aconbury (Herefords) where a blocked doorway indicates the former existence of an upper-storey gallery entered from the west range (Gilchrist 1994: 107–8).

In most cases, the west range was used for guest accommodation, arranged as a secular manor house, with ground-floor hall, private parlour at the upper end and buttery at the lower end, such as Davington (Kent) (Tester 1980: 210). A two-storey range survives at Polsloe (Exeter); it is bisected by a stone wall at ground-floor level in order to divide guest accommodation from the chambers used by the convent (figure 77). The division of space between the guest-hall and a private lodgings for the prioress was common. The central importance of hospitality seems to have resulted in the rebuilding of many west ranges in the 15th or 16th centuries, such as at Kington St Michael (Wilts) where the ground floor provided a central guest hall, upper-end parlour and buttery at the lower end, divided by a screens passage. Above the parlour end was accommodation for the prioress, and a chamber above the buttery might have provided accommodation for a priest (figure 72) (Brakspear 1922). At Carrow (Norwich) the extant west range was rebuilt by prioress Isabel Wygun in the 16th century as a range set back from the cloister (figure 67). Resistivity survey has suggested that the original west range flanked the cloister and was demolished in order to make way for the new building, which originally consisted of a hall, north parlour and spiral staircase to an upper chamber with oriel window.

Figure 78 Minster-in-Sheppey (Kent): the gatehouse to the west of the nuns' church and cloister has arches for pedestrian and waggon traffic and residential chambers above.

Attached to the cloister to the east was the infirmary – provided for the sole use of the monastic inmates of the convent. At Burnham (Berks), the infirmary is largely extant and consists of a large hall with its axis north–south, a small latrine at its northern end and a possible chapel towards the east. A meat-kitchen, or *misericorde*, was sometimes provided in the infirmary in order to supplement the diet of the old and infirm nuns. Excavations at Barking (Essex) suggested this was located at the western end of the hall, where a large hearth was screened from the main infirmary hall (figure 73) (Clapham 1913: 85).

An inner court was sited beyond the nuns' cloister. This was a service court and sometimes contained accommodation for secular people living within the precinct, including servants and corrodians. The priest or chaplain of the nunnery was often resident here, and may have lived in a chamber above the gatehouse into the court or in free-standing lodgings (figure 78). At St Helen Bishopsgate, London, in 1344, Walter Dieuboneye established a chantry within the church and provided a salary for a chaplain together with a 'suitable house within the priory such as the parish priest had' (Reddan and Clapham 1924: 5). A chamber to the west of the church at Killone (Clare, Eire) may have served such a function; western priests' chambers are known to have existed at parish churches in Ireland. Additional features of the court are shown on a late-16th-century plan of Marrick (N Yorks), which shows the position of the convent's buildings surrounding three sides of the cloister, and a 'greate court' which contained a gatehouse, stranger's stable, soke house, slaughter house and other animal houses (figure 79). A similar survey of Crabhouse (Norfolk) was made in 1557, and allows a reconstruction of the inner court buildings based on a perambulation moving from the west range of the former nunnery (figure 80). The 'courte' was of one acre, three parts and more; ranged around it were houses, stables, a cattle pen, an old mill house, a malting house, a store house and the parson's chamber, together with its kitchen and buttery, adjacent to the 'old sepale' (steeple) of the former church, with its walls of stone (Dashwood 1859).

Rarely did the arrangement of buildings around the nunnery cloister depart from the standard patterns. At the decrepit and overgrown remains of the Augustinian nunnery of St Catherine d'O'Conyl (Limerick, Eire) the church (*c*24.6 by 5.4m) projects from the east at right angles from the cloister court (*c*22.2m sq) (figure 76). The identification of this building as the church is confirmed by the presence of a piscina with quatrefoil basin in its south wall. The windows and doors indicate that the church, cloister and refectory to the south are largely dated to the 13th century. The church was entered from the cloister court by a fine west door with keeled piers and moulded capitals, one with dog-tooth ornament (figure 81). The cloister was formed by a pentice supported on corbels which survive on all inner sides of the ranges. The refectory joined a roughly constructed building to the south, possibly a kitchen, sited between the cloister and a stream running to the south. There are no surviving remains of a north range, or indication of the situation of the major accommodation for the nuns. Excavations by Sir Alfred Clapham at the Dominican nunnery at Dartford (Kent, founded *c*1356) were interpreted as indicating a similar plan. Clapham suggested that the nuns' church projected from the east side of the cloister, and measured *c*30.6 by 6.15m

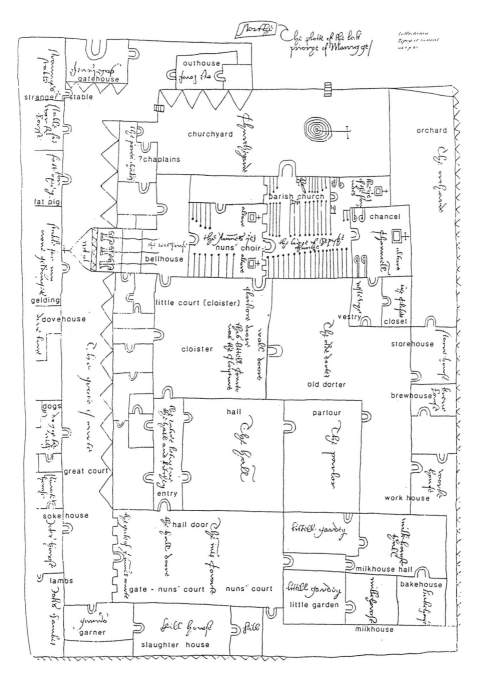

Figure 79 Marrick (N Yorks): a late 16th-century plan of the former nunnery, from *Collectanea Topographica et Genealogica* 5 (1838).

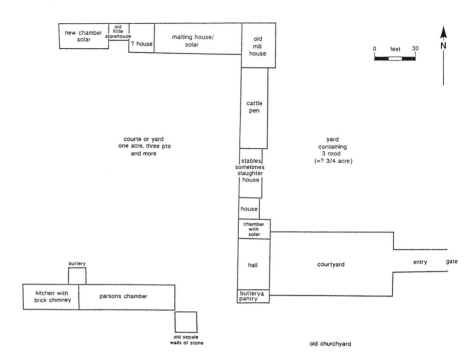

Figure 80 Crabhouse (Norfolk): reconstruction plan based on a survey made in 1557.

(Clapham 1926: 76–77). A close parallel is the Franciscan nunnery at Provins (Ile de France), a 13th-century monastery which retains a long rectangular chapel at right angles to the east walk of the cloister. Such variations on the monastic plan seem to have been considered acceptable for late-founded female houses of the 13th and 14th centuries.

Modifications subsequent to the main phases of claustral building included the addition of sacristies to those nunneries which were without them initially, and the construction of new chapels, such as Lady Chapels at Romsey (Hants) and Lacock (Wilts). Shaftesbury (Dorset) gained 14th-century chapels to the north and south side of the chancel, resulting in the demolition of the transeptal apses (RCHME Dorset 4 1972: 59). Private chantry chapels were added to St Helen Bishopsgate in 1371 and to St Sepulchre, Canterbury, in 1369, the latter motivated to provide the nuns with their only daily mass (Cook 1947: 26). In some cases such chapels proliferated, such as Chester, where 13 chapels are listed in a processional of *c*1425 (Legg 1899).

Substantial rebuilding of the cloister was rare in the case of the nunneries, although excavations at Elstow have shown that the cloister and south and east ranges were substantially replanned, including the lengthening of the chapter-house as far east as the main east end of the church (Baker 1971). At Lacock, the windows of the original buildings (1232–38) were blocked in places by the erection of buildings over the cloister and the erection of a gallery over the south walk after the late 14th century (Brakspear 1900: 131–2). In addition to

Figure 81   St Catherine d'O'Conyl Shanagolden (Limerick, Eire): western door to the nuns' church.

Figure 82 Bungay (Suffolk): the tower of the parish church which joined the church of the nuns to the west.

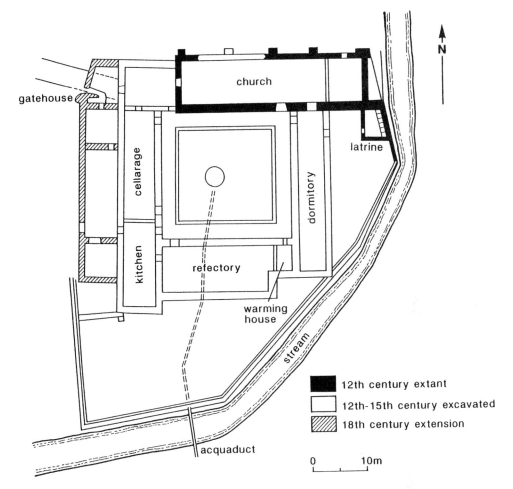

Figure 83 Coyroux (Limousin, France): excavation of the Cistercian nunnery. Based on Barrière (1992).

the renovation of the west range (discussed above), programmes of new building frequently reflected the interests of the parish, including the addition of towers to the parochial nave, as at Bungay (Suffolk) (figure 82), and porches and new aisles, for instance at Usk (Monmouths [Gwent]).

More fundamental changes related to developing perceptions of the monastic community. The impetus towards individual, private space in monasteries is shown in the partitioning of dormitories (above p. 129) and the tendency for the female religious community to splinter into smaller households, or *familiae*. Such groups are reported in bishops' visitations from the late 13th century and with growing frequency by the 15th (Power 1922: 317). They were particularly common in the group of wealthier nunneries with royal and aristocratic connections, perhaps indicating that higher-status nuns craved the lifestyle of their secular peers from the same social milieu – women who lived in the 'inner household' of castles (Gilchrist 1994: 168). The breakdown of the communal dormitory and refectory resulted in smaller groups of women residing together in religious community. Such groups may have been accommodated at Elstow in converted outbuildings, within the partitioned refectory, or in timber-framed buildings just outside the precinct (Baker and Baker 1989: 270). At Godstow (Oxfords), three households replaced the traditional monastic cloister in a radical reordering of monastic space. The households were described and drawn in the 17th century (Ganz 1972), and indications survive of their arrangement. They were concentrated in the southern part of the walled enclosure, towards a two-storey chapel tucked in the south-east corner. Two parallel ranges were aligned east–west around a conduit which ran through the enclosure. A third building abutted the outer court to the west (Gilchrist 1994: 123).

It seems that the majority of smaller British nunneries were modestly constructed in a manner more in keeping with small manor houses or non-conventual ecclesiastical establishments. This tradition was observed also by the nunneries of medieval Denmark and by smaller female houses in France. Excavations at Cistercian Coyroux (Limousin), for example, have revealed a convent markedly similar to smaller British nunneries (figure 83). The in-hospitable, isolated site was prone to frequent flooding, and was poorly constructed with stone bonded by earth rather than mortar, in contrast with the nearby male house at Obazine, established by the same founder, Etienne of Obazine. The aisleless parallelogram church contained a nuns' choir with a screen pierced by a small grille for communication. The cloister was created by a pentice with timber roof and no proper warming-house was provided. In the words of the excavator:

> No function was neglected, no element was missing, all the necessary technical services were there, yet nothing was conceived to last; the daily conditions of use were difficult and precarious, as if any possibility of comfort, even the most rudimentary, had been thoroughly ruled out (Barrière 1992: 81).

Filiation and iconography

The gender of monastic inmates seems to have been more significant in the planning of nunneries than the order to which a house subscribed. The role of patron can be elucidated in a handful of cases, particularly those in which a female founder took an active interest in promoting a particular order or established a nunnery into which she herself could retire. Excavations at the site of the Franciscan Minories (London) suggested an unusual semi-octagonal east end. The foundress, Blanche of Navarre, may have modelled this first Franciscan nunnery in England, established 1293–4, on the church at Winchel-sea Franciscan Friary (Sussex). The only substantial remains of a Franciscan nunnery in Britain are those at Denney (Cambs), where from c1339 Mary de Valence, the Countess of Pembroke, altered an existing monastic complex, instituting an open-court cloister typical of Franciscan architecture.

An aisleless cruciform church was first built at Denney by a cell of Benedictines c1159, which was transferred to Knights Templar by 1170 (see p. 75), following their suppression, to the Countess in 1324 (figure 38). She received

Figure 84   Denney (Cambs): the blocked crossing and transepts of the church. The foundations of the former nuns' chancel are marked out on the foreground.

a licence to transfer the nuns from nearby Franciscan Waterbeach in 1339. De Valence demolished the chancel of the Templar church and had erected a more spacious aisled choir for the nuns, placing the western responds of the arcades against the blocked arches to the transepts of the Benedictine church (figure 84).

In the nave and south transept she constructed private apartments at ground- and upper-storey level, with a gallery in the crossing enabling sight of the nuns' choir through a squint. The Countess herself is likely to have resided in these apartments until her death, after which time they would have been used by subsequent prioresses. The 14th-century alterations consist of new doorways inserted through blocked Norman arches. The work is of high quality but shows little adornment; the only exceptions are carved female heads, one *in situ* supporting the vaulting of the eastern chamber in the former nave, the other now resited in the north transept. The north transept seems to have contained the night stairs from the nuns' dormitory range to the north, which was one of three ranges sited around an open court cloister to the north of the church (Christie and Coad 1980).

At a number of sites the patronage of women founders appears to have influenced the visual iconography of the church and claustral buildings. In some cases, such as the work commissioned by Mary de Valence at Denney, this resulted in the greater prominence of representations of women. At Nun Monkton (N Yorks), founded jointly by Juetta and William de Arches, *c*1147–53, a corbel in the form of a female head, wearing a decorated headband and flanked by two birds, marks the junction of the nave and choir. At Killone (Clare, Eire), founded *c*1189 on lands of Donal Mor O'Brian, a corbel at the

Figure 85   Killone (Clare, Eire): a corbel in the shape of a female head is placed at roof level at the external south-eastern angle of the church. Drawing by Ted West.

external south-eastern angle of the church is a female head, with hair worn loose and held by a headband; the woman's hands are raised in a gesture to support the roof of the church (figure 85). Such figures may represent the female founders of nunneries, or perhaps female saints. Those at Nun Monkton and Denney are flanked by birds, possibly referring to the life of St Scholastica, to whom the dove appeared in a vision. Representations of women or female saints are not uncommon in male houses but their occurrence would seem to be particularly noteworthy at female houses, which are otherwise unembellished by sculpture or iconographic schemes.

Ela, Countess of Salisbury, founded Lacock (Wilts) *c*1230 and became the community's first abbess in 1239–40. The corbels supporting the vaulting survive *in situ*, and their subjects seem to have been determined according to the spatial rules which governed access to various rooms in the nunnery. Those in the sacristy – the area of the priest – are male heads, the *Agnus Dei* and foliage; the chapter-house contains both male and female heads, whereas the parlour, deeper within the female space of the convent and accessible only to the sisters of the house, contains two decorated corbels, both female heads. Similar rules governed the imagery at Marham (Norfolk), established by Isabel of Arundel in 1249. Only one sculptural figure survives in the north end of the west range, an area most likely to have contained the guest accommodation. The figure supported the rib-vaulting of the former range and represents a bearded man holding a sword or gauntlet – a secular image appropriate to this less sacred area (Gilchrist 1994: 159–60).

Devotion within nunneries was directed primarily towards Christ and the Virgin Mary. In the sacristy and church were images associated with the sacrifice of Christ, appropriate for areas linked with the eucharist. These included the *Agnus Dei*, the Lamb of God shown with a nimbus or halo, depicted on a corbel at Lacock, and wall-paintings from the Minories (London) and at Marcigny (Autun). Medieval stained glass at Llanllugan (Montgomerys [Powys]) includes a Crucifixion in the east window, with a hooded figure of an abbess in prayer in the left light (RCHM Montgomery 1911: 119). Monastic seals of the 13th and 14th centuries from the nunneries of Flixton and Bungay (Suffolk) depict Christ on the Cross; that from Flixton and a second, prioress's seal from Bungay, show the *Agnus Dei*. The Lamb of God is shown on a number of other seals from nunneries, including those of Ellerton (N Yorks), Esholt (W Yorks), Godstow (Oxfords), Kilburn (Middlesex), Lambley (Northumb) and Stamford (Lincs). Both of these images suggest a strong interest in the Passion and the sacrifice of Christ, a predilection associated with female piety. A carved sacred heart from the site of Dartford Dominican Nunnery (Kent), possibly associated with the medieval convent, shows the pierced heart of Christ encircled by a crown of thorns. At Usk (Monmouths [Gwent]) remains of a 16th-century range of the convent include a panelled room with emblems of the Passion: the nails, ladder and scourge (Williams 1980). Religious women were associated with aspects of the medieval mystical tradition, and are known to have focused on the heart and blood of Christ in their devotions.

Devotion to the Virgin Mary was articulated through material culture such as ceramic tiles and monastic seals. Tiles excavated from Campsey Ash (Suffolk) bear the initials 'BM', *Beata Maria* (Sherlock 1970: 133). The dedications of nunneries favoured the Virgin overwhelmingly. Of the Benedictine nunneries in England and Wales listed by Knowles and Hadcock (1971) some 39 were dedicated solely to the Virgin and a further 13 were to the Virgin and one or more other saints (52.5 per cent). Although Mary Magdalene was a favoured patron saint for hospitals, she was invoked by only five nunneries, second in popularity to the Virgin. Next in frequency of

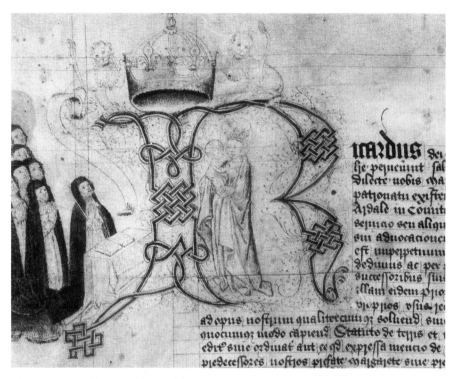

Figure 86   An illuminated initial from the Esholt Priory Charter, 1 June 1485, showing the nuns of Esholt praying to the Crowned Virgin with the Child. Reproduced with permission of the West Yorkshire Archive Service (acc 3429).

dedications were St Margaret, St Helen, St John the Baptist and St Leonard, each with three nunneries dedicated to them; St Catherine, St Andrew, St Giles, St Edward, St James, St Edmund, the Holy Cross, St Peter and St Bartholomew with two dedications each; and single nunneries dedicated to St Sepulchre, St Stephen, St Michael, St Patrick, St Laurence, St George, St Clement, the Holy Trinity and the early medieval saints, St Elfleda, St Ethelburga and St Radegund (Knowles and Hadcock 1971). A similar preference is revealed by nunnery seals. In a sample of 136 surviving seals, more than half relate to the life of the Virgin, with particular emphasis placed on images related to her role as mother: the Annunciation and, more especially, the 'Throne of Wisdom', in which the crowned Virgin holds the Christ Child resting on her knee (Gilchrist 1994: 143–6). This maternal imagery is repeated in psalters commissioned for nunneries, such as those of Amesbury and Shaftesbury, and the 1485 charter of Esholt Priory (W Yorks), which shows the nuns of the convent kneeling before the altar in adoration of the crowned Virgin Mother and Child (figure 86).

Iconographic messages were sometimes signalled through the ground-plan and form of the claustral buildings. For instance, the two-storey refectories, which were common to nunneries, may have contained a specific meaning for religious women. The upper-storey refectory may have been a reference to the 'upper room' which housed the Apostles, the Virgin Mary, Mary Magdalene and the other Holy Women after Christ's death (Acts 1: 13–14). The upper room, or *coenaculum*, identified with this event was the upper chapel at St Mary Mount Sion (Palestine), which was rebuilt in the 11th and 12th centuries (Pringle 1986: 345). The *coenaculum* represented the early stages of the Church at Jerusalem which acknowledged the active participation of women in the Pentecost. The nuances contained in such an iconographic archetype would have been particularly appropriate to the nunnery refectory: the one context in which public reading and speaking by women was encouraged (Gilchrist 1994: 116–17).

In some cases, iconographic undertones may have determined even the placement of the cloister. Approximately one-third of nunneries were established with their cloisters to the north of the church, in contrast to the usual ordinances which placed the cloister to the south. While in some cases the siting of the cloister may have resulted from restrictions relating to drainage or water supply, in others, the north cloister may have been chosen for particular iconographic associations. Indeed, when mapped, north cloisters cluster in certain regions: the south-east, East Anglia and Yorkshire. Each cluster may have taken its cue from a house with particular relevance to female religious. For example, Barking (Essex) was a Saxon double house which was praised by Bede (*Historia Ecclesiastica* 4: 6–10) It was refounded and rebuilt in the early 12th century with a north cloister which may have served as a model for nunneries subsequently founded in the region. Surrounding nunneries with north cloisters included St Helen Bishopsgate (–1216), Clerkenwell (*c*1144), and Haliwell (–1158), (London), Burnham (Berks) (1266), and Minster-in-Sheppey (Kent) (*c*1130), the last house itself having been a Saxon female community. Nostalgic connotations of female piety, together with more general tendencies to associate women with the northern regions of churches, may have been taken into account in the layout of the cloister and its buildings (Gilchrist 1994: 128–49).

Economic production and standards of living

In comparison with their monastic brothers, nuns were provided with relatively crude systems of sanitation (above p. 129). The results of recent excavations at nunneries suggest that these lower standards included less regular clearance of domestic waste from the cloister. Modern archaeological investigations of monasteries for men have come to anticipate the scrupulously high standards of cleanliness appropriate to monastic living. At nunneries, greater quantities of refuse have been encountered, such as the deposits of animal bone excavated at Elstow and Polsloe (Exeter), at the latter site from contexts including the cloister garth and dormitory as well as kitchen and garden areas (Levitan 1987).

The diet in nunneries was fairly simple in comparison with the richer fare known to have been served in wealthier monasteries. Indeed, it has been proposed that the diet observed in smaller nunneries had closer affinities with that of the better-off peasantry, known to have been cereal based, consisting largely of bread and pottage, fruit and vegetables, fish, dairy produce, beef and bacon (Dyer 1989: 157–8). The accounts of Marrick (N

Yorks) show purchases of grain for bread, which represented a substantial element of the diet, and malt for brewing into ale. Large quantities of salt were purchased, presumably to preserve meats, and only small amounts were spent on fish and dairy produce, both of which would have been supplemented by the nunnery's own outer court and home farm. Vegetables were provided by the convent's cole or cabbage garden, the *Kalgarth* (Tillotson 1989: 15–16). Evidence from the animal bones at Polsloe suggests an increasing reliance on beef over mutton in the nuns' diet at this house. Carcasses were purchased either whole or halved, and butchered on site at the priory (Levitan 1987). The aristocratic connections of St Mary, Winchester, resulted in a richer diet, represented by the animal bones of farmed and wild game and 20 types of fish and bird species, including rare types such as sturgeon, porpoise, crane and whooper swan (Coldicott 1989: 77–8). Excavations at Denney recovered some evidence for fruit in the nuns' diet. A garderobe built onto the west wall of the south transept, which formed part of the chambers of the foundress, and subsequent abbesses, contained seeds of elderberry, blackberry, fig and grape (Christie and Coad 1980: 155). A surviving charter of the cellaress at Barking adds dried peas and beans to our impression of the nuns' diet, which at this wealthy house included figs, raisins, almonds and salt fish as Lenten fare (Power 1922: 566). In Franciscan nunneries it was expected that the healthy sisters would refrain from eating meat, instead consuming fish (Bourdillon 1926/1965: 70), a tenet of monastic life which was broken by most communities of nuns and monks alike.

At a number of nunneries, cemeteries have been partly excavated, many of which remain unreported. Interim statements on the human bones from Clementhorpe (York) indicate that the majority of the 139 adults identified were female (67 per cent) and that they enjoyed good dental health and a low incidence of arthritis. Individuals from St Mary, Winchester, and Denney Abbey, by contrast, showed a more common occurrence of degenerative joint disease, and at the latter site, an inflammatory condition indicating a low resistance to infection (Christie and Coad 1980: 271). Predominantly female groups of skeletons have been excavated from Chester and Carrow (Norwich), but generally both men and women seem to have been accepted for burial in the convent cemetery and church, in contrast to male houses which have yielded assemblages primarily of male skeletons.

Beyond the cloisters and inner court the monastic outer court contained appurtenances essential to the subsistence of the nunnery. The nunnery's home farm, which supplied garden and dairy produce, is likely to have been situated nearby, so that the outer court and home farm may be indistinguishable archaeologically. These elements can be reconstructed from extant buildings, earthworks, documents and the results of excavation. Most houses would have held fishponds, represented today by earthworks such as those at Marham (Norfolk) (figure 87). Extensive systems of fishponds are indicated at larger houses like Campsey Ash (Suffolk), although self-sufficiency was seldom achieved, and the cellaress of Campsey regularly purchased large quantities of fish in the 13th century. Areas of ditched or embanked closes within the precinct may have contained livestock, gardens or orchards. Water or windmills were common features and each nunnery would have possessed a bakehouse and brewhouse. Excavations at the Fontevraultine double house

Figure 87   Marham (Norfolk): earthworks mark the site of the cloister to the south of the extant south wall of the church. Further to the south is a possible inner court and to the west an infirmary court. Possible fishponds are indicated to the extreme south. Reproduced with permission of the Norfolk Air Photographs Library of the Norfolk Museums Service and Derek Edwards.

of Nuneaton (Warwicks) uncovered a brewhouse, with a sunken, round, mortar-lined vat from which an iron pipe passed through the wall (Andrews *et al* 1981: 64).

Light industrial activity may be expected in the outer court, although as yet only limited evidence has come to light. At the Gilbertine double house of Shouldham (Norfolk), a medieval tile kiln was used in the production of roof tiles from local sources of clay (Smallwood 1978), and at the Cistercian nunnery of North Berwick an excavated kiln contained ornamented relief tiles (Richardson 1928); excavations in the outer court at St Mary Clerkenwell, London, located tile kilns (Sloane in prep). Outbuildings at Elstow (Bedfords) yielded copper-alloy trimmings, and bone-working may have been carried out at Haverholme (Lincs). Excavations inside the precinct at St Helen Bishopsgate, London, revealed deposits of garden soil, rubbish pits and the chalk-lined cellars of two buildings. A ditch which ran parallel to the precinct boundary contained extensive dumps of waste possibly from bell-founding (*Medieval Archaeol* 35 1991: 152). At St Mary Clerkenwell, London, an inner court developed north of the main cloisters, which were situated to the north of the church, and included a stone building at least 22m in length, which extended from the east range, and a kitchen which formed part of the north range; a metalled yard surface separated the two buildings (Sloane 1992 unpub). Within the courtyard, a number of chalk-built structures were served by drains and cesspits. A lead conduit crossed the outer court from the north, linking it with the water supply, illustrated by the famous Charterhouse plan (see pp. 202–4).

Insights provided by excavations at Clerkenwell suggest that the inner court was used for small-scale industry, gardening and refuse disposal and burning. The presence of latrines implies that some structures in the inner court were used for domestic occupation, possibly by servants, priests, corrodians or even *familiae*. A similar perspective has been provided by excavations at Elstow (Bedfords), where stone outbuildings stretched from the dormitory of the nuns' cloister to a possible jettied structure towards the stream. The only agricultural building was the stable; the remainder were service structures containing drains, sloping stone floors, water tanks and wells, while others were more domestic, having been provided with hearths and latrines (Baker and Baker 1989: 267). Elstow gives the impression of the inner court as an area frequently renewed and rebuilt, a perspective provided by excavation in the outer courts of male houses such as Thornholme (Lincs) (Coppack 1989). The evidence of archaeology and documents, however, confirms that nunneries would not have achieved the self-sufficiency originally expected of enclosed monastic communties.

Beyond the bounds: the diversity of female monasticism

Nunneries represent the most formal and well-documented type of religious life for medieval women. The vocation of the hospital sister was more actively charitable and was open to women in towns and those from a broader social spectrum (see pp. 14–17). A wide variety of alternatives existed for those who wished to follow a communal or solitary religious life, some of which fell beyond the bounds of ecclesiastical orthodoxy and therefore outside ecclesiastical documents. In the 12th century, women banded together to form eremitic groups or lived as women hermits (see p. 175). An eremitic life for religious women was not deemed acceptable by patrons and churchmen, and references to such communities had ceased by the end of the 12th century. However, similarly fluid communities sprang up spontaneously in the 15th century.

These informal communities of religious women can be recognised in the wills of townspeople and clerics, referred to by such terms as 'women dedicated to chastity' or 'sisters under religious vow'. These women have been identified as having lived in later medieval East Anglia: nine informal communities of women were located in Ipswich (Suffolk) and five in Norwich (Norfolk). Other women described as nuns, *moniales*, are recorded as having resided in places in Norfolk where no formal nunnery is known to have existed: at Dereham in 1527, Grenecroft in 1280, Hingham in 1385, Swaffham in 1242 and 1280 and Yarmouth in 1291 (Gilchrist and Oliva 1993: 101). John Bale, a Carmelite priest, wrote in some detail of a 15th-century community of women who lived in Ipswich. His account tells that they lived by an informal rule which dictated that: they rise at midnight from September

Figure 88   Elmhill, Norwich (Norfolk): a 15th-century building which may have housed an informal community of religious women, known to have been associated with the church of St Peter Hungate (to the south). Note its close proximity to the church of the Blackfriars to the west (in the background), and their anchorhold for female recluses to the north of the chancel.

14 until Easter and at dawn in the summer; refrain from eating meat; fast on bread and ale on Fridays and Saturdays; wear hairshirts; and above all, say a prodigious number of prayers (Gilchrist and Oliva 1993: 71–3). These communities suggest a possible indigenous tradition of female piety, which flourished outside the theological and spiritual practices ordained by the Church. Such informal groups may have resembled beguinages. It seems likely that their occurrence in East Anglia in the 15th century was stimulated by the region's close contacts with northern continental Europe. Yet the 'women dedicated to chastity' may have been part of a wider English tradition of women living under vows of voluntary poverty.

The unstructured nature of these communities meant that they were often short-lived, established in ordinary tenements within towns or in dwellings set up in churchyards, such as those at St Peter Hungate and St Lawrence in 15th-century Norwich. These women may have drawn support through the spiritual munificence of the friars; they resided close to the Carmelite Friary in Ipswich and the Blackfriars in Norwich. The community at St Peter Hungate, Norwich, would have been situated immediately to the east of the friars' church. A possible candidate for their accommodation is a 15th-century building backing onto the churchyard of St Peter Hungate. A door from the churchyard provided direct access to the house, a jettied, timber-framed building which originally consisted of three, self-contained floors reached by an external stair on the east side (figure 88). The tenement would have provided an ideal set of stacking chambers or cells for the religious women.

Figure 89 Vowess's brass from Witton (Norfolk): Dame Juliane Anyell, 1500.

Beguinages developed from the 13th century as groups of secular women in towns of the Low Countries, northern France and the Rhine valley, banded together in order to serve the needs of the poor and sick. They supported their communities through their own labours and by begging for alms. By the 14th century these women lived increasingly in enclosed communities and were forced to rely on patronage for their subsistence. In Italy, particularly in Rome, women succeeded in living a communal life as *pinzochere* or *bizoche* in open monasteries, *monasteri aperti*, until the end of the 16th century. These women participated especially in the penitential movement (Gill 1992: 16–18). Women in almshouses or *maisons dieu* across Europe lived a semi-religious lifestyle, as bedeswomen. They were not necessarily professed or celibate but carried out charitable works, prayed and attended funerals for a pittance in order to offer their prayers for the souls of patrons. In Germany, these women, or *Seelfrauen*, lived in 'soul-houses', often supported by the largesse of secular women. In Augsburg, there were six soul-houses and seven convents of nuns (Roper 1989: 245).

Women who lived solitary lives of prayer were also part of an international movement of medieval female religious. Female recluses lived in their own homes in France and Italy, and in England widows took the veil, were given a ring and took vows to lead chaste lives dedicated to prayer as vowesses –

unenclosed solitary religious women. Occasionally, these women are recognised by their funerary brasses, such as those of Joan Braham and Juliane Anyell at the parish churches of Frenze and Witton (Norfolk) (figure 89). Some individual holy women were remembered in the wills of medieval townspeople. In 16th-century Norwich, these women were singled out by the term 'Mother', and may have been midwives, healers, or some other religious personae outside our modern terminology (Gilchrist and Oliva 1993: 80).

Large numbers of religious women lived solitary lives as anchoresses attached to parish churches. Theirs was the most extreme of religious vocations (see pp. 183–93). This ascetic lifestyle attracted both men and women, but English recluses were predominantly female (Warren 1985: 20). This movement was not specifically English in origins, but only in England did the independent ascetic life remain formalised and widespread into the 16th century.

When the diversity of female religious experience is considered it becomes clear that the map of nunneries represents only a small fraction of the opportunities through which women could express their piety. This can be demonstrated graphically by mapping the variety of female religious in medieval East Anglia (figure 90). While there were only 11 nunneries in medieval Norfolk and Suffolk, the geography of religious women included an additional 14 informal communities (at 6 known sites), at least 14 hospitals that accommodated women staff and inmates, 73 anchoresses (at 42 parish churches), 7 vowesses, *moniales* at 5 sites not previously known as nunneries, and the intriguing 'Mothers' noted in Norwich.

Women were essential to an international religious movement which was not confined to orthodox monasticism. Women's religious lifestyles were characterised by fluidity and variety. The vitality of their devotions continued to attract the support of local laity through testamentary bequests and gifts right up to the Dissolution and beyond. Nuns continued to reside together and receive support even after the suppression of individual nunneries. Pensioned nuns from the priory of Carrow in Norwich congregated in the parish of St Peter Hungate, while the parish of St Stephen in the same city attracted nuns from as far afield as Shouldham in Norfolk and Bruisyard, Bungay and Campsey Ash in Suffolk. Elizabeth Throckmorton, the last abbess of Denney, retreated to her family's manor in Coughton, where, with two of her fellow sisters, she continued to live a monastic life (VCH Cambridge 2 1948: 301–2). In Augsburg, Germany, the nunneries were the least receptive to the German Reformation. The convents outside the city walls had to be forcibly closed and the nuns billeted in the intramural Dominican nunnery, while the nuns themselves were forbidden to hear mass, go to confession or receive the sacrament (Roper 1989: 213–15).

Conclusions: the character of female monasticism

The vast majority of post-Conquest British nunneries were established by middle-ranking founders. Their architecture and landscapes indicate that nuns lived a frugal and modest existence. But were nunneries simply impoverished monasteries or was their material culture specific to female piety?

In certain respects nunneries resembled manorial settlements, which would

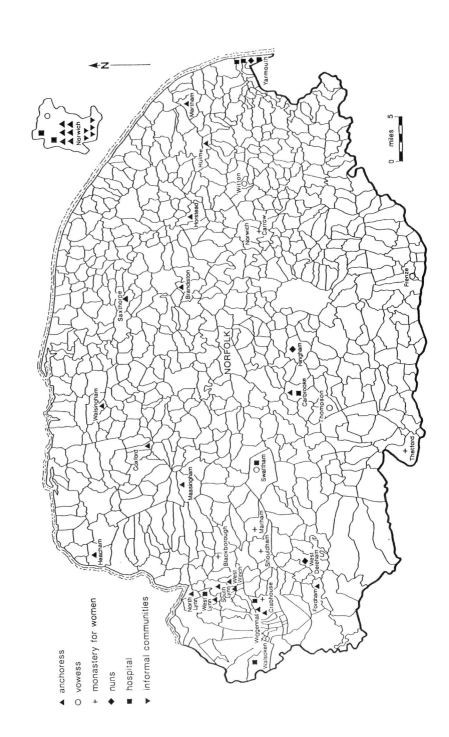

N

NORFOLK

Yarmouth
Martham
Hulme
Witton
Horstead
Norwich
Carrow
Saxthorpe
Brandiston
Frenze
Walsingham
Hingham
Carbrooke
Thompson
Coxford
Thetford
Massingham
Swaffham
Heacham
Marham
Blackborough
Shouldham
North Lynn
West Lynn
South Lynn
West Winch
Wiggenhall
Crabhouse
West Dereham
Fordham
Walsoken

Norwich

▲ anchoress
○ vowess
+ monastery for women
◆ nuns
■ hospital
▼ informal communities

0   miles   5

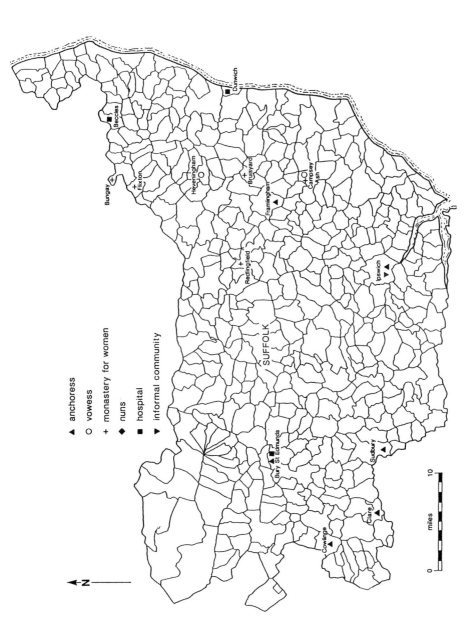

Figure 90 Distribution of known religious women in medieval East Anglia (Norfolk and Suffolk). From Gilchrist and Oliva (1993).

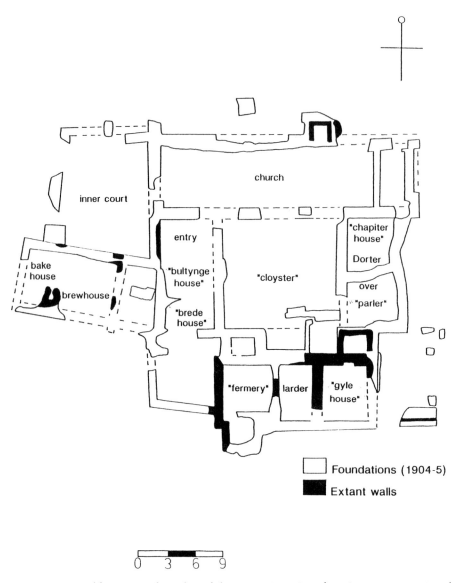

Figure 91   Kirklees (W Yorks): plan of the excavations. Based on Armytage (1908) and his interpretation of buildings and rooms taken from documentary sources.

have formed the most familiar model for the gentry founders and inmates of nunneries. Like manor houses, many nunneries were surrounded by moats, ordered as discontinuous ranges around courtyards formed by pentices and constructed in local materials, such as timber and cob. Some nunneries seem to have developed domestic and service facilities within the cloister, lending them a secular appearance. At Kirklees (W Yorks), for example, a service wing was added to the west range in order to accommodate the brewhouse

Figure 92   Priory seal of Ankerwyke (Bucks) *c*1200: showing a timber-framed and thatched building, possibly a hermitage. Drawing by Ted West.

and bakehouse, identified by its excavated oven, and the refectory was subdivided to serve domestic functions (figure 91) (Armytage 1908).

The situations of some nunneries indicate that they were intended by their founders to interact closely with the local community. Nunneries were established adjacent to existing villages or planned in conjunction with them, and many shared the nave of their conventual church with a parochial congregation. At times, nunneries must have seemed rather worldly places: with corrodians taking up residence in the inner court and visiting secular guests living in the hall of the west range. This integration brought about the continued financial support of the nunneries by local people. The intercessory prayers of the nuns were held in high esteem, and represent an appropriate religious role for women who seem to have modelled their piety on images of the Virgin Mary as mother. Such support may have been anticipated by the founders of nunneries when endowing them with lands and holdings too meagre to achieve self-sufficiency.

Yet, many other nunneries were established in remote and isolated situations, far from worldly distractions. These nunneries appear to have catered for women with a more penitential vocation. Some, like Crabhouse and Markyate, had their origins in hermitages for women. The modest construction of these nunneries may have related not just to the social origins of those associated with the house, but may have commented on the spiritual aspirations which they practised. Like the French nunnery of Coyroux, these

British houses were constructed in order to preclude any degree of comfort or luxurious living. Many had cloisters placed to the north of the church, rendering their domestic ranges unnecessarily cold and dark. They consumed relatively modest diets and spurned the usual standards of monastic sanitation, preferring, it seems, more basic garderobes and less regular disposal of refuse. These women may have sought a more ascetic lifestyle, occasionally reflected in the iconography of the nunnery seal. That of Ankerwyke (Bucks), dedicated to the model penitent, Mary Magdalene, depicts a hermitage shown as a timber-framed rectangular building with a thatched roof (figure 92). The eremitic priory of Crabhouse was represented by the eagle of St John the Evangelist; an image portrayed also at Hampole (W Yorks), a nunnery which hosted an anchoress and the renowned hermit, Richard Rolle.

It seems that there were many monasticisms from which religious women could choose. Royal and aristocratic women could spend their lives in the handful of wealthier houses which operated at a level more akin to male houses, or like Godstow, developed the *familiae* more typical of the lives of upper-status secular women. The remaining nuns could choose between either a nunnery which fostered close links with the local community or one which followed the ascetic lifestyle of the penitent. More private lives, elusive to the historian and archaeologist, were pursued by informal communities of religious women, while women seeking the severity of individual enclosure followed the vocation of the anchoress. It is to the motivations and archaeology of the most austere monastics that we now turn.

5 A desert place: the archaeology of hermits

'The wilderness and the solitary place' (Isaiah 35: 1)

The later middle ages witnessed a variety of monastic lifestyles for the hermit, a calling which demonstrated sanctity through the denial of comfort and companionship. The hermit sought distance from worldly distractions in order to establish a closer communion with God, through isolation and the practice of extreme asceticism. This austerity often involved trials of the mind and body, including the denial of pleasure and sustenance, and rites of self-mortification. These men and women could choose between the life of the recluse or that of a member of an eremitic community. This chapter considers the material culture of hermitages, eremitic monasteries (including those of the Carthusian and Grandmontine orders) and anchorholds – the dwellings of permanently enclosed solitaries. The meaning of the eremitic vocation is explored in relation to changing religious mentalities among the monastic and lay population.

The calling of the hermit was motivated by, and modelled upon, the example of biblical hermits, such as Elijah, Elisha and John the Baptist, and the hermits of 3rd- and 4th-century Egypt and Syria, ascetics who lived singly or in groups at the edges of the desert. These desert fathers and harlots, as they have come to be known, practised a penitential, contemplative solitude after having been converted to a Christian life. The first Christian hermit was Antony of Egypt (*c*251–356), whose influential *vita* brought about the conversion of Augustine in 384, among many others. In solitude, Antony battled the devil through fasting and prayer until he was able to achieve a kind of spiritual perfection which was thought to represent a return to 'man's *natural* condition' (Chitty 1966: 4). Many exemplary men and women of the desert tradition were thought previously to have led sinful lives, such as the former prostitutes Mary of Egypt, Pelagia and Thaïs (Ward 1987). Through the penance of the desert these sinners could be reborn, and the desert itself came to represent the birth of a new form of religious life, the precursor to the eremitic monasticism of western Europe from the 5th to 16th centuries.

In Britain, the first hermits were solitary holy men who frequented the fringes of human settlement: in Roman ruins, caves, coastal promontories, islands and marshes (Morris 1989: 104). Eremitic monasteries, or groups of hermits observing some form of communal life, were established from the 7th century, especially in areas influenced by the Celtic church: Ireland, Scotland, Northumberland, Wales and Cornwall (Thomas 1971: 44). The memory of this indigenous tradition continued to influence the character and incidence of eremitic living throughout the later middle ages.

A revival of monastic interest in the anchoritic life of the desert began in Italy in the 10th and 11th centuries and flourished in Ireland, England, France,

Germany and Switzerland. Monks left regular monasteries to pursue a life of solitude and voluntary poverty. The most charismatic proponents of this new monasticism invariably attracted followers, so that from the chrysalis of the hermitage emerged the hermit orders of the 11th century. Although devoted to a retreat from the world, these hermits lived a form of communal monasticism dedicated to extreme poverty and a life motivated by the Acts of the Apostles, the *Vita Apostolica*. Their vocation was considered by contemporaries to be the most challenging and developed form of monasticism.

The earliest hermit order was initiated by Romauld of Ravenna (*c*950–1027), who trained solitaries at a hermitage on Mount Camaldoli for the eventual order of Camaldolese. The order of Grandmont was inspired by the activities of Stephen of Muret, who from 1076 attracted a small group of hermits at Muret, 19km from Limoges; after his death the expanding group moved to nearby Grandmont (Haute Vienne), a rocky site on the side of a mountain (Hutchison 1989: 13). Although living in community, the Grandmontines regarded themselves as hermits who sought places of solitude in which to fulfil a contemplative vocation. They were committed to poverty and were forbidden to own lands outside the immediate enclosure of the 'cell', or monastery. All members of the community were expected to engage in physical labour and to observe a frugal diet. The model lives of the Grandmontines attracted impressive patrons, including the English king, Henry II.

The Carthusians formed around St Bruno, who, with six followers, established a hermitage in the Alps at La Grande Chartreuse, above Grenoble (Haute Savoie), in 1084 (Thompson 1930: 8). Bruno died in 1101 after having founded three eremitic communities. Shortly afterwards, his followers began to organise their number into a monastic order, with their customs and observances regularised by the fifth prior, Guigues du Pin. These customs ensured that the monks could continue to withdraw from the world in pursuit of the hermit's vocation. The Carthusians were unique among monastic orders in eschewing the communal life. Each monk lived, worked and prayed alone in his cell, with food brought to him by the lay-brothers. Only the nocturnal office and vespers were sung in common in the church; meals were taken together in the refectory on Sundays and feast days, and speech was allowed after the refectory meals or during a walk, taken once a week, outside the cells. Initially, lay-visitors were discouraged and were allowed into the cloister only during an hour allowed on feast days for conversation (Thompson 1930: 118). Even to the present day, the Carthusians continue to observe their strict rules of solitude, silence and abstinence.

These orders emerged as part of an 11th-century movement in which monks rediscovered the concept of the desert. They sought strength in the wilderness, just as Christ, John the Baptist and the desert fathers had done. Like Pachomius (*c*286–346) in 4th-century Egypt, the Carthusians and Grandmontines aimed to combine the eremitic and cenobitic vocations. Their desert was found in harsh and lonely mountain regions, and their reinterpretation of the monastic life spread quickly across Europe.

In England, a contemporary eremitic movement was inspired by a desire to return to the monasticism chronicled by Bede. This nostalgia led to a 'northern revival' in which prominent Northumbrian houses were refounded

by monks dissatisfied with the luxurious living of their Benedictine monasteries. Symeon of Durham described how in 1073–4 three monks from
Evesham (Worcs), Aldwin, Reinfrid and Aelfwig, travelled to Jarrow to begin
their new observances. From there they re-established Wearmouth and Whitby.
The first decades of the 12th century saw the spontaneous founding of a
number of eremitic monasteries which would eventually be absorbed into the
reformed monastic orders. At Nostell (W Yorks) and Llanthony (Monmouths
[Gwent]) hermitages had become Augustinian monasteries by 1120. In 1133,
Fountains (N Yorks) was founded by 13 monks from St Mary's, York, and
similar hermitages were established at Kirkstead (Lincs), Kirkstall (W Yorks)
and Radmore (Staffs); these communities quickly adopted the Cistercian Rule
(Leyser 1984: 36–7). In the 12th-century, hermitages came under pressure to
adopt a formal rule and to conform to the standards of regular monasticism.
No less than 30 Augustinian priories began as hermitages only to transform
themselves into priories as a response to persuasion from benefactors (Herbert
1985: 131, 140).

During the 12th century, England, together with Italy, had more followers
of the eremitic life than any other country (Dauphin 1965: 303). In addition
to the hermitages which were destined to be absorbed into the reformed
orders, there were individual hermits who achieved great acclaim. There were
many whose existence is attested only by a single reference to a name or the
site of their hermitage, but others drew hagiographers who popularised their
cults through the writing of saints' lives. These hermits attracted reputations
as mediators in their particular localities, acting as counsellors and healers
and using their distance from the world to adopt the powerful role of arbi-
trator (Brown 1971/1982; Mayr-Harting 1975). The respect and awe which
they engendered has been examined by Peter Brown in relation to the hermits
of Late Antiquity:

> Here was a man who had conquered his body in spectacular feats of mortification.
> He had gained power over the demons, and so over the diseases, bad weather, the
> manifest disorders of a material world ruled by demons (Brown 1982: 106).

In England the promotion of eremitic personalities was at its peak from 1115
to 1170, years which produced Henry of Coquet, Wulfric of Haselbury,
Christina of Markyate, Godric of Finchale, Bartholomew of Farne and Robert
of Knaresborough (Holdsworth 1990: 58). It has been observed that the
majority of famed 12th-century ascetics had Anglo-Saxon or Anglo-
Scandinavian names (Holdsworth 1990: 58; Herbert 1985: 138; Clay 1955:
202). They lived in remote, rural regions and were supported by Anglo-Saxon
gentry (Hughes 1988: 65). As well as living on the physical margins of human
habitation, these Saxon hermits were living on the fringes of Norman society.
Christopher Holdsworth has proposed that for 150 years after the Conquest:

> There were discontinuities in the social and religious worlds which [the hermit]
> could fill and so we find another age of Holy Men and Women, not too dissimilar
> to that in Late Antiquity (Holdsworth 1990: 71).

The very liminality of the hermit made him or her a bridge between social
groups within Anglo-Norman England.

The decline in the hagiography of hermits, together with the pressure exerted on hermitages to adopt a regular monastic rule, may reflect increasing conformity in English society and a change in religious mentalities. However, less-celebrated hermits continued to dwell in towns and the countryside. Some were hermit-priests, acting as chaplains to wayside or bridge chapels; others established their own hospitals for good works. One such example petitioned the prior of Butley (Suffolk) for recognition of his foundation at Earl Soham:

> John Beket, hermit of the diocese of Norwich, that he who is a priest has newly, *de novo*, founded and built a hospital with a chapel in the place of *SOHAM COMITIS* in the said diocese, and has given to it a chapel and certain parcels of land (Twemlow (ed.) 1933: 501).

A more extreme version of the eremitic vocation took root in England from the 12th century, and gathered momentum in the 13th century. Anchoresses and anchorites, or female and male recluses, tooks vows of permanent en-closure and were walled up for the rest of their lives within cells attached to parish or monastic churches. The anchorite's cell was a metaphor for the desert caves of the early ascetics and represented the passage to a mental desert. Enclosure within a cell promoted the most contemplative of monastic vocations. The anchorite was, however, dependent upon patrons for mainten-ance, which included the provision of food, sanitation, clothes, fuel, servants and confessors for up to 40–50 years (Warren 1985: 13). At first this vocation was dominated by holy women, and many anchoresses were drawn from the Anglo-Saxon aristocracy, in keeping with the supposed Saxon ethnic prefer-ence for this way of religious life. This movement expanded in the 13th century with new anchorholds built for Norman noblewomen and an in-creasing number of male anchorites (Warren 1985: 21, 25).

Although the eremitic movement in general had begun as a rural phenom-enon, anchorites were sponsored increasingly in town and city churches. Support of an anchorite was an expensive business, but benefactors invested in return for the anticipated efficacy of the anchorite's intercessory prayers. The contemplative life continued to be valued above other forms of monastic-ism and drew the patronage of monastic houses, clerics, merchants, citizens and guilds in London and towns like Norwich and York. Jonathon Hughes has proposed that in the Diocese of York this patronage came chiefly from the nobility and was of a personal nature, indicating that nobles cultivated relationships with particular recluses (Hughes 1988: 71). He suggests that by the 14th century the meaning and function of the eremitic life had changed. Later ascetics influenced lay society by communicating their experience of the contemplative life through counselling and writing (ibid.: 88). They replaced the earlier emphasis on penitential practice and mortification of the body with an approach more influenced by mysticism. The *Form of Living* (*c*1348), a guide for an anchoress written by the hermit Richard Rolle (*c*1300–49), advised quiet seclusion and prayer to achieve a union with God through contemplation, in contrast to the 'flamboyant ascetic practices' of early solitaries (Brown 1971/1982: 109).

In 15th- and early-16th-century England, some male hermits found an altogether more utilitarian form of eremitic calling. Men from lower social ranks followed the Rule of St Paul, the First Hermit, in living an unenclosed

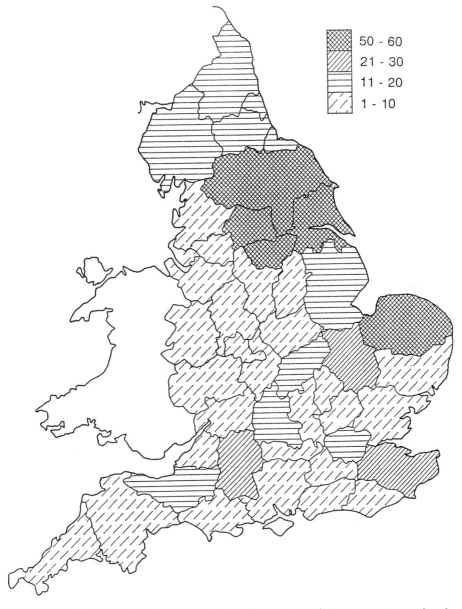

Figure 93 Concentrations by county in the distribution of Hermitages in medieval England. Based on Clay (1914).

solitary existence which aimed to perform useful tasks. The Rule referred to the hermit Paul, who was encountered by St Antony after a dream revealed that his desert existence was shared by another hermit. Those who followed the Rule were seldom educated and their functions included the keeping of town gates and coastal lighthouses, and the repair of bridges and highways;

indeed, they are referred to simply as bridge hermits in many episcopal registers and public records. This vocation was based on a version of St Jerome's *Life of St Paul* in the *Golden Legend* by Jacob of Voraigne (Davis 1985: 204). These hermits were professed by bishops; they were distinguished by their simple garments and sandals. Their subsistence was assisted by travellers who contributed alms as they passed by the hermitage.

The most successful hermits lived in one place for 20 to 30 years or more. If a hermitage or anchorage became particularly renowned it might have continued to be occupied sporadically, or even continuously, for several generations. These sites may have been constructed more substantially so that evidence of their former existence may survive today. In general, however, the archaeology of hermitages is especially fragmentary. According to their self-denying ordinances, hermits cannot have generated much in the way of either archives or material culture. As a result, the history and archaeology of hermits, much like their own lives, has remained on the margins. Rotha Mary Clay's work, while sometimes anecdotal, remains the only synthetic study to consider the history and material remains of hermits and anchorites (Clay 1914). She listed the approximate sites of 750 hermitages in medieval England (figure 93); this figure represents a minimum estimate and further sites may become known through modern historical research.

While the vocation of the hermit was equally significant in Scotland, Wales and Ireland, no comparable work has been attempted in either country (although see McRoberts 1966 for a survey of Scottish evidence); in Ireland, scholarship has concentrated almost exclusively on the Early Christian phases of the eremitic movement. Only a few British hermitages have been excavated or recorded using modern archaeological techniques; anchorages have been subject only to antiquarian curiosity and probing. Recently, the documentary evidence for anchorites has been re-evaluated (Warren 1985), and 12th-century solitaries and eremitic communities have been discussed (Holdsworth 1990; Leyser 1984; Elkins 1988). By monastic standards the eremitic monasteries in Britain devoted to the Grandmontine and Carthusian orders were occupied for a relatively short time, allowing a more precise archaeological evaluation of their chronological development and sequences of occupation. These houses have received considerable archaeological attention in recent years (Hutchison 1989; Aston 1993b; Coppack 1991; Soden 1992; Burrow and Burrow 1990).

Solitary hermits

For medieval people the hermit possessed a kind of mystique: an otherness. The intensity of the hermit's vocation sustained the severities of deprivation of food, comfort and companionship. In rising above earthly needs the hermit was thought to attain powers of healing, prophesy and wisdom. Moreover, asceticism was used to forge a new identity, 'a long drawn-out, solemn ritual of dissociation – of becoming the total stranger' (Brown 1971/1982: 131). Such liminality was emphasised further by the topographical siting of hermits' dwellings. Hermitages were built on the physical and psychological margins created by boundaries, rivers, roads, coasts and cliffs, and in inaccessible pockets provided by forests, islands or fens. Rotha Mary Clay proposed seven categories of hermit based on the siting of their hermitages: island and fen recluses, forest and hillside hermits, cave dwellers, light-keepers, highway and bridge hermits, town hermits and anchorites (Clay 1914). Topographic and archaeological evidence sometimes combine to suggest the sites of possible hermitages uncorroborated by documents.

Typically, Scottish hermits were provided with three acres to support themselves, possibly supplemented by the milk of one cow, as in the case of 13th-century hermit Gillecmichel; in 1236, the intriguing Gyllecrist Gartanach, hermit of Ruthven, was granted the life-tenure of his hermit's croft by King Alexander II (McRoberts 1966: 201). Unenclosed hermits avoided entering into relationships of obligation; saints' lives suggest that they moved away from their family and kin and practised self-sufficiency (Holdsworth 1990: 65–6). Godric of Finchale cleared woodland to make a garden, and Bartholomew of Farne and Robert of Knaresborough fished and raised crops, cultivating a little field with his own plough drawn by tame deer (Bottomley 1993: 8, 14). In the absence of environmental deposits associated with hermitages, we can discern from written sources that hermits avoided eating meat and drinking wine, preferring a staple diet of cereals and vegetables, wild fruit, herbs and roots (Leyser 1984: 66). According to the life of Robert of Knaresborough, 'A dish of salt, and nothing else, gave savour to his food; for drink he had water and bread was the only filling for his belly. Meat, when he recognised its smell, he entirely refused to eat' (Bottomley 1993: 12). Medieval hermits followed the desert fathers in achieving a close link with nature, wilderness and animals. According to Athanasius's *Life of Antony*, the hermit sowed grain in order to make bread, and persuaded the animals not to disturb his garden (Chitty 1966: 16). St Jerome's *Life of Paul* in the 14th-century *Golden Legend* describes how Antony met Paul in the desert and they fed on bread brought by two ravens; when Antony learned of Paul's death he returned to bury him and was aided by two lions who obligingly dug the grave (Davis 1985: 204–5).

Celtic hermits settled on coastal islands from an early date. Hermitages, such as those on Scattery Island in the estuary of the River Shannon (Clare, Eire) and Skellig Michael off the coast of Kerry, were perched quite literally on the edge of the known world. St Cuthbert's 7th-century hermitage on Inner Farne, off the Northumbrian coast, was reported to have been built with a stone enclosure wall surrounding the dwelling and a latrine built overhanging the cliff edge. His basic requirements were an oratory and a small room for general accommodation, a well and a small area of cultivated ground (Cramp 1976: 201). Bede described how the hermitage was built:

> almost round in plan, measuring about four or five *perticarum* 'poles' from wall to wall; the wall itself on the outside is higher than a man standing upright; but inside he made it much higher by cutting away the living rock, so that the pious inhabitant could see nothing except the sky from his dwelling, thus restraining both the lust of his eyes and of the thoughts by lifting the whole bent of his mind to higher things. He made this same wall, not out of stone nor of bricks and mortar, but just of unworked stone and of turf which he had removed from the excavation of his dwelling (Bede, *Life of Cuthbert*, 17, trans. Colgrave 1940).

The twin elements of oratory and domestic accommodation were to remain the standard requirements for hermits throughout the middle ages. The oratory, or chapel, was the more substantial element which survives more frequently today.

Hermits continued to inhabit Coquet Island, south of Farne, after the death of the renowned hermit Henry of Coquet (1120). In the 13th century, the hermitage consisted of two isolated cells and a chapel with attached tower, the latter surviving until the early 19th century (Clay 1914: 7). Solitary hermits occupied islands off the Welsh coast and islands in the River Severn, such as Chapel Island at the mouth of the River Wye. The supposed oratory of St Tiriac was recorded in the 19th century as measuring 9.6 × 4.26m (Clay 1914: 12). Two sites are associated with the Pembrokeshire hermit St Caradoc (d. 1124), whose life was described by Gerald of Wales. Caradoc is said to have built an oratory and cell on the low-lying island of Burryholms, off the Gower Peninsula. Above the beach at Newgale is the site of a chapel founded by, or at least dedicated to, him. In the 19th century it was described as a long, narrow building constructed from smooth beach pebbles and mortar (Davis and Lloyd-Fern 1990: 60, 87). Hermitages were established in the lakes of Cumbria from the 7th century, when Herebertus settled in Derwentwater at a site which continued to attract hermits into the 14th century. Two hermit-priests served a chapel on Lady Holm, near Bowness on Windermere (Clay 1914: 13). Harlside Chapel, Allithwaite, was built on a site made inaccessible due to channels and quicksands. The roughly built limestone chapel was 'gothicised', or artificially ruined, in 1823.

Comparable isolation was sought in the fens, where hermitages were built on prominences surrounded by swamps or flooded rivers, and are recorded at Crowland, Peakirk, Thorney, *Huneia* (possibly Honey Hill, Chatteris) and Bethney (Clay 1914: 14). The most famous fenland hermit was Guthlac, who, in the 8th century, sought a desert in the fens and whose life was recorded by Felix, a monk of the later Crowland Abbey, in the south Lincolnshire fens. Guthlac's sister Pega established a hermitage at Peakirk, where a later church now stands. According to the *Liber Eliensis* a hermitage was established near Chatteris by Huna, chaplain of Etheldreda of Ely. Medieval pottery and a scatter of building material mark the assumed site of this hermitage at Honey Hill (Haigh 1988: 18).

The most celebrated forest hermit was Godric of Finchale who lived first in the forest of Inglewood, near Carlisle, and later in a forest near Whitby, then in a turf-covered log hut in Eskdale, and finally at Finchale (Durham). Accounts of Godric suggest that he communed peacefully with animals, protecting them and nursing them (Clay 1914: 24–5). Clay outlined the patchy evidence for forest hermits, including many solitaries in royal forests sponsored by the king. In the Forest of Dean, for example, there were cells at Ardland, St Briavels and Taynton. In 1255, Panye de Lench became a recluse at Ardland and Henry III granted her four acres of land and two oaks for the construction of her dwelling (Clay 1914: 28). Such timber-built dwellings have left little trace in the archaeological record. Clay described how a 12th-century hermit on the island of Higney, near Ramsey, surrounded his hermitage by a dyke, spanned by a drawbridge; he also attempted to build an outer dyke (Clay 1914: 21). Occasionally, evidence for such enclosures survives, as at Yarls Wood (Bedfords), where the medieval hermitage occupied an isolated site within a double-ditched moat (Hutchings 1969: 75). At Coppingford Wood (Sawtry, Cambs) a single moat *c*20 × 25m has been identified as the site of a hermitage founded by Simon of Costentin between 1225 and 1233; a scattering of medieval pottery was recovered from the site (Haigh 1988: 78–9). Another potential site is Hermitage Wood, Alconbury Weston (Cambs) where there is a well-preserved rectangular ditched enclosure (Haigh 1988: 1).

In Somerset, a considerable number of hillside hermits were recorded (Clay 1914: 17). On the steep slope of a secluded coombe the remains of Burgundy Chapel may represent one such example. A two-room hermitage consisted of a chapel and attached western chamber, constructed of well-mortared walls. Associated with the site were fragments of medieval pottery, tiles, glass, animal bones and the head of a 15th-century arch. The chamber had a window for light and a vent tile to allow smoke to escape through the roof (Huish 1941: 141).

In emulation of the hermits of the desert many were drawn to natural caves or chambers excavated from the living rock. The 4th-century hermits of Palestine lived in the caves and limestone caverns of the Judaean wilderness (Chitty 1966: 15). In Britain, caves and rock-cut chambers served as hermitages and chapels. Their ruggedness provided the close link with nature sought by many hermits. Natural caves and associated cliffs were occupied especially in Scotland, Northumberland, Derbyshire, Shropshire, Hereford and Worcester and Warwickshire. Many were hollowed out by rivers at the base of rock faces, such as Gratcliff Rocks, Stanton in Peak (Derbys), where a carved cross stands in a recess at the eastern end of the cave (Clay 1914: 32). Anchor Church (Derbys) is a rock-face containing four chambers in a semicircle, assumed to have been associated with a hermit. A site at Hastings (Sussex) was carved in the west side of East Hill. Three chambers, each measuring 2.7 × 1.2m, were entered by three square-headed openings cut in the rock. A niche in the east wall of the central chamber has a cross cut over it (Gattie 1892). These examples have been assumed to be medieval, but have no documentary evidence which confirms their function or date.

At Southstone Rock (Hereford and Worcester), a hermitage dedicated to St John the Baptist was recorded from 1140 to 1206. The chapel stood at the summit of the rock, 60m above the River Teme and the rock-cut cells below, and was approached by rock-hewn stairs which still survive (Winnington 1863–4). A hermitage known as Guy's Cliffe (Warwicks) was occupied by many solitaries, possibly as early as the 10th century, and during the 14th to 16th centuries. A system of caves was excavated in the sandstone rock-face next to the River Avon. There is a series of cells in the upper and lower cliffs, some with square-headed windows. Opposite is the chapel of Mary Magdalene, founded for hermits by Richard Beauchamp in 1422–3, now incorporated into a Palladian house of *c*1751. In keeping with other types of hermitage, cave hermitages typically provided the twin elements of the chapel or oratory together with domestic accommodation. At Bridgnorth hermitage (Shrops), occupied throughout the 13th century, a long, narrow chapel joined a cave which had access by stairs to an upper cave cut out of the rock (Smith 1878). At the red sandstone caves of 'Isis Parlis', the site of a presumed hermitage near Brougham (Cumb), the walls of the main cave have been polished smooth, while those of two smaller caves show signs of rough tooling (Heelis 1914: 340).

Figure 94   St Robert's Cave Hermitage, Knaresborough (N Yorks). Photograph courtesy of Jane Grenville.

At Knaresborough (N Yorks) a hermitage cave and chapel are associated with St Robert (d. 1218), originally Robert Flower, a York merchant's son. The cave was cut out of the magnesian limestone bedrock above the River Nidd, on the outskirts of the medieval town (figure 94). The cave is between 1.8 and 1.9m in height and is entered by three steps leading down into it; ledges and recesses survive in two of the corners. The development of the hermitage was described in the *Life of St Robert*,

> Little by little the building rose, made from the living rock and from well-cut and polished stone. The hermitage was extended so that it could receive the poor and the pilgrims making a voluntary journey as well as those hastening to the heavenly Jerusalem (Bottomley 1993: 10).

Outside the cave entrance, between the face of the cliff and the edge of bedrock, a domestic area was added, retaining evidence for a bench along the cliff face and a drain running from the cave to the edge of the site. A chapel was established at the base of the stairs that were cut into the cliff face. A surviving altar platform and the southern wall of the chapel are formed by irregular blocks of magnesian limestone. Together the chapel and domestic area measure 5.5 × 11.7m (figure 95).

The hermitage at Pontefract (W Yorks) has recently been re-examined by Peter Ryder (Ryder 1992 unpub.). Two medieval chambers were cut in the soft sandstone face created by a natural escarpment, where Southgate runs today (figure 96). This hermitage was first noted in 1368 when Robert de Laythorpe gave the site to brother Adam. The site was later held by Nostell Priory, itself having originated from a hermitage. An old walled garden (23m

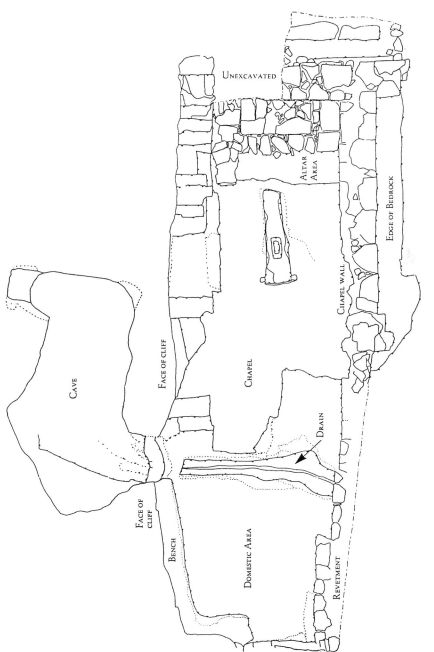

Figure 95 St Robert's Cave Hermitage, Knaresborough (N Yorks): plan. Reproduced with permission of the Harrogate Museums and Art Gallery Service.

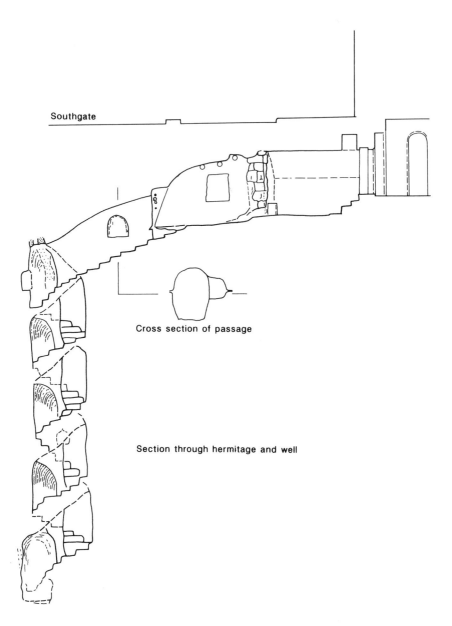

Southgate

Cross section of passage

Section through hermitage and well

Figure 96   The Hermitage, Pontefract (W Yorks): section. Based on Ryder (1992 unpub).

square) associated with the site was destroyed in 1880. The two chambers are known traditionally as the Hermitage and the Oratory (figure 97). They are entered from a chamber 4.7 × 1.53m with an arcade of three four-centered arches on its north side. The Hermitage has a trapezoidal antechamber with walls of coursed stone and a segmental vault in brick. The rear wall of the

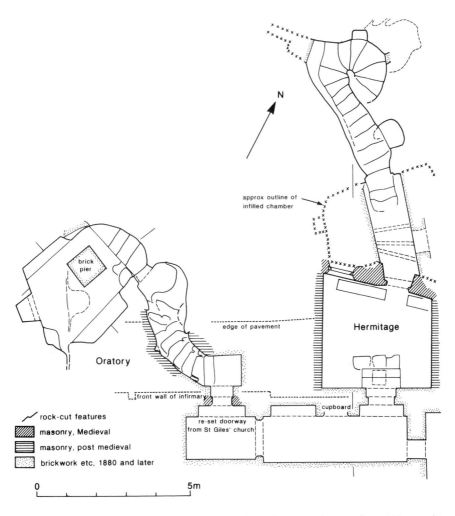

Figure 97 The Hermitage, Pontefract (W Yorks): plan. Based on Ryder (1992 unpub).

antechamber forms the front wall of the original hermitage. A door from the antechamber leads to a passage descending to a second doorway with a rock-cut passage descending to a vertical newel staircase of 57 steps, leading to a well chamber. The Oratory has a curving flight of steps leading to a rock-cut vestibule which gives access to the oratory itself – a domed chamber of 2.3 × 3–4m. Its eastern wall has an altar shelf or mensa and a plain square-headed fireplace with a flue rising through the rock (Ryder 1992 unpub.).

A number of cave hermitages in Scotland and Northumberland were sited perhaps to allow their incumbents to act as light-keepers. On a promontory at Lossiemouth, a cave destroyed in the early 19th century is reported to have measured 3.65m square and to have had an arched doorway and mullioned window (McRoberts 1966: 213). At St Medan's Cave, Kirkmaiden (Dumfries), a chapel was formed in a natural cave on the western shore of the Bay of

Luce (Trotter 1886: 78). A chapel approximately 4.26m square was formed by extending the space of the small cave by building walls and a gable end of stone bonded with red boulder clay or a mixture of lime from whelk and limpet shells and stalactites.

The most elaborate cave hermitage is at Warkworth (Northumb): a combined rock-cut and masonry structure, ornately carved and rib-vaulted (figure 98). The hermitage was sited in the park of Warkworth Castle and was under the patronage of the Earls of Northumberland (Honeyman and Hunter Blair 1954/1993: 28–33). Located on the River Coquet, it was originally approached by a flight of steps cut into the cliff. When built in the 14th century it consisted of three chambers hewn out of a projecting part of the cliff on the north side of the river. During the 15th century, living rooms were added to the face of the cliff. The ground floor of these living rooms included a kitchen with an oven, adjacent to a hall (4.6 × 5.5m) with a fireplace and window overlooking the river. Above the hall was a solar, or upper chamber, with a garderobe and fireplace. A smaller rock-hewn chamber preceded this hall, which contained four small windows looking into the chapel. The chapel is entered through a porch joining its west bay. The shafts, capitals and ribs of the roof were carved from the living rock. To the south of the altar is a recess or tomb chapel which contains a sculpture of a reclining woman. The sacristy was entered by a doorway from the western bay of the chapel, and an inscription above the door was once traceable: 'They gave me gall for my meat: and in my thirst they gave me vinegar to drink' (Psalm 69: 22). At the eastern end of the sacristy there is a small oratory with a squint sighted on the altar in the main chapel.

In the 15th and 16th centuries hermits were found most often at bridges, highways and ferries, many devoted to the Rule of St Paul, the First Hermit, and others acting as hermit-chaplains. These hermits, together with the light-keepers considered below, valued service to others above the calling for strict solitude (Clay 1914: 49). Hermits maintained the ferry terminus at Gorleston (Norfolk) and at Witham (Lincs), among others. Road-hermits were common in the 14th and 15th centuries and assisted in keeping new highways in good repair. Bridge-hermits were at times responsible for raising revenues through alms and tolls to assist in the construction of the bridges in their care (Clay 1914: 58–9). Eamon Duffy has commented on the Christian symbolism of bridges and bridge-building which may have appealed to learned patrons, including imagery likening Christ, bishops and popes with bridges (Duffy 1992: 367–8). The hermit himself may have represented a bridge between worldly and religious states, between the familiar and the wilderness. Hermits built bridges for John of Gaunt at Singleton (W Yorks), and at Skipwith and Stainforth they collected money for the repair of roads (Hughes 1988: 76). Maintenance must have been a challenging vocation in most regions, perhaps particularly so in the fens. At Earith (Cambs) a hermitage stood on the causeway from Ely to Aldreth, and in the 14th century the hermits were responsible for its repair and that of the bridge (Haigh 1988: 22).

At Doncaster bridge a *reclusarium* for two anchoresses was founded in 1270 by the FitzWilliam family; it continued to be supervised by the family and received bequests up to 1382 (Hughes 1988: 69). Bridge and causeway chapels were established at some hermitages, where hermit-priests or chaplains

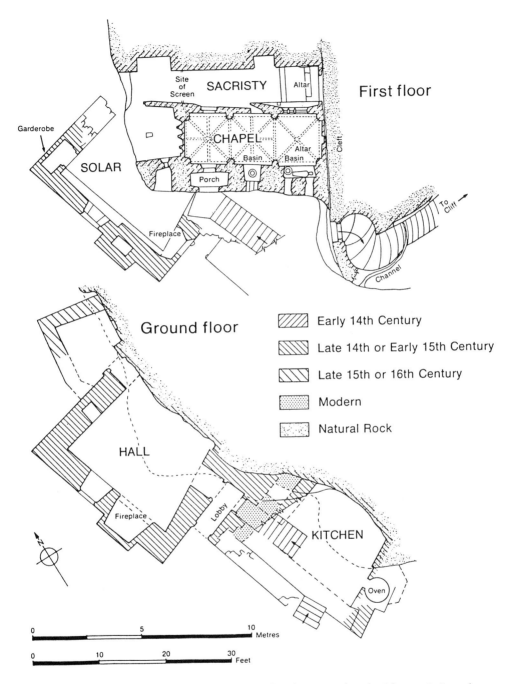

Figure 98 The Hermitage, Warkworth (Northumb). Reproduced with permission of English Heritage from H. L. Honeyman and H. Hunter Blair (1954/1993) *Warkworth Castle and Hermitage.*

Figure 99   St Catherine on Chale Down (Isle of Wight): the lighthouse hermitage, from *The Gentleman's Magazine* 27: 176.

were responsible for collecting alms or tolls and ministering to travellers. Many of these were timber structures built on a starling or extended pier to one side of the bridge; others spanned its length.

Many of the hermits residing on islands, cliffs and in coastal caves served as coastguards and light-keepers to assist mariners on their journeys. Hermits lived adjacent to chapels or in purpose-built towers which acted as lighthouses. The tower at the hermitage of St Catherine on Chale Down, Isle of Wight, was erected before 1328, when a letter referred to the structure. The hermitage stood 230m above sea level and comprised a tower and attached oratory. Parts of the 10.6m tower remain; it is octagonal with a piscina reincorporated into the walls (Clay 1914: 52) (figure 99). A chapel on St Aldhelm's Head, a promontory which forms the southern edge of the Isle of Purbeck (Dorset), may have been kept by a hermit-priest who also acted as a light-keeper.

Architecturally, the 7.62m square chapel dates from the mid- to late 12th century (figure 100), with its north door elaborated by billet ornament. No records survive to suggest that it was served by hermits, but it was recorded

Figure 100 St Aldhelm's Head (Dorset): a mid- to late-12th-century chapel, possibly associated with a hermit-priest or light-keeper.

as a chapel in 1291 (Clay 1914: 52). Perhaps the most substantial remains of a hermitage in Scotland, known as St Anthony's, is situated under the crags of Arthur's Seat, outside Edinburgh, overlooking the port of Leith and the Firth of Forth. The site consists of a chapel of three bays (13.1 × 5.57m), with remains of vaulting and pictorial evidence for a former western tower, and a nearby hermit's cell (5.12 × 3.90m) (Coles 1895–6) (figure 101). At Gilean Mor, Kilmory (Argyll) a 15th-century cross-shaft may have formed part of a monument intended to guide mariners (McRoberts 1966: 204). Its inscription reads: *M[ARGARITA] D[R]OS INSULARUM DOMINA ET JOHANNES PRESBITER AC HEREMITA ISTE INSULE ME FIERI FECERUNT*: Margaret, Lady of the Island, and John, priest and hermit of the island, had me made. Clay noted evidence for a comparable case near King's Lynn on the east coast of the Wash. The 14th-century hermit John Puttock erected at his own cost 'a certain remarkable cross of the height of 110 feet' to assist seamen sailing up the Wash (Clay 1914: 50).

Hermits were associated with later medieval towns, often inhabiting their outskirts near town walls or gates. Clay reported that hermits were sometimes given the charge of disused parish churches, such as St Margaret Colegate, Norwich, and St Giles, Thetford (Clay 1914: 71). Hermits inhabited chambers next to or over the gates of St Stephen, St Giles, Bishopgate, Berstreet and Magdalen Gates, Norwich, and next to Cripplegate, Aldgate and Bishopsgate in London. At Aldgate, for example, the cell was built in a turret of the city wall (ibid.: 67). At Cripplegate a chantry was founded in 1399 by Mary, Countess of Pembroke, at the Hermitage of St James-in-the-Wall (Cook 1947/1963: 44). In Norwich the hermit Robert Godard was given lodgings over St

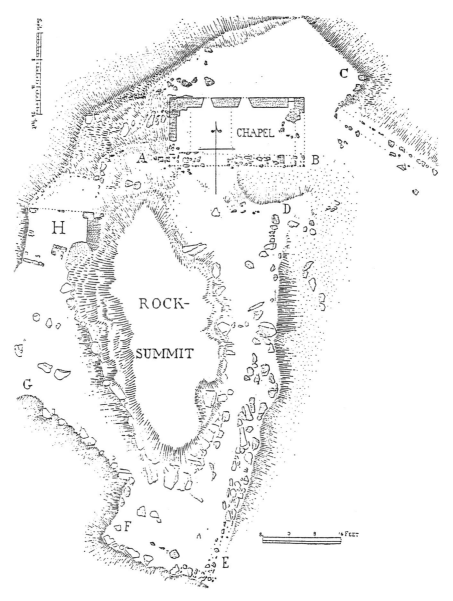

Figure 101 St Anthony's Hermitage, Edinburgh, Lothian (Scotland): remains of the chapel and hermitage. From *Proceedings of the Society of Antiquaries of Scotland* 30 (1895–6).

Stephen's Gate by the city government in 1483 in return for his work as keeper of the ditches in the subward of St Stephen's (Tanner 1984: 62). At Winchester, the Hermit's Tower, first recorded as such in the late 14th century, may commemorate a hermit who lodged high in the tower overlooking the city and the north-west angle of its walls (Keene 1985: 128).

Like medieval lepers, these hermits helped to define the edges of the medieval town and concerned themselves with travellers coming or going, whether to beg for alms or to pray for their safe journeys. The hermit at Magdalen Gate, Norwich, was directly connected with the nearby leper hospital at Sprowston, and at Bristol a cave hermitage was built near the Hospital of St John. St John's Hermitage at Redcliffe, Bristol, was founded in 1347 by Thomas Lord Berkeley for the hermit John Sparkes. The 2.74 × 2.43m hermitage was cut out of the red sandstone cliff; an arched opening in the rock led to a chamber with two roughly hewn seats (Pritchard 1911). Hermits seem to have been commonplace in English towns by the 13th or 14th century, including examples at Canterbury, Colchester, Durham, Ely, Leicester and Shrewsbury. In contrast, David McRoberts noted the surprising absence of references to hermits near the major towns of Scotland, such as Glasgow, Aberdeen and Dundee, suggesting that they may have been described in documents simply as chaplains (McRoberts 1966: 215). He proposed that place-name evidence may provide further potential sites, particularly those containing *anker*, such as Ankerlaw, south of Edinburgh.

Group hermitages

As outlined above, the eremitic movement in England experienced something of a renaissance in the 12th century, with evidence for both charismatic solitaries and groups of hermits living communally. The group hermitages of which we have some knowledge were destined to be short-lived. Increasingly, patrons either pressured communities of eremitic men and women to adopt a regular monastic rule, or formal monasteries were established on the site of existing hermitages. It seems that the life of a hermit was considered by patrons and churchmen to be particularly unsuitable for religious women. During the 12th century we know of four groups of women hermits having been regularised into nunneries through the actions of male ecclesiastics: Sopwell (Herts) *c*1135, Kilburn (Middlesex) by 1139, Crabhouse (Norfolk) *c*1180 and Markyate (Herts) in 1145. The last example concerns the enclosure of the women hermits who had been drawn to the holy recluse Christina of Markyate. The events described in her *vita* occurred around *c*1140, when she was assisted by a network of hermits to flee from a forced marriage. The informal nature of the female community which developed around her is suggested by the terminology of the text, referring to Christina as *domina*, rather than prioress, and to her followers simply as girls, *puellae*, instead of *sanctimoniales*, or nuns (Thompson 1991: 21). Sally Thompson has suggested that a number of other nunneries may have originated as communal hermitages, including Armathwaite (Cumb), Delapré (Northants) and Flamstead (Herts), the eremitic origins of the last perhaps reflected in its dedication to St Giles in the Wood (ibid.: 28).

Some semblance of the communal hermitage seems to have survived, either as retreat houses of monasteries, or as hermitages supported by secular patrons. The hermitage at Bodsey House (Hunts) became a rest house for monks of Ramsey Abbey from the 14th century (*Medieval Archaeol* 13 1969: 246). One example of a communal hermitage has been excavated at Grafton Regis (Northants) (Parker 1981–2; *Medieval Archaeol* 10 1966: 202–4) (figure 102).

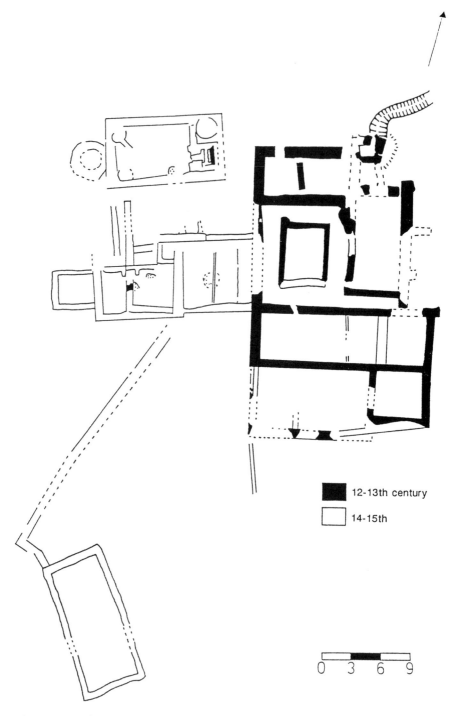

12-13th century

14-15th

0   3   6   9

Figure 102   The Hermitage, Grafton Regis (Northants): plan of the excavations. Based on *Medieval Archaeology* 10 (1966): 202–4.

Its continued existence was owed to its patronage by the Woodville family, who retained the right to elect the master. The hermitage was first noted when a hermit of the house, Helia, witnessed a charter of Abbot Walkelin (1180–1205) of St James's, Northampton (Parker 1981–2: 247). In 1313, the register of Bishop Oliver Sutton referred to the 'brothers and sisters and other ministers of the house', suggesting a form of monastery seldom evidenced in ecclesiastical records: a mixed, or double, hermitage of men and women. In the 15th century monastic occupation of the hermitage seems to have ceased, with the function of the site devolved to that of a chantry. However, Grafton still possessed lands and revenues in seven villages which yielded 35s annually. (Parker 1981–2: 251). The site consisted of a 13th-century cloister (10.4 × 7.3m internally) to the north of a chapel (14.6 × 4.6m). The chapel contained burials in the east end and was screened into a short chancel and a long, aisleless nave. Some of the ranges flanking the cloister were two-storey structures, approached by a staircase in the east cloister walk. A square, external projection to the north of the domestic ranges was situated over a drain, appropriate for a garderobe. Beyond the cloister was a 14th- to 15th-century service complex with ovens, drying kiln and foundations for a brewing vat. To the south-west of the cloister was a rectangular building, perhaps a guest-house or hospice, and beyond the enclosure were the foundations of a round structure, most likely a dovecote. In the late 15th century the cloister was sealed off and a new room was built which contained two hearths. The chapel continued in use and was refloored with tiles showing the coat-of-arms of the Woodville family and the royal house of York. Clay listed 42 private foundations in her list of 750 hermitages (Clay 1914). Some of these, like Grafton Regis, were reminiscent of the family monasteries of the sub-Roman and early medieval periods; they may have been short-lived or liable to revert to secular use (Gilchrist 1994: 186).

In Celtic areas of Britain the eremitic movement kept a tenacious foothold alongside newer forms of monasticism. Hermitages continued to be occupied, particularly where they were enhanced by an early medieval tradition, attracting pilgrims to the sites of shrines or holy wells. Excavation at group hermitages has demonstrated a continuity of purpose and occupation, linking later medieval hermits with their more celebrated predecessors in Wales, Ireland, Cornwall and Scilly.

At Burryholms on the Gower Peninsula (Glamorgans), a communal hermitage developed around an island shrine associated first with the early medieval solitary St Cennydd, and later with the 12th-century holy man, Caradoc of Rhos. The site occupies a tidal island in the Rhossili Bay, which would have been accessible only at low tide. In the 12th century, a timber oratory was replaced by a masonry church with an apsidal east end; stone-built domestic buildings were also added. In the 14th century, the church received a longer square-ended chancel and more substantial domestic buildings, including a hall to the south side of the church, measuring 10.36 × 4.57m and containing a central hearth, with an enclosure to the east and an annexe on its south side (*Medieval Archaeol* 10 1966: 184) (figure 103).

At St Tudwal's Island, Absersoch (Gwynedd), the site of a 6th-century hermitage was reused as a Celtic hermitage from the 13th to 15th centuries (figure 104). On the sheltered side of the island a group of domestic buildings

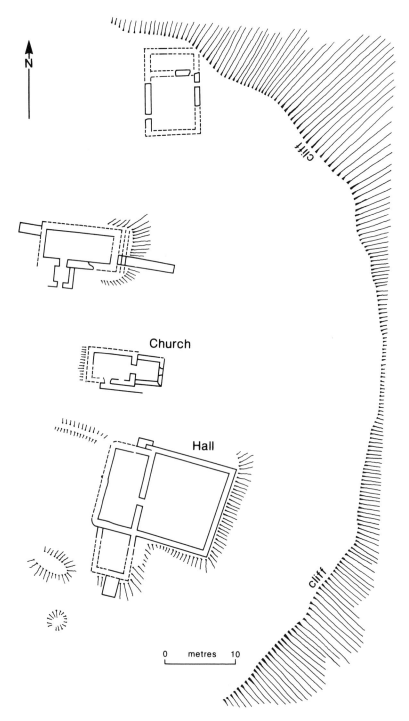

Figure 103   Burryholms Hermitage (Glamorgans, Wales): excavations of the church and domestic buildings. Based on *Medieval Archaeology* 10 (1966): 184.

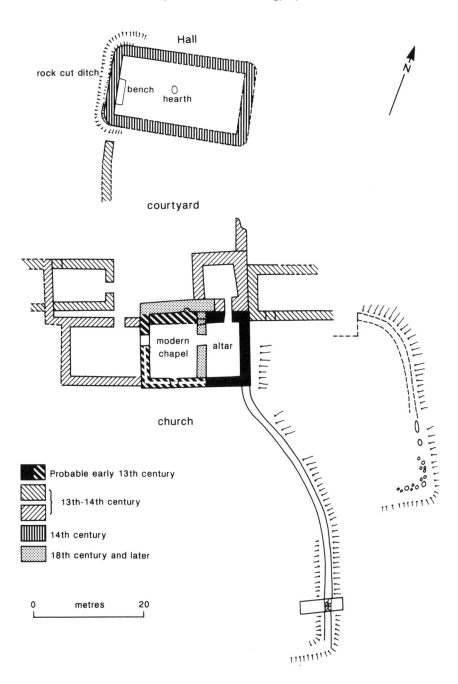

Figure 104 St Tudwal's Hermitage (Gwynedd, Wales): excavations revealed domestic buildings surrounding the 13th-century church, including a partially rock-cut hall. Based on *Medieval Archaeology* 6–7 (1962–3): 318–19 and 8 (1964): 246–8.

was arranged around the early 13th-century church. During the next century the church was enlarged and given a sacristy with an upper floor, as evidenced by the base of a stone staircase. An impressive hall of the mid-14th century was built to the south of the church with a walled courtyard between the two. The hall was partly rock-cut, with its western end sited over a rock-cut drainage ditch and its walls formed of free-standing rock. The hall had benched seating created by the interior walls, and a central hearth, with nearby post-holes suggestive of a rack or loom. One rock-cut mortice and a carefully rock-cut platform suggest that the hall was formed by cruck-trusses, providing a hipped, thatch roof (*Medieval Archaeol* 6–7 1962–3: 318–19; 8 1964: 246–8).

At Puffin Island (Anglesey), a ruined church and tower of the 12th century mark the site of the 6th-century monastery of Seiriol. The 12th-century chronicler, Gerald of Wales, described the island as having been inhabited by hermits who allowed no woman to enter (Davis and Lloyd-Fern 1990: 156). Such gynophobia had weighty precedents among hermits, and was one means of suggesting sanctity. Similar tales enhanced the holiness of St Kevin, in relation to Glendalough (Wicklow, Eire), and St Senan, regarding Scattery Island (Clare, Eire).

Many of Ireland's Early Christian hermitages, while disrupted by the Anglo-Norman presence, may have continued to be occupied throughout the later middle ages. The hermitage on Ardoileán (Galway, Eire), for example, dates mainly to the period *c*625–725; buildings continued to be refurbished and repaired into the 15th century (Herity 1990: 79). At Reask on the Dingle peninsula (Kerry, Eire), an Early Christian site of the 5th to 7th centuries experienced a second main phase of occupation, extending possibly from the 7th or 8th to the 12th century. In common with other famous sites, such as Skellig Michael or Church Island (Kerry), a stone enclosure contained a small oratory and foundations of *clochauns*, the round, beehive-shaped, stone huts of the hermits. In the second phase of occupation the sanctuary area was divided from the domestic area by a low stone wall (Fanning 1981: 158).

Excavations at St Helens, Isles of Scilly, suggested that a group hermitage may have evolved from a solitary's site with oratory and single round hut (figure 105) (O'Neill 1964). Dates from excavated pottery suggested that the site may have originated in the 11th century; by the 12th century it was a hermitage associated with Tavistock Abbey (Devon), known as *Insula Sancti Elidii* (ibid.: 40). Pottery from the site dated its occupation from the 11th century right up to the Dissolution. The oratory and round hut were built within an enclosure (*c*48 × 34m), into which three further cells of rectangular shape were built (figure 106). The hermits were provided with maximum seclusion by placing each of the huts at different levels on the granite cliff. Within the enclosure were both the oratory and later chapel, with a level courtyard to its south. The oratory was situated as the highest building on the slope, with the chapel below. The buildings were constructed in natural boulders and beach pebbles, with the exception of the chapel, which was built in freestone and Purbeck marble. Delabole slates from Cornwall were imported for the roof. The chancel of the chapel was extended and a north aisle was added; associated with the site was the gable end of a shrine in Purbeck marble (O'Neil 1964: 67). Burials were excavated within the church

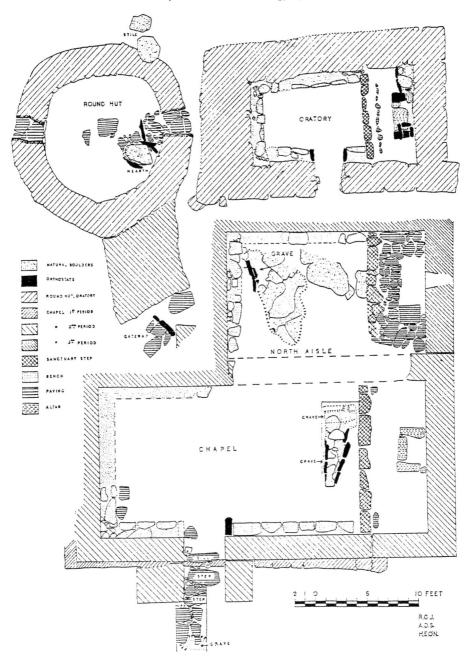

Figure 105 St Helens (Scilly): plan of the oratory and round hut. Reproduced with permission of the Royal Archaeological Institute from H.E. O'Neill, 'Excavations of a Celtic hermitage on St Helens, Isles of Scilly', *The Archaeological Journal* 121 (1964).

and outside its south door. A well was located outside the enclosure to the east at the foot of the granite cliff.

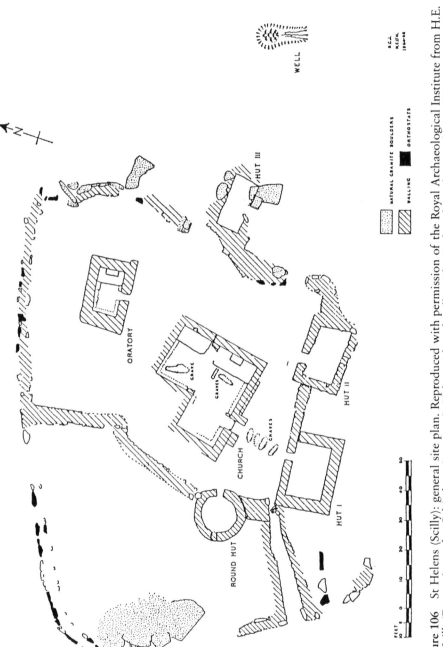

Figure 106 St Helens (Scilly): general site plan. Reproduced with permission of the Royal Archaeological Institute from H.E. O'Neill, 'Excavations of a Celtic hermitage on St Helens, Isles of Scilly', *The Archaeological Journal* 121 (1964).

Anchorites

The office of the anchorite was distinct from that of the hermit in that he or she took vows to remain permanently enclosed and solitary. While the hermit was dedicated to self-sufficiency, and often to manual labour, the anchorite was dependent upon patrons to support a life of contemplation and prayer. An anchoress attached to the parish church at Whalley (Lancs), for example, was provided for by Henry, first Duke of Lancaster, who gave lands to Whalley Abbey to finance her two female servants, her food, maintenance of her cell and a chaplain (Hughes 1988: 66). Anchorites, such as Wulfric of Haselbury, may have earned their keep in part through the production of books, while anchoresses like Christina of Markyate were encouraged to carry out needle-work for their church. But the largesse of benefactors was thought to have been repaid by the efficacy of the intercessory prayers of the recluse.

Ann Warren has shown that English anchorites were sponsored from the 12th century up to the 16th, with the highest incidence occurring from the 13th to 15th centuries. The anchoritic institution was particularly important for women. While occasional references to unenclosed female hermits (*virago; ancilla domini*) are found in the later middle ages, they are extremely rare after the end of the 12th century (Warren 1984: 201). The economic, spiritual and physical self-sufficiency of the office of the hermit seems to have been considered inappropriate for women, in contrast to the enclosed life of the anchoress. Throughout the period, women were more commonly enclosed in anchorholds than men, with particularly disproportionate numbers in the 13th and 14th centuries (Warren 1985: 19–20). Women drawn to this vocation seem to have come mainly from a secular background, whereas men more often had some existing clerical status, enabling them sometimes to serve as anchorite-priests.

The anchoritic movement was popular in different regions at different times, and was entirely absent from some areas, including Buckinghamshire, Rutland, Cumberland and Westmorland. Anchorites were found in Oxford-shire, Sussex, Worcestershire and Hampshire only in the 12th and 13th centuries. They were popular from the 13th to 15th centuries in Yorkshire, Middlesex, London, Lincolnshire, Kent and Norfolk, and from the 14th to 16th centuries they were most likely to be found in the eastern counties of England (Warren 1985: 36), in Yorkshire and Norfolk in particular.

Anchorholds were an integral element of the ecclesiastical topography of medieval towns. In 13th-century Winchester anchoresses were recorded in outlying suburban churches. These churches played a special role in popular devotion through their prominent siting in relation to the routes of liturgical processions, such as that on Palm Sunday (Keene 1985: 128). In York, support of anchoresses was found throughout the city and suburbs but focused especi-ally on the parish of St Saviour, within the city walls, where it has been suggested that merchants and parishioners were influenced by Adam Wigan, a scholar of Balliol College, who was rector of St Saviour's from 1390 to 1433 (Hughes 1988: 69–70). The city of Norwich supported anchoresses at some 14 parish churches and three monastic ones. Some parishes demonstrated a remarkable continuity in their sponsorship of an anchorhold. St Edward, Conisford, and St Julian, Conisford, supported anchoresses from the 13th to the 16th centuries, and from the 14th to the 16th centuries respectively (Gilchrist and Oliva 1993: 75). Some urban monasteries seem to have forged strong links with the anchoritic tradition. The Dominicans and Carmelites, in particular, sponsored anchoresses' cells attached to their churches. At the London Blackfriars a cell was built for Margerie Elyote in 1521. This substantial house abutted the north aisle of the friars' church near the porch; it measured a generous 7.3 × 9.14m and was surrounded on three sides by the cemetery (Clay 1955: 213). Norwich Blackfriars sponsored a cell occupied from the late 15th century; from at least 1531 until long after the suppression of the friary it was occupied by Katherine Mann. Her devout and learned reputation secured the continuing support of the mayor and city of Norwich. Her cell was located to the north of the friars' chancel, where, today, three blocked brick archways suggest a single-storey cell of more than one room (Gilchrist and Oliva 1993: 76).

In common with members of monastic communities, anchorites took permanent vows and followed some kind of rule or guide. Warren lists a total of 13 English anchoritic rules, ranging from letters to comprehensive guides to daily life, dating from Goscelin's *Liber confortatorius c*1080, to works by Walter Hilton, dating to the second half of the 14th century (Warren 1985: 294–8). The most influential rules were written for anchoresses, including a letter composed by the Cistercian Aelred of Rievaulx for his sister, *De institutus inclusarum, c*1162, and the very popular *Ancrene Riwle*, written by an Augustinian canon for three sisters, *c*1220. Aelred's rule divided the anchoress's day into three parts: manual work, reading and prayer, the last including meditation and short and frequent periods of worship. He urged simplicity of food and clothing for the female recluse and a cell purged of ornaments, paintings and embroidered hangings or cloths. The altar in her cell was to have on it only a white cloth, 'whiche bitokeneth both chastite and symplenesse' and a crucifix 'of cristis passion' (Clay 1955: 203; 1914: 80). The author of the *Ancrene Riwle* outlined the requirements of the cell. It was to have three windows: one looking into the church for observing the sacrament, one for light or for communicating with priests or visitors, and a third to receive food from the servant. These were to remain shuttered or curtained:

> Have curtains made of two kinds of cloth, a black ground with a white cross showing both inside and outside ... The black cloth is not only symbolic, but also less harmful to the eyes than other colours and it is much stouter against the wind and other things. See the parlour window is fastened and well locked on every side, and when you are near it guard your eyes (Salu (ed.) 1955/1990: 21–2).

Later rules included more spiritual guides such as Richard Rolle's *Form of Living c*1348 (Allen 1931), written most likely for the anchoress Margaret de Kirkeby, and the *Scale of Perfection* by Walter Hilton (Underhill (ed.) 1923). Both Rolle and Hilton were renowned mystics who found disciples among female solitaries. Anchoresses gained reputations for their high standards of learning and literacy; they were both given books and bequeathed books themselves (Clay 1953: 79). Anchoresses shared much in common with the mystic traditions associated with the Carthusians and Bridgettines. Without doubt the most famous mystic among anchoresses was Julian of Norwich, born around 1343 and enclosed as an anchoress from the mid-1370s until at least 1415, in St Julian's, Conisford, Norwich. In common with other professed mystics Julian experienced visions, or 'showings'. She recorded her 16 'showings' in her collected writings, the *Revelations of Divine Love*, considered remarkable both for the degree of theological learning which they demonstrate and for their elegance of literary style. Like many female mystics, Julian focused on the suffering of Christ during the Passion, with visions of his blood and heart, and likened her own vocation to an enclosure with Christ (Colledge and Walsh (eds) 1978).

In general, anchorites lived alone in their cells but occasionally a group of two, or less often, three recluses shared a churchyard. The sisters for whom the *Ancren Riwle* was written each had her own cell but were served by the same two maids and a kitchen boy (Warren 1985: 33). It seems, however, that most cells were designed to accommodate a single recluse. Anchorite's cells might contain an oratory or altar and sometimes had a small garden attached in which the recluse could meditate and take exercise. Purpose-built cells were positioned either next to the church, in order to view the high altar, or within the churchyard. Recluses (or hermits) may also have occupied chambers above porches or in church towers. Chambers in towers sometimes retain fireplaces and latrines, as at Great Witchingham (Norfolk) (Cattermole 1990: 68–9); an anchorhold is one possible function that they may have served.

For the enclosed recluse visibility of the high altar was fundamental, allowing sight of the elevation of the Host. From the end of the 12th century it was customary for the consecrating priest to elevate the Host high above his head after the sacring (Duffy 1992: 95). To the medieval mind, at this moment the bread quite literally became the body of Christ. Viewing the Host was believed to assist in achieving individual salvation and to provide spiritual and physical nurture. The significance of this moment for the anchoress was explained by Julian of Norwich, 'our precious Mother, Jesus, feeds us with Himself and does so very courteously and tenderly with the Blessed Sacrament, which is the precious food of life itself' (Colledge and Walsh (eds) 1978: Chapter 60, Long Text).

In order to view the Mass the cell was positioned most often to the north or south of the chancel and was provided with a hatch, or squint, through which to view the high altar. The cell may often have been constructed in timber as a lean-to abutting the chancel. This arrangement may be suggested on the basis of evidence surviving in chancel walls of holes which supported timbers for roof beams. At Bengeo (Herts), two holes were found blocked with clay above the squint in the north wall (Micklethwaite 1887: 28); similar arrangements have been recorded at Chipping Ongar (Essex) and East Ham (Essex) (Deswick 1888: 286; Hodson 1940: 346).

The squint was generally widely splayed toward the east and fitted with a shutter in order to ensure the privacy of the recluse. At St Anne, Lewes (Sussex), for example, the small square window was still fitted with the iron pin for a shutter hinge when uncovered in 1927 (Godfrey 1928: 165). At East Ham (Essex), the squint is 0.30 × 0.20m, with the sill set 1.03m above the ground. It is rebated on the cell side for a small shutter, for which the hinges and bolt-hole were traced. The stone forming the head of the squint contained small holes which held wooden pegs, possibly for the hanging of a wickerwork

Figure 107   Compton parish church (Surrey): squint of the first anchorhold.

Figure 108   Saxthorpe parish church (Norfolk): blocked squint in the north wall of the chancel. A funerary brass of 1534 positioned at the entrance to the chancel commemorates a possible anchoress, 'the Venerable Cecily'.

screen which would have shielded the recluse when the shutter was open (Hodson 1940: 346). Elsewhere, the squint was formed by a quatrefoil opening, as at Shere (Surrey), or a cruciform opening, such as at Compton (Surrey) or St John the Baptist, Newcastle upon Tyne. Some squints were positioned very low down in the chancel wall and must have been used in a kneeling position for prayer, such as Hardham (Sussex) set 0.76m above the floor, and Compton (Surrey), where a squint for the first of two anchorholds at the church was positioned to enable sight of the high altar only when lying on the floor of the cell (figure 107) (Gibson 1950: 154).

Once anchorholds had fallen into disuse some were converted into vestries. Only some half dozen or so stone-built examples survive which can be corroborated by documents. Further examples can be proposed on the basis of archaeological evidence, such as Saxthorpe (Norfolk), where a squint opens from a vestry on the north side of the chancel and a funerary brass commemorates 'the Venerable Cecily', perhaps once an anchoress (figure 108).

At Staindrop (Durham), the vestry to the north of the chancel retains an upper-storey chamber with a fireplace and a blocked window. At the top of the newel staircase is a square-headed trefoiled window which was wide enough to view the nave and chancel (Clay 1955: 208). From his cell the anchorite would have kept guard over the Sacrament, which once blessed, could not be touched by a lay-person.

At Compton (Surrey), the second anchorhold at the church is a two-storey cell located to the south of the chancel; it measures 2.04 × 1.31m (André 1895) (figure 109). In its south wall there is a small window with a semi-circular head, possibly of the 12th century, and a rebate on the outside for a shutter. In the same wall is a blocked doorway. In the north wall of the cell there was a squint through which to view the high altar, and a doorway from the chancel into the cell (Gibson 1950: 154). Over the sanctuary in the east end of the chancel is an upper chapel which may have served as the oratory for an anchorite-priest. Today the oratory is accessible by modern stairs in the upper level of the cell. At Compton, the anchorite would have been ideally situated to keep watch over the Blessed Sacrament at night.

A slightly larger cell was provided for an anchorite at Leatherhead (Surrey), where excavations to the north of the chancel revealed foundations of massive flint walls 0.91m thick forming a chamber 2.43m square, set flush with the east end of the chancel (Johnston 1908: 223). The north wall of the chancel retains a blocked doorway and a square opening rebated for a shutter on the cell side and placed high up in the wall, suggesting a two-storey cell (figure 110).

The majority of cells were placed on the north side of the chancel, as evidenced mainly by the presence of blocked squints. Indications of anchorholds to the north survive at Leatherhead, Shere (Surrey), East Ham, Chipping Ongar, Chickney, Lindsell (Essex), Staindrop (Durham), St John's, Newcastle upon Tyne, Gateshead (Tyne and Wear) and Bengeo (Herts); evidence for anchorholds to the south of the chancel survives at Compton (Surrey), Hardham, Lewes (Sussex) and Polesworth (Warwicks). Positioning of the cell to the north may have been necessary in order to avoid the priest's door, the piscina and sedilia, placed most often in the south wall of the chancel. Exceptions might therefore include the cells of anchorite-priests, as proposed

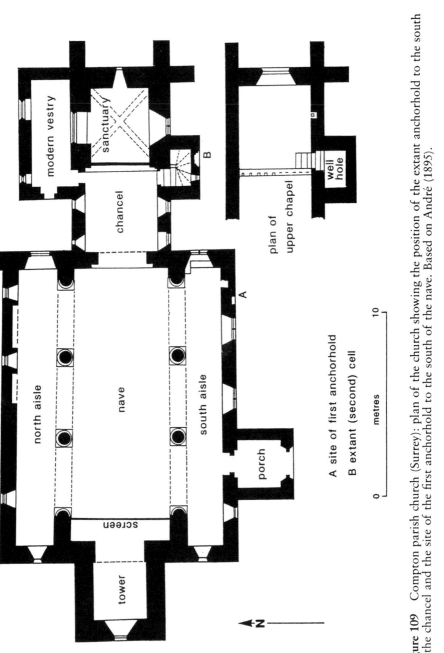

Figure 109 Compton parish church (Surrey): plan of the church showing the position of the extant anchorhold to the south of the chancel and the site of the first anchorhold to the south of the nave. Based on André (1895).

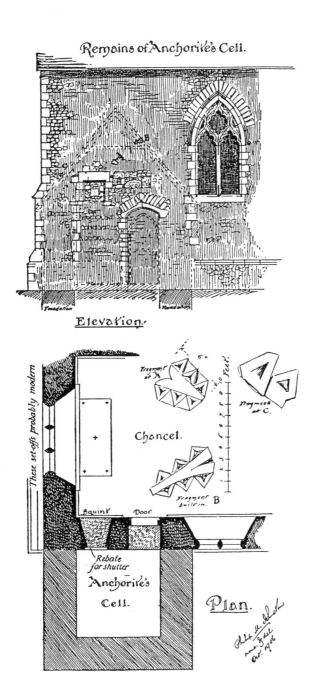

Figure 110 Leatherhead parish church (Surrey): blocked squint and conjectural roof-line of the former anchorage. From *Surrey Archaeological Collections* 20 (1908).

for Compton, where the usual ordinances did not apply. Symbolically, a northern situation was more fitting for the penitential vocation of the recluse, placed on the colder aspect in an area of the churchyard less popular for burial. In this respect the siting of anchorages can be likened to the positioning of nunnery cloisters to the north of the conventual church, and may comment on the greater incidence of female recluses for whom the north side would have held particular significance (above p. 45).

Placement of the cell may have varied according to the gender of the anchorite; certainly spatial rules were closely observed in some enclosure ceremonies. The 12th-century ceremony contained in the Pontifical of Magdalene College requires the postulant to lie prostrate in the mid-choir, if a male cleric, at the entrance to the choir for unordained men, and towards the west end of the church for women (Wilson 1910: 243–4). Evidence for the western siting of women's cells survives at St Marwenna, Marhamchurch (Cornwall), where Celia Moys's cell window looked into the church from the west (1403–5). At All Saints North Street, York, Emma de Raughtone's cell was built at the western end of the south aisle. At the ground floor is a small oblong opening with chamfered reveals and remains of the original wrought-iron grill, with an archway above. An upper-storey opening was positioned to observe the high altar. Male anchorites were recorded at Hartlip (Kent), where a two-storey cell still survives at the west end of the north aisle (figure 111), and at Chester-le-Street (Durham), where a very substantial anchorhold still exists at the west end of the church on the north side of the tower. Four rooms were provided for the anchorite, two at each level of the cell. The anchorage was formed by partitioning the western bay of the north aisle and extending it as an annexe to the tower. An upper room contained a squint sighted on the south aisle altar; this chamber may have been entered by an external stair. Windows included a small slit looking into the church and an external window to the west formed by a stone slab pierced by five openings. A well has been located in the foundations (Clay 1914: 83).

Siting of the anchorage within the parish cemetery was one means of signalling withdrawal from the living world to that of the desert. Anchorites inhabited a liminal plane between the living and the dead: to be immured in a cell represented a kind of symbolic death. In many cases it was expected that the anchorite would eventually be buried in the cell. Indeed, the rite outlined in the Exeter Pontifical (*Reclusio Anachoritarum*) indicates that the grave was dug as part of the enclosure ceremony, and remained open through-out the anchorite's life. In the *Ancrene Riwle*, the anchoresses were advised to remind themselves daily of their own mortality, she 'should scrape up earth every day out of the grave in which she shall rot … the sight of her grave near her does many an anchoress much good … She who keeps her death as it were before her eyes, her open grave reminding her of it … will not lightly pursue the delight of the flesh' (Salu 1955/1990: 51).

At East Ham (Essex), excavations have taken place in the area of an anchorite's cell indicated by openings in the north side of the chancel. Two burials were uncovered: one skeleton was close to the north wall of the church, and one was further north contained within a lead shell (Hodson 1940: 346). At St Anne's, Lewes (Sussex), previously known as St Mary Westout, a female recluse was recorded in 1253 when she was left 5s in the

Figure 111 Hartlip parish church (Kent): the extant anchorhold at the west end of the north aisle.

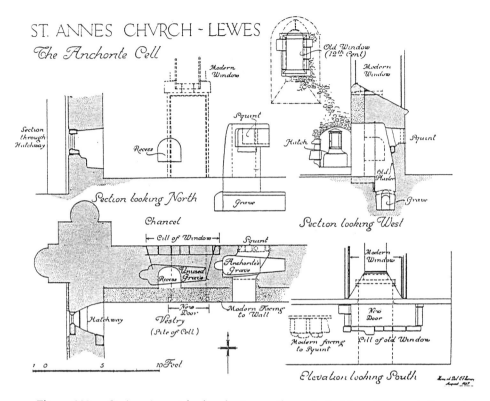

Figure 112   St Anne's parish church, Lewes (formerly St Mary Westout) (Sussex): excavation of the anchoress's cell. From *Sussex Archaeological Collections* 69 (1928).

will of Richard de Wych, Bishop of Chichester. Excavation of an anchorage on the south side of the chancel revealed the remains of a woman's skeleton dug into the foundations of the cell. Within a semicircular recess in the south wall of the church was a squint which slanted towards the high altar; at its base a grave had been tunnelled into the sides to allow space for the hands and feet of the skeleton (figure 112). Below the squint the plaster of the recess continued to the bottom of the grave, which formed the back of the shaped coffin (Godfrey 1928: 166–8). In order to view the high altar through the squint the recluse would have had to kneel daily in her own grave. Such morbid practices were integral to the penitential aspect of anchoritic life in the 12th and 13th centuries.

Evidence for anchorholds was compiled by antiquaries who stripped render and unblocked openings in search of 'low side windows' and the mythical lepers' squints in chancel walls (e.g. Johnston 1899). Once piqued, their curiosity often led to digging in the area of the anchorite's cell. Unfortunately, such pastimes were seldom recorded accurately, or even at all. We therefore have little evidence on the average dimensions of anchorholds, the nature of their construction or whether they were surrounded by a garden or enclosure. We have no evidence of artefacts or food remains associated with the cells, or of whether they were provided with garderobes or drains. Certainly, sanitation must have been difficult, with refuse and human waste most likely passed out to the servant by the external window. The author of the *Ancrene Riwle* reminded anchoresses to 'Wash yourselves wherever necessary as often as you wish, and your things as well. Filth was never dear to God, although poverty and plainness of dress are pleasing to him'. The nature of the anchorhold and the standards of living of its incumbents is surely one area in which church archaeology still has much to contribute.

Eremitic monasteries

The revival of the eremitic movement in the 12th century led to the birth of monastic orders which attempted to combine cenobitic and eremitic ideals (above pp. 157–9). In England, an indigenous response included the 'northern revival' in the late 11th century and the foundation of a number of eremitic communities in the first decades of the 12th century which would eventually adopt the Augustinian or Cistercian Rules (Leyser 1984: 36–7). In 1133, Fountains (N Yorks) was founded by 13 monks from St Mary's, York, who left the abbey with the help of the archbishop of York, Thurstan, in order to follow the truth of the Gospel. Their first years were lived out in extreme poverty until gifts from a deacon in York helped them to improve their hermitage (ibid.: 94). Excavations at Fountains, beneath the south transept of the later Cistercian abbey church, revealed an early phase which may have corresponded with this stage in the community's development. Two timber buildings were identified, consisting of a structure of four bays orientated east–west (4.9 × 7.6m) and joined at right angles to the south by a structure with substantial post-pits (Gilyard-Beer and Coppack 1986: 175). These buildings have been interpreted as an oratory and a domestic structure of possibly two storeys: the twin components necessary for any hermitage. This modest stage in the life of the abbey was short-lived; in the first 70 years the monastery experienced three major phases of development (ibid.: 183).

In France and Italy, monastic orders specifically devoted to the eremitic life emerged in the late 11th century. The French orders of Grandmont and La Chartreuse (Carthusians) established a small number of houses in Britain during the 12th and 13th centuries; the Carthusians enjoyed an 'Indian summer' of popularity in the late 14th and 15th centuries (figure 113). Like earlier ascetics, the Grandmontines and the medieval English Carthusians excluded women from their orders. In common with the early practices of the Cistercians, both orders had *conversi*, or lay-brothers, amongst the members of their communities.

Grandmontines

The Grandmontine order developed rapidly after the death of Stephen of Muret in 1124: by 1163, 39 houses had been founded in France (Hutchison 1989: 13). Only three daughter houses of Grandmont were founded in Britain, all in England. Grosmont (N Yorks) was established *c*1204 by Johanna, daughter of William Fossard; Alberbury (Shrops) *c*1221–6 by Fulk Fitz Warine;

Figure 113 Distribution of Grandmontine and Carthusian monasteries in medieval Britain. Based on Knowles and Hadcock (1971), Gwynn and Hadcock (1970) and Cowan and Easson (1976).

and Craswell (Herefords) *c*1225 by Walter de Lacy, Lord of Ewyas Harold. As alien priories they were confiscated in 1414, but continued in use until *c*1536, 1441, and 1462, respectively (Knowles and Hadcock 1971: 108–9).

　Grandmontines lived together in a 'cell' of up to 13 members of the order, including contemplatives, choir monks and lay-brothers. Both the monks and lay-brothers shared the choir, chapter-house, refectory and dormitory, the last divided into cubicles by wainscotting. In common with other hermits, the Grandmontines favoured woodlands and upland sites for their monasteries.

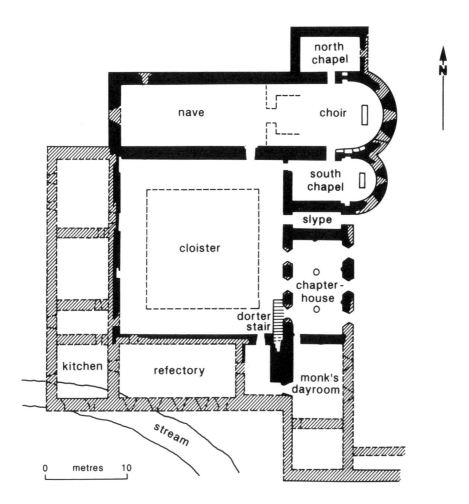

Figure 114 Craswell (Herefords): plan of the Grandmontine priory. Based on Hutchison (1989) and Graham and Clapham (1924–5).

Their choices reflected the hermit's craving for liminality: often Grandmontine monasteries were placed on the borders of states, provinces, dioceses and parishes (Hutchison 1989: 84). The English sites were no exception. Craswell and Alberbury were located on the Welsh border and Grosmont was a desolate site in the North Yorkshire moors. The monastery at Alberbury was contained in an oval enclosure formed partially by the River Severn together with a moat. The initial grant to the prior of Grosmont included 200 acres of wood with timber rights, a mill at Egton, pasturage and a house in York (Graham and Clapham 1924–5: 171). Grandmontine buildings were modestly constructed in local stone; at Craswell a well-worked quarry is located above the site (Hutchison 1989: 287).

In her survey of Grandmontine architecture, Carole Hutchison commented on the remarkable uniformity of style and ground-plans at their monasteries across Europe. Priories of the order appear to have resisted any variations in building which would normally have resulted from factors such as stylistic change over time, regionalism and developments in technology. The great majority of Grandmontine churches were aisleless parallelograms, terminating in a semicircular apse slightly broader than the nave, and lit by a triplet of round-headed windows (Hutchison 1989: 290). The apsed church at Craswell is typical in this respect, measuring 34m in length (figure 114).

Craswell was unique, however, in its two chapels flanking the chancel and for its exceptionally large and ornate chapter-house. Alberbury was one of only a few Grandmontine churches with a square-ended chancel, having originally been built for Arrouaisian (Augustinian) canons. Grandmontine churches were characterised by their high vaults – perhaps raised in an effort to improve acoustics – and the greater width of the apse. Hutchison has proposed that a symbolism of light played a significant role in the design of the Grandmontine churches (ibid.: 302). The nave was lit by a single west window, creating a dark cavern, perhaps in emulation of a hermit's cave. Morning light would have entered through the triplets in the apse and evening light through the west window, uniting the daily round of services with the natural cycle of the day.

In keeping with the hermits' desire to serve others, the Grandmontines were dedicated to providing hospitality, and would greet their visitors in a parlour located at the lay entry. Often this was a lean-to annexe projecting from the church to the north. At Craswell there are indications that the parlour was built in stone. A bull of Pope Clement V notes that women were only allowed as far into the church as the altar at the pulpitum (Graham and Clapham 1924–5: 191). Larger French priories, such as St Michel de Lodève (Herault), had side chapels with annexes specially provided for the laity, in particular for women (Hutchison 1989: 321).

Carthusians

In Britain the eremitic vocation seems to have been served more by hermits and anchorites than by the initiation of eremitic monasteries. However, while only three Grandmontine priories were founded in England in the early 13th century, the Carthusians enjoyed a late, but substantial, degree of lay support. Eventually nine charterhouses (monasteries of the Carthusian order) were established in England, one in Scotland and one in Ireland. The first English charterhouse was sponsored at Witham (Somerset) 1178–9 by Henry II in expiation of his part in the murder of Thomas Becket. A second house was founded by William Longespée at Hatherop (Gloucs) in 1222, which was later moved and refounded in 1227 at Hinton (Somerset) by his widow, Countess Ela of Salisbury, founder also of the nunnery at Lacock (Wilts). Houses were planned at Exeter and Horne (Surrey) but never materialised. The Irish charterhouse was established at Kinalehin (Galway, Eire) c1252, but was deserted by c1341 and shortly afterwards resurrected as a house of Franciscans. The two Somerset houses were to remain the only outposts of the Carthusians in England until the middle of the 14th century. While charterhouses had been founded across Europe from the 1160s onward (Aston

1993b: 143), English patterns of benefaction had favoured the reformed order of the Cistercians or the solitary life of the recluse.

In England, a third charterhouse, Beauvale, was founded by Sir Nicholas de Cantilupe in his park at Gresley in Nottinghamshire in 1343. Beauvale, like the earlier charterhouses at Witham, Hinton and Kinalehin, was modelled on arrangements at La Grande Chartreuse. All four sites accommodated communities of lay-brothers at 'lower houses', or *correries*. Lay-brothers were necessary in order to isolate further the Carthusian monks from the secular world. At La Grande Chartreuse the *correrie*, or *Domus Inferior*, of the lay-brothers was sited lower down the mountain side (hence, 'lower house'), at the entrance to St Laurent-du-Désert, the wilderness which contained the charterhouse. At the *correrie* visitors were received, a hospital tended the sick and industries such as tanning, milling and carpentry were carried out; a gate at the Entrée du Désert was the point beyond which women were not allowed. The *correrie* was a miniature charterhouse: the community had its own church and each lay-brother had his own cell. At Hinton, the charterhouse was established on a hilltop within the park of Countess Ela. The 'lower house' was situated about 1km away on the River Frome (Gee 1897: 528; Aston and Bettey 1990). Witham's *correrie* later developed into the village of Witham Friary, where the former lay-brothers' church survives today (McGarvie 1989), a late-12th-century aisleless, stone-vaulted structure. The 'lower house' at Witham evolved into a community of families acting as servants to the charterhouse, and its church received its own font and cemetery in 1459. The unmarried lay-brothers may have moved to the site of the main charterhouse, perhaps accommodated in a dormitory built by Thomas Bekynton in the mid-15th century (Dunning 1991: 34). At Beauvale, the 'lower house' seems to have been located on the opposite side of the valley from the charterhouse, where medieval remains include a gatehouse, burials and a possible altar slab (Du Boulay Hill and Gill 1908: 92).

In the 14th century, the Carthusian order expanded considerably in Europe: monasteries were founded in close association with magnate families and new charterhouses were established near towns and cities (Aston 1993b: 143), in stark contrast to the remote, rural sites of earlier years. In England, the Carthusians benefited from a change in religious mentalities. In the 14th and 15th centuries there was an increase in interest in the solitary religious life; this extended to the foundation of seven charterhouses by courtiers between 1343 and 1415, including Beauvale (Hughes 1988: 72). Several of the new houses were suburban, located outside town walls, including London (1371), Hull (1377) and Coventry (1385); the new rural charterhouses were Axholme (Lincs) in 1397–8 and Mount Grace (N Yorks) in 1398. The expanding reputation of Carthusian spirituality resulted in two royal foundations. Henry V established Sheen (Surrey) between 1406 and 1415, across from his Bridgettine double house at Syon and close to his royal palace at Richmond. Henry bequeathed 1000 marks for the completion of Sheen for 40 monks, making it the richest and largest of the charterhouses (Cloake 1977: 150). In 1426, James I of Scotland endowed a charterhouse for 13 monks near the burgh at Perth (Ferguson 1909–12: 183).

The later charterhouses in England, and elsewhere in Europe, might be seen as an extension of the growing chantry movement, in which prayers were believed to relieve the pains of those in Purgatory. The primary motivation in establishing a charterhouse would have been to receive the intercessory prayers and masses of the monks. After the Black Death, the prayers of the eremitic, mystical Carthusians were especially esteemed at a time when the Benedictines and Cistercians had lost their reputation for spirituality. The foundation charter of Mount Grace states that the monks were obliged to perform masses for a number of leading courtiers (Hughes 1988: 77). At the London Charterhouse, individual nobles and rich merchants each sponsored the building of a cell (Knowles and Grimes 1954: 26), in effect establishing their own private chantry. Charterhouses were founded to serve as mausolea for a particular person or family. The grave of the founder of the London Charterhouse, Sir Walter Manny, was located in the centre of the choir of the church, at the foot of the steps to the high altar. The stone and brick-lined tomb contained an anthropomorphic lead coffin (Knowles and Grimes 1954: 49). Excavations at Coventry Charterhouse uncovered a possible founder's grave beneath the foundations for the altar (*Medieval Archaeol* 13 1969: 248). Lesser bequests were repaid by burial in the conventual church. At Coventry the skeletons of 59 individuals were excavated in the church, including four women and seven children, and 12 skeletons were located to the north of the church (Soden 1992: 80).

Originally, the Carthusians had intended their monasteries to be entirely self-sufficient, with the estates within their boundaries worked by servants bound to the order (*redditi*) (Thompson 1930: 123). Both Hinton and Beauvale were surrounded by an outer wall with earthworks surviving beyond it; at Beauvale this was suggestive of fishponds and possibly a coalpit, and at Hinton indicative of quarries (Aston 1993: 101). Witham held granges at Charterhouse on Mendip, Hydon, Bellerica and Green Ore, the last associated with lead mining. In common with other monasteries, later houses relied mainly on cash from rents and bequests. Fourteenth-century houses rejected the *correrie* in favour of accommodating their lay-brothers in a separate cloister adjacent to that of the monks. The eremitic roots of the order continued to be signalled through the choice of site, even in suburban locations. The London Charterhouse was founded on the site of a former plague cemetery, where a chapel was served by two hermits, and Coventry was established at the hermitage of St Anne. The rural charterhouse at Axholme was sited at an existing shrine, known as the 'ancient priory of the wood' (Hills 1961: 3).

The observances of the Carthusians were clearly expressed by the layout of their cloisters. Each monk lived alone in a cell, not dissimilar to the houses of chantry priests. The cells of the individual monks were laid out around a great cloister, while the buildings used for communal purposes, such as the church and chapter-house, were much smaller than in other types of monastery (figure 115).

Little is known of the arrangements at the charterhouses of Axholme or Hull; Sheen has been reconstructed on the basis of documentary evidence (Cloake 1977); and the earthwork site of Witham has been partly excavated (Burrow and Burrow 1990). The best surviving example in Britain is Mount Grace (N Yorks), founded in 1398 on a manor of the Ingilby family in the Cleveland hills (figure 116). The individual cells were substantial two-storey

Figure 115 Mount Grace Priory (N Yorks): aerial view showing foundations of the individual cells of each monk arranged around the great cloister.

dwellings with enclosed gardens attached. At Mount Grace each of 15 cells with their garden plots required about 15.25m, so that a large cloister was required measuring 70.4m on three sides and 83m on the fourth. The cloister itself simply provided covered walkways from the cells to other parts of the cloister, and was built as a lean-to, much of it remaining in timber until the dissolution of the monastery (Coppack 1991: 15).

The earliest cells on the site were first built in timber and gradually replaced in stone. Each cell faced onto the cloister alley and was contained in its own garden. The cell itself measured from 6m square at Beauvale (figure 117), to 8.2m square at Mount Grace. The door from the cloister had a hatch positioned next to it, through which the lay-brothers would pass food to the monks. The L-shaped hatch turned within the thickness of the cell wall in order to preclude any eye contact between the lay-brothers and the incumbent of the cell. The entrance lobby had a mortared, tiled or timber floor, and was separated from the other ground-floor rooms by timber partitions. At Mount Grace the ground floor has been interpreted as a living room or hall, an oratory and bedroom, and a study. The living room had a fireplace and the rooms had raised wooden floors. A wooden stair led to a workroom above, where the monk would practise book production, weaving or some other trade. The interior of the cell was limewashed; some were plastered and some were panelled in their latest phases of occupation. From the entry passage a door led to a small, private cloister used for meditation. Excavation at Mount Grace showed that this small cloister had a wooden floor and glazed windows. A second door led to the garden, which had penticed walkways leading to a latrine and a wall-niche for a tap for drinking

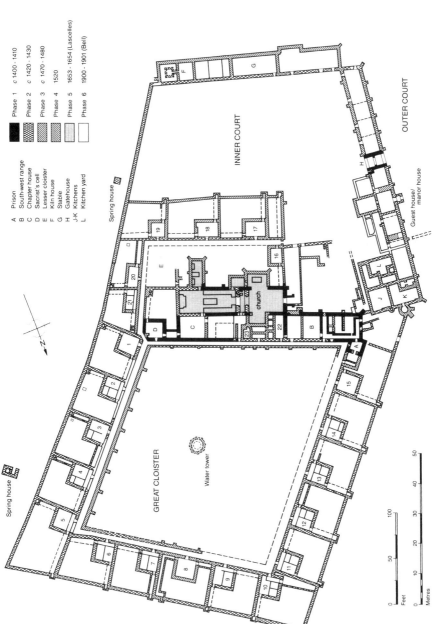

Figure 116 Mount Grace Priory (N Yorks): plan showing the monks' cells around the great cloister, the communal church and refectory, the lay-brothers' cells around the little cloister and service buildings in the inner court. Reproduced with permission of English Heritage from G. Coppack (1991) *Mount Grace Priory.*

A   Prison
B   South-west range
C   Chapter house
D   Sacrist's cell
E   Lesser cloister
F   Kiln house
G   Stable
H   Gatehouse
J-K   Kitchens
L   Kitchen yard

Phase 1   c 1400 - 1410
Phase 2   c 1420 - 1430
Phase 3   c 1470 - 1480
Phase 4   1520
Phase 5   1653 - 1654 (Lascelles)
Phase 6   1900 - 1901 (Bell)

Spring house

Spring house

GREAT CLOISTER

Water tower

INNER COURT

OUTER COURT

Guest house/
manor house

church

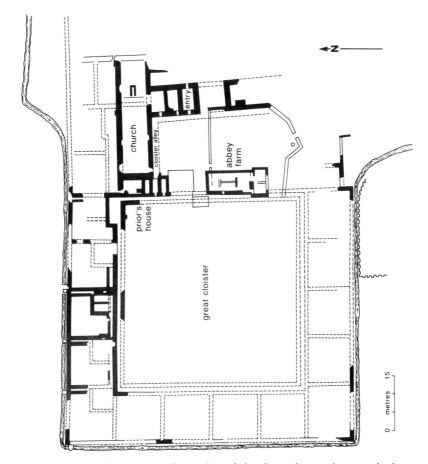

Figure 117 Beauvale Priory (Derbys): plan of the charterhouse showing the layout of cells. Based on Du Boulay Hill and Gill (1908).

water (Coppack 1991: 18). Several gardens were excavated and each was arranged differently. Cell 8 had rectangular beds defined by paths of roof-slate; Cell 9 had small square beds edged with stones (Coppack 1990: 78). When the number of monks at the charterhouse increased it became necessary to squeeze additional cells into the space available. At Mount Grace, two cells were built in an open space on the north side of the church, to the east of the prior's cell and refectory.

The necessity of providing each cell with water-flushed latrines and fresh drinking water resulted in elaborate systems of water supply. Charterhouses channelled water into the main cloister, from where it was redistributed to the individual cells. At Chartreuse de la Verne, Collobrières (Var), the charter-house was constructed on a series of aqueducts draining from the River La Verne and carried by two conduits to a basin in the centre of the great cloister (*Archéologie Médiévale* 23 1993: 362–3). Witham had a central conduit in the cloister garth from which water was fed by lead pipes (Bond 1989: 88). At Mount Grace, three natural springs on the hillside were tapped and covered by well-houses to the north-east of the monastery in order to provide drinking

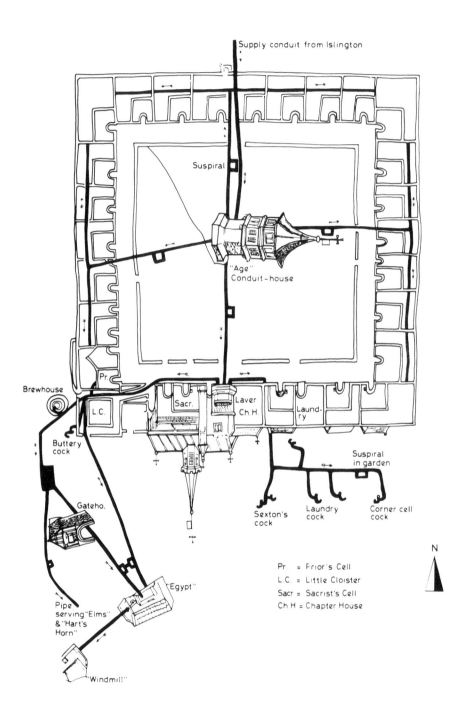

Figure 118   The water supply to the London Charterhouse. A redrawing by C. James Bond based on the plan of *c*1500. Reproduced courtesy of C.J. Bond from Bond (1993).

Figure 119 Hinton Priory (Somerset): the two-storey chapter-house of the charter-house.

Figure 120 Hinton Priory (Somerset): the medieval refectory and kitchen area survive as part of a later service court.

water. An octagonal water tower was situated in the garth of the great cloister and received the water via underground pipes. The tower redistributed water through lead pipes to each cell, where a latrine was set over a channel flushed by running water. A similar arrangement was required at urban houses, such as the London Charterhouse, where water was piped from Islington (3.2km away) by an underground conduit. The internal water system is clearly indicated on a surviving plan of *c*1500 (figure 118). The supply pipe led to a large conduit-house from where it was redistributed by four branch pipes, each of which passed by a small tank to different parts of the great cloister (Bond 1993: 55, 65, 66). Before the construction of the conduit the latrines were simple garderobes positioned over pits, as excavation has suggested at the site of cells on the north side of the great cloister (Barratt and Thomas 1991: 287).

The communal buildings of the charterhouse were small in comparison with those of other orders, and included the church, chapter-house and refectory. The chapter-house was located in order to allow access to the church and great cloister. At Hinton, it survives as a two-storey structure, with the upper storey perhaps having served as a library (figure 119) (Hogg 1975). During the 13th century, its east end appears to have been heightened and lengthened. The refectory was sited on the great cloister, adjacent to the kitchen (figure 120). At Hinton the refectory was placed over a vaulted undercroft, next to a kitchen with a large hearth and serving hatch.

Carthusian churches were simple in plan and decoration. At Mount Grace the church was begun *c*1400 and was subject to three principal phases of building, elucidated by excavation and study of the standing fabric (St John

Hope 1905). It began as a simple rectangle (27 × 7.7m) divided in two by a cross-passage defined by timber screens; the western section would have been used by the lay-brothers. When the charterhouse received new endowments in 1415 the church was altered accordingly. The cross-passage was replaced with stone screening walls that carried a bell-tower. A rood-loft at the eastern end of the nave would have been flanked by altars (Coppack 1990: 52–4). Excavations at Coventry Charterhouse revealed a long, aisleless church with the nave and choir divided by screens and a crossing tower (figure 121).

Both churches resembled those of friars, with the monastic choir screened from the nave by a tower or walking place. The church of the London Charterhouse began as a simple rectangle and, like Coventry, had later chapels added to it. Three chapels to the south side of the church were dedicated to St John the Evangelist, SS Jerome and Bernard and SS Michael and John the Baptist; to the north were those of St Catherine and St Agnes (Knowles and Grimes 1954: 29). Between the church and the little cloister was a chapel dedicated to St Anne and the Holy Cross, built as an extension of the church intended to accommodate women, before they were later banned from it entirely (ibid.: 60).

The later charterhouses were built with little cloisters in which lay-brothers were accommodated. At London, the little cloister has been excavated to the west of the site of the great cloister. The slight foundations of the cells suggest that they may have been timber-framed. Additional accommodation was provided in a second court located to the west. Its extant 16th-century ranges are constructed of red brick with some ragstone rubble. At Mount Grace, Yorks, the little cloister was to the east and south of the church. The cells of the little cloister were built in stone, but seem to have replaced earlier timber structures. They were smaller than those of the monks and likely to have been a single storey. They consisted of an entry passage, living room and bedchamber, each with a private cloister, walled garden and latrine (Coppack 1991: 28).

In common with other monasteries, charterhouses had an inner court where services were located and guests housed. At Mount Grace, three ranges of the inner court survive to the south of the little cloister. The inner court was entered via a gatehouse which controlled access to the monastery. To the north of the gatehouse was a substantial range which is likely to have served as the guest-house. It was rebuilt in stone in the later 15th century and divided at ground floor into four units by timber-framed partitions. Higher-quality accommodation was provided by an upper-level suite, and a hall was located to the north. The close ties which the monastery maintained with noble families required that they should extend a comfortable degree of hospitality. Beauvale and Mount Grace had lay fraternities associated with the monasteries, and Mount Grace served as a place of temporary retreat for clerics in the Diocese of York (Hughes 1988: 122). At some houses the entertainment of guests may have taken place in the prior's cell. Excavations at La Cartuja, outside Seville (Andalucia, Spain), yielded remains of 20 different bird species in the prior's cell, in contrast to the fish bones and marine molluscs identified in the cesspit deposits associated with the monks' cells. At Mount Grace, the inner court also contained service structures such as a granary, kiln-house and stables. Additional agricultural and industrial

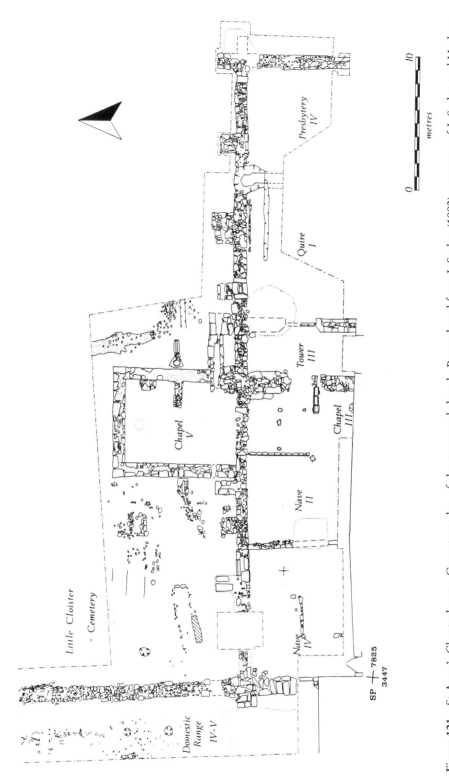

Figure 121 St Anne's Charterhouse, Coventry: plan of the excavated church. Reproduced from I. Soden (1992), courtesy of I. Soden and Herbert Art Gallery and Museum, Coventry.

activities were performed in the outer court, on the lower terrace to the west of the monastery. Here there was a mill, a farm, fishponds and a guest-house.

In the later middle ages the Carthusians enjoyed the patronage of the highest-ranking members of the English aristocracy. For some, Carthusian spirituality may have represented a revival of the old contemplative ideals at a time when Benedictine and Cistercian monasticism was viewed with increasing scepticism (Hughes 1988: 73). The monks continued to observe the ascetic tradition in their solitude and frugalness of diet. In certain respects, however, they enjoyed a lifestyle above average standards, with heated, spacious accommodation and excellent sanitary provisions. The wealth of the Carthusians has been confirmed by the evidence from excavations. For example, the garden of a single cell at Mount Grace (figure 116, number 8) produced fragments of 24 pottery vessels thrown out at the closure of the monastery, together with copper-alloy book mounts. The assemblage consisted of fragments of vessels of six local wares, three regional imports and 15 continental imports (Roebuck and Coppack 1987).

Revived interest in the Carthusians corresponded with an increased sympathy for mysticism. The order took an active role in transcribing and studying the major works of the English mystics and in providing copies for others. Carthusian scribes at Mount Grace and Beauvale copied devotional literature for those engaged in a more active life in the world, while the monks of Sheen produced books for the libraries of the Bridgettine house at Syon. It seems that Mount Grace may even have lent books to local nobles (Hughes 1988: 111). Certainly, excavations at Mount Grace have produced substantial evidence for book production, including pens, parchment prickers, styli, coloured pigments and a stone mould used for casting type for book printing. Examples of their work contained mystical references and illustrations of subjects closely linked with the mystical and eremitic traditions, including the sacred heart, the Yorkshire mystic Richard Rolle, Mary Magdalene and Mary of Egypt (Hogg 1981).

In addition to providing intercessory prayers, hospitality and disseminating devotional literature, the later Carthusians engaged in charitable works. The Coventry Charterhouse maintained a school within the precinct from c1396 and distributed alms at the gate of the Carmelite friary. Hull Charterhouse was initially established with a hospital for 13 poor men and women. By 1383 the priory had separated from the hospital, but their precincts remained adjacent, separated only by a road. These urban charterhouses fulfilled social roles more usually associated with the friars (see Lawrence 1984: 207–12). This, together with the increasing accessibility of the Carthusians to their lay-patrons, may account for the similarities between later Carthusian and friars' churches.

Conclusions: 'the desert a city'

> There he saw old men, glorious in the life of action and also of contemplation, fervent in spirit, serving the Lord (The Life of St Mary of Egypt, Chapter 4, trans. Ward 1987: 38).

In the story of Mary of Egypt, the priest Zossima enters a Palestinian desert thick with ascetics. He joins an eremitic monastery where the monks are committed simultaneously to a life of contemplation and action. The biblical and desert traditions continued to shape religious mentalities and were crucial in forming the monastic landscape of later medieval Britain. While seemingly disparate, the vocations and lifestyles described in this chapter stemmed from this unifying legacy. Like the desert of the fathers and harlots, the towns and countryside of Britain in the later middle ages were busy with hermits.

Solitary hermits practised an active vocation providing service to others: maintaining roads, ditches, bridges and town walls, and lighting cliffs for seafarers. Recluses living in caves or enclosed as anchorites in parish churches fulfilled a more penitential life of contemplation. Hermits in western Britain continued to live together in monasteries of the early medieval tradition, often placed wistfully at the sites of Celtic monasteries or the shrines of early saints. All of these hermits, together with those living as monks at Grand-montine and early Carthusian houses, were united in their search for liminality. All of them in their different ways lived on the physical and social boundaries of existence: their vocation was served through distance from the world.

From the 14th century, anchorites and Carthusians were fired by a life more devoted to mysticism, and their intercessory prayers took on a new value in the spiritual turmoil which followed the Black Death. Moreover, they were committed to communicating their spiritual insight to a lay audience. In the later middle ages, the role of the recluse adapted itself to suit changing religious and social needs. While other monastics lost favour, the contemplative life took on a renewed significance, in its way as vital and accessible as that of the friars.

6 Conclusions: 'the other monasticism'

This book began by recalling the images of medieval monasticism considered most frequently: the agricultural workings of the Cistercians, the extravagant lifestyles of the Benedictines and the more modest existence of the urban friars. In examining the ideas and material culture of 'the other monasticism', we have taken a physical journey through the medieval countryside. The medieval traveller through this landscape would encounter the hermit of the road, bridge or forest, to whom he or she might offer alms, and stop at the hospice in search of food and rest. Passing through secular and monastic estates, the traveller would see dozens of parish churches, perhaps stopping to seek counsel from a resident anchoress. When approaching the town, the traveller would first glimpse the hospitals, and perhaps a nunnery, in the fields at the edge of the urban hinterland. Lepers would beg alms as the traveller walked the last distance of the journey, passing beneath a hermit resident in the town wall. These are a few of the sights common to the medieval traveller or pilgrim, to whom 'the other monasticism' was highly visible and constant.

Certain patterns can be discerned in the changing social and economic functions of hospitals, preceptories, nunneries and hermitages, and in the nature of patronage which they attracted from different groups within medieval society. Initially, hospitals were established by wealthy individuals or by monasteries dedicated to providing charity. Motivations for their foundation varied from the provision of welfare for the poor to the more personal desire to attract intercessory prayers from the inmates and patients. From the 14th century charitable provision was more collective: hospitals were founded by merchants, parish groups, fraternities and guilds. Their hospitals represented an emerging secular concern with the poor, while, increasingly, charity was considered to be of spiritual value only if given and received by those perceived to be in a state of grace.

Support for the Military Orders came from all social levels and remained strong into the 13th century. Gifts to the orders kept step with their success in the East, with donations of land and programmes of church rebuilding corresponding to the period during which Jerusalem was recaptured (1229–44). When Acre was lost in 1291, the Military Orders gave up their last foothold in the Holy Land. Unlike other monastic orders the vocation of the knight-monks could be seen, by their medieval contemporaries, to succeed or fail. The final loss of Jerusalem and the Holy Land was considered to signal the displeasure of God (Nicholson 1993: 134). The military vocation disappeared from the range of monastic options. Increasingly, the Hospitallers concentrated their wealth and efforts on charitable relief, while the more redundant Templars left themselves ripe for suppression in 1312.

The majority of British nunneries were established in order to make a more regional impact, often founded by local lords who held neither title nor high office. Hermits had private patrons in the aristocracy or, more often, relied on support from passing travellers who contributed alms for their upkeep. Anchorites attracted popular support, especially in eastern England, in particular, Yorkshire and Norfolk, while from the late 14th century the Carthusians gained the patronage of kings, nobility and baronial families, in addition to wealthy merchants and more modest townsfolk.

Archaeological summary

Certain patterns can be discerned in the siting, forms and economies of hospitals, preceptories, nunneries and hermitages. Because the poor were attracted to medieval towns, most categories of hospital were strongly urban in their distribution, while hospices were sited on rural routes associated with pilgrimage. Hospitals were placed on bridges, at gates, at the boundaries between parishes and at the frontiers between urban, suburban and rural. Their situations on major thoroughfares indicate that not even *leprosaria* or hospitals founded for the sick poor were placed in order to guard against infection. Instead, hospitals were located in order to display the charity of founders and patrons to the widest audience, and to gain the intercessory prayers of travellers passing the hospital. The liminal siting of leper hospitals reminded the onlooker of the terrible divine retribution for sin, particularly sexual sin, which was thought to cause leprosy. The leper took on the role of the penitent. In common with anchorites, he or she was ritually separated from society and regarded as symbolically dead; both groups engaged in ceremonies of dissociation which involved the digging of their own graves.

Preceptories were largely rural in their distribution, associated especially with regions of arable agriculture which appear to have been deliberately sought by the Military Orders. The preceptory estate was often built up in piecemeal fashion through the donations of small parcels of land by local patrons. Nunneries were often sited in marshlands, so that water was used to delineate the boundaries of the monastery and to reinforce the strict enclosure of the nuns. The inhospitable settings of nunneries in marsh, fen and moorland may have contributed to the penitential vocation of some houses of religious women. Others were established in close proximity to villages and parish churches, an indication of the close links between the nuns and the local community. Such connections included the nuns' provision of schools, hospitals and alms for the local poor. The mingling of religious and laity resulted from the sharing of convent and parish churches and the practice of accepting paying guests in monastic houses.

The siting of hermitages varied according to the precise nature of vocations. The most eremitic were sited on islands, in fens, or in forests, while those following a life of physical service to others established their hermitages on bridges, roads or causeways. Bridges may have been considered particularly poignant sites, representing the liminal status of the hermit. Some lodged in chambers in town walls, assisting in the physical maintenance of the fabric of the city and helping to define its identity. Hermitages were placed on boundaries, such as the Grandmontine monasteries of Craswell, Alberbury and

Grosmont, located respectively on the Welsh borders and the Yorkshire moors. Even in urban contexts the liminality of 'the other monasticism' was re-inforced by the siting of hospitals, nunneries, preceptories, hermitages and charterhouses at the boundaries of towns, on the suburban fringe. While such positions may have resulted largely from the availability of land, especial-ly in the case of latecomers like the Carthusians, medieval people must have viewed these monastics as defining the edges of urban life, beyond the bound-aries of the familiar.

Documentary and archaeological evidence suggests a fluidity of functions and forms in the medieval hospital. The basic elements were the infirmary hall and its chapel attached to the east, often arranged with other buildings around a quadrangle, close or cloister. In mixed hospitals for men and women, sexually segregated infirmary halls were provided either on separate floors, arranged as parallel halls, or placed in a T-shape plan with the two halls meeting a central chapel. Lepers were accommodated in cells grouped around a chapel or, more typically, in common halls which, by the 15th century, were partitioned into separate rooms. Hospitals adopted a more regular arrange-ment in the 14th and 15th centuries, sometimes involving the separation of the infirmary hall and chapel, and the more regular ordering of buildings around a cloister. Almshouses built in the 15th and 16th centuries were based on the collegiate plan, with separate dwellings arranged around a quadrangle. In larger monastic hospitals cloisters were provided for different groups within the house, possibly including canons, sisters, corrodians and male and female inmates. Even at smaller hospices, like St Giles by Brompton Bridge (Brough, N Yorks), care was taken to segregate the chapel and the travellers' hall from the main hospital. Larger establishments had gardens and service buildings beyond the central complex, in some cases including a bakehouse, brewhouse, dovecote and mill.

Preceptories consisted of religious, domestic and agricultural buildings contained within a precinct defined most frequently by a moat. Few had formal cloisters but the conventual buildings of larger preceptories were sometimes grouped around a central space or courtyard. The churches of these larger houses were often shared with a parochial congregation, resulting in the spatial separation of the church and the conventual buildings. The components of the preceptory may be best reflected by the development of South Witham (Lincs) in the 13th century, expanded to include a great and lesser hall, chapel, kitchen and dairy or brewhouse, all in the central court, with agricultural buildings and fishponds to the north and west. Smaller preceptories consisted of a hall with integral chapel, often arranged as a chamber-block with the hall, or chapel over an undercroft. Two-storey halls and chapels appear to have been particularly typical of Hospitaller pre-ceptories.

Nunneries were ordered around the standard monastic cloister or court, although frequently the cloister was formed only by the creation of lean-to roofs against the church and domestic buildings. Most often, the nunnery church was without aisles, transepts or additional chapels; its simplicity reflected the liturgical prohibitions on religious women. In many cases the nuns' church was shared with a parish, with segregation of the two groups achieved through the provision of parallel aisles. Two-storey refectories were common and west ranges were arranged as ordinary domestic halls in order to serve as guest accommodation. The west range was the area of the nunnery most often renewed in the 15th or 16th centuries, reflecting the significance of hospitality. Often, the inner court of the nunnery accommodated secular lodgers and visitors, while the outer court contained light industry, storage and gardens.

The forms of hermitages were varied, but all required the twin elements of oratory and domestic accommodation. Many were sited in caves or carved from the living rock, demonstrating continuity with the early hermits of the desert and showing a strong link with nature. The eremitic monasteries of the Carthusians (charterhouses) had a distinctive plan in which the cells of the individual monks were laid out around a great cloister, while the communal buildings, such as the church and refectory, were smaller than those in other monasteries. The inner court of the charterhouse was devoted partly to hospitality, an important priority in all categories of monastery. Grand-montines were provided with a communal dormitory, despite their status as hermit-monks. Their monasteries observed strict filial guidelines in the design of buildings, including dark, cavernous churches, which may have been intended to emulate the hermit's cave.

While distinctive in many respects, these monasteries shared common traits with other categories of medieval settlement, monastic and secular. The basic infirmary hall and chapel was similar in plan to the nave and chancel of a parish church. The domestic buildings of smaller hospitals, preceptories, nunneries and communal hermitages, such as Grafton Regis (Northants), were constructed in timber, earth, or from local sources of stone. In this respect they may more closely have resembled lower-status urban or rural buildings than those of other monasteries. Smaller rural nunneries might have been mistaken for manor houses: their ranges were ordered as discontinuous courtyards, formed by pentices and constructed in local materials; the entire complex was often surrounded by a moat. In the 15th and 16th centuries, hospitals adopted arrangements like those of secular colleges, while the cells of anchorites and Carthusian monks were similar to the houses of chantry priests. These parallels were no coincidence: all of the individuals living in such accommodation were devoted to a life of contemplation and intercessory prayer. Ground-plans of the churches of the later charterhouses, such as Coventry and Mount Grace, closely resembled those of friary churches in the screening of the choir and nave, perhaps reflecting the more public character of the later Carthusians.

Smaller preceptories were similar in form to other rural settlements dedicated to arable production, including alien priories, monastic granges and manor houses. This analogy may be especially apt, since preceptories in the West were, in fact, alien houses of the Hospital and Temple in Jerusalem. Larger preceptories adopted features which, at least in the 12th century, were more indicative of castles and palaces. These included the provision of a detached chapel, often two-storeyed, the tendency for central planning, the grouping together of buildings within defensible enclosures, extensive moats and two-storey halls. The use of first-floor halls is generally thought to have been common in a number of types of masculine institution in the 12th century, including early castles, aristocratic residences and bishops' palaces.

Two-storey or galleried chapels were used at hospitals, nunneries and preceptories. At hospitals this arrangement facilitated the accommodation of inmates at the upper level, where the high altar of the chapel would still be visible to them. Within preceptories the more general aim may have been to segregate social groups; for example, accommodating the preceptor and brethren in a gallery, and the servants below. This means of segregation was used at nunneries to divide the nuns from male religious (at some double houses), parochial congregations, or from secular women visiting or boarding in the house. Such galleried chapels were common in castles and manor houses and suggest the extent to which these monasteries borrowed from conventions used in the planning of high-status secular settlements. The types of building which occurred at a preceptory, such as South Witham, were equally characteristic of secular manors and monasteries. However, the domestic and agricultural buildings were constructed on an exceptional scale, and space was carefully regulated, with religious and industrial areas clearly separated.

By the 15th century, the ordering of space in the monastery had altered to favour privacy and personal devotions over the concept of community which had been central to cenobiticism. This growing desire for privacy can be observed first in higher status secular contexts, with private households occurring in palaces from the 12th century, and ranges of private lodgings replacing the great and lesser hall from the late 14th century. Hospital infirmaries were partitioned by the 14th to 15th centuries, or rebuilt as collegiate almshouses in the 15th to 16th centuries. Hospital inmates seem to have guarded their personal property keenly. Private cupboards or lockers are suggested by the assemblages of copper-alloy keys from St Mary Spital, London, and St Bartholomew, Bristol. Many preceptories provided individual quarters for the preceptor by the 14th century, while in the 15th century some nunneries rebuilt their dormitories as individual cubicles, such as Littlemore (Oxfords). The more aristocratic nunneries, such as Elstow (Bedfords) and Godstow (Oxfords), witnessed the splintering of the communal dormitory and refectory into smaller households (*familiae*) from the late 13th century, and with growing frequency from the 15th century. Such arrangements resembled the permanently resident 'inner households' of women residing in castles. In England, the resurgence of interest in the Carthusians during the late 14th century corresponded with a time when their emphasis on individual space and private devotions was in keeping with lay and monastic attitudes.

The economies of these monasteries varied considerably, but only the preceptory or the 12th-century charterhouse corresponds with the model proposed by archaeologists of the monastery as a self-sufficient unit of production. Preceptories of the Military Orders actively built up estates which specialised in arable agriculture. The larger preceptories administered outlying estates and holdings, and served as central places for the storage of agricultural products, as evidenced by the massive barns which survive at Temple Cressing (Essex) and those which have been excavated at Skelton (W Yorks). A number of sites possessed impressive mills and fishpond complexes, evidence of the considerable impact which these monasteries had on their surrounding landscapes.

Hospitals were endowed with property or rents from which to earn income.

Some were established with extensive precincts and scattered rural estates, but few could have achieved surplus or self-sufficiency in food production. The endowments of nunneries were relatively meagre, consisting of concentrated estates and small manors. With the exception of the female houses established before the Conquest, and the small number of aristocratic Norman foundations, few nunneries would have been able to achieve economic self-sufficiency. In contrast, hermits eked out their modest livings in avoidance of dependence on others. Evidence from saints' lives suggests that they kept cows for milk, raised crops, fished and gathered wild foods for themselves. The contemplative lifestyles of anchorites and Carthusian monks required absolute reliance on others; both groups were brought food in their cells by servants or lay-monastics. The 12th-century charterhouses were established with estates, granges and separate settlements for the lay-brothers (*correries*) to work and administer these holdings, while later foundations relied on cash from rents and substantial bequests.

Recent archaeological and historical research has contributed to our knowledge of medieval standards of living, adding to our understanding of diet, disease, treatment of the sick and sanitation. Diet in hospitals consisted of coarse bread, meat or fish, cheese, beer and fruit and vegetables such as leeks, onions, pears and apples, in keeping with the lower-status diet of the time. The predominant source of meat varied according to local economies. For instance, greater quantities of mutton were consumed in areas of sheep husbandry. Most nunneries would have consumed a simple diet resembling that of the better-off peasantry, while aristocratic communities like St Mary's, Winchester, enjoyed a greater variety of foods, especially a diversity of marine and freshwater fish. Remains of fruit have been recovered from the nunnery of Denney (Cambs) and the hospital of St Mary Spital, London, in both cases consisting of soft fruit, such as berries and figs. Hermits, anchorites and Carthusians observed frugal diets, generally eschewing meat in favour of vegetables, pulses and fish.

From hospital cemeteries comes evidence of the contrasting standards of diet and health of different social groups. Individuals buried within the church at St Mary Spital, London, were found to be taller than those buried outside, perhaps indicating that they had been better nourished throughout their lives; it was suggested also that their diet had been more likely to lead to dental disease and perhaps to a condition linked with obesity (DISH). At St Saviour, Bury St Edmunds, some of those buried outside the hospital chapel seem to have suffered from chronic anaemia; these individuals, together with the cases identified from St Bartholomew, Bristol, must have suffered a poor diet in childhood. The age profiles of the skeletal populations sometimes indicate the function of a particular hospital: the elderly group from St Bartholomew, Bristol, reflects its purpose as an almshouse, while the early phases of the cemetery at St Mary Spital, London, suggest that the hospital catered for migrant workers and the young, mobile poor attracted to London (see p. 33). A small group of skeletons excavated to the north of the nave of the Hospitaller headquarters at Clerkenwell, London, included women and a number of individuals with rickets, suggesting that the infirmary at the site served the general poor.

Some treatment of the sick poor at hospitals may be indicated by the presence in concentrated occurrence of plants with medicinal properties, or by the recovery of specialised implements or vessels, such as urinals, or jordans, used in the diagnosis of patients, or pottery or wooden vessels used to feed the infirm. Excavations at hospitals have suggested a high standard of cleanliness, including the provision of a fresh water supply and the regular clearance of drains. A building at the Templar site of Denney (Cambs), thought to have been the infirmary, was kept immaculately clean. At the hospital of St John the Baptist, Oxford, an ashlar-lined culvert was located at the east end of the infirmary chapel, with steps leading down into it. Leper hospitals were sited at wells thought to have medicinal properties, perhaps in reference to the case of Naaman the Syrian, the leper who was cured by God after bathing in the River Jordan. It seems that water was considered to have healing qualities, with treatment through immersion perhaps linked with the rite of baptism. Its connotations of rebirth and cleansing of the soul would have been appropriate to the perceived connection between physical and spiritual afflictions.

Arrangement of the individual cells at charterhouses necessitated an elaborate system of water supply and redistribution. In marked contrast to hospitals and charterhouses, nunneries seldom directed their resources towards the provision of sanitation. Fresh drinking water was supplied by a well or piped source, but few nunneries had latrines flushed by flowing water. Excavations at Polsloe (Devon) and Elstow (Bedfords) suggested that domestic refuse, such as animal bones, was allowed to accumulate in the cloisters. Some anchorites were provided with wells, but most relied on their servants to bring fresh water for drinking and occasional cleansing, and must have passed refuse and human waste to the servant by the external window of their cell. As part of their penitential observances, some hermits and religious women may have deliberately rejected the usually meticulous standards of monastic cleanliness.

Excavations at charterhouses have produced evidence for high standards of living, including diverse assemblages of imported medieval pottery. The daily lives of the Carthusians were much concerned with literacy, reflected by archaeological evidence from Mount Grace (N Yorks) for book ownership and book production. More secular pastimes may have been typical of the Military Orders. At South Witham, hunting and gaming were indicated by the assemblage of horse furniture, arrowheads and blades, and bone gaming pieces excavated from the great hall.

Tales from the edge

Material culture helped to create meaning for each of the different monastic vocations. Identities were maintained through distinctions in the siting of monasteries, the artefacts and food remains associated with particular lifestyles and the forms chosen for their buildings. For instance, a military iconography can be glimpsed at some preceptories, including symbols on artefacts, graffiti and architecture reminiscent of the Holy Land. This is demonstrated most graphically in the round-nave churches of the 12th century, built in reference to the Holy Sepulchre in Jerusalem. This iconography, together with elements of planning borrowed from castles, and the pre-dominance of secular pastimes such as hunting and gaming, would have strengthened the highly masculine identity of the Military Orders.

In contrast, nunneries often exhibited female images and iconographic architecture relevant specifically to women, such as the two-storey refectory suggestive of the *coenaculum*, or 'upper room', where the Holy Women and the Apostles met after Christ's death. Hermits frequently signalled their withdrawal to the wilderness by incorporating living rock into their dwellings: its ruggedness a reminder of nature. The symbolism of the hermit's cave seems to have been invoked in the planning of Grandmontine churches. The occasional incorporation of flowing water into hospital buildings, most markedly at St John the Baptist, Oxford, may have resulted as much from the penitential identity of inmates as a deliberate concern with hygiene.

The Christian symbolism of rebirth through baptism and repentance was reflected by the dedications of hospitals, predominantly to Mary Magdalene and John the Baptist. In contrast, the intercessory role of nuns, Grand-montines and Carthusians was indicated by the dominance of the Virgin Mary in the dedications of their churches. Both the Carthusians and the Military Orders showed a strong interest in the lives of female saints, such as Mary of Egypt. This preference may be seen as another aspect of liminality, in which male monastics used feminine images in order to express denial and the inversion of reality (Bynum 1984: 110). Religious women drew from biblical models for their images: women serving in hospitals had chosen the active life of Martha, those in nunneries and anchorholds had followed the contemplative calling of Mary.

Patterns in the relative popularity of these vocations reflect wider changes in religious mentalities. While the impetus behind the crusading movement had disappeared by the end of the 13th century, lay-people never lost their belief in the efficacy of charity or intercessory prayers. Bequests left in wills continued to demonstrate lay support for religious in hospitals, nunneries, charterhouses and anchorholds, together with the friaries, right up to the Dissolution. The liminality of these groups was perceived to be effective in following lives of prayer for the salvation of others' souls.

In the later 14th and 15th centuries the strength of lay sympathy for these vocations was shown through new foundations of charterhouses, hospitals, informal communities for religious women and the sponsorship of increasing numbers of anchorites. In contrast, foundations of Benedictine, Cistercian and Augustinian monasteries had ceased entirely by the late 13th century, and friaries largely by the late 14th century. More than other monastic groups, religious in hospitals, hermitages and institutions for religious women con-tinued to interact with changing popular belief. A greater fluidity can be perceived for these categories than in more conventional monastic structures, for example in the developing range of formal and informal vocations for religious women. Hermitages and hospices continued to be linked with pilgrimage and popular religious devotions focusing on shrines, wells and bridges. Certain changes in the meaning of the monastic life were stimulated by the experience and expectations of lay society, especially in the wake of the high mortality caused by the plagues of the mid-14th to 16th centuries: after the Black Death of 1348–49 there were 12 more outbreaks of plague before the Dissolution, in addition to regional plagues and diptheria. The penitential aspects of certain lifestyles in the 12th and 13th centuries, such as nuns, anchorites, lepers and the sick poor, were replaced by a more mystical way of life by the 15th century. The Carthusians and anchoresses, in particular, elevated quiet seclusion and prayer over extreme ascetic practices. Interest in mysticism, together with the increased importance of chantries and intercessory prayer, brought about renewed interest in the contemplative life. Such mentalities fostered lifestyles outside more mainstream monasticism and encouraged an engagement with the material world which brought meaning to 'the other monasticism'.

The religious men and women of 'the other monasticism' were vital to medieval people and embedded in the daily life of town and countryside. They were an alternative to the more self-absorbed houses of Benedictine and Cistercian monks, which have formed the subject of the vast majority of historical and archaeological scholarship on monasticism. It is clear that the current models which dominate monastic archaeology fall short of grasping the complexity and variety of the medieval religious scene. Monasteries were far more than economic units, and must be placed within the context of medieval belief and society. The material culture of monasticism was concerned as much with ideologies as with economic production.

Gazetteer

Many of the sites described in the text are in private ownership and cannot be visited. The gazetteer contains a selection open to the public, or which can be visited by prior arrangement (denoted *).

Amesbury Abbey, Wilts
The parish church belonged to the Fontevraultine nunnery founded in 1177 by King Henry II. A cruciform church survives with evidence of a former pentice on its north side. The church is considered to be that of the parish and the brothers of the community.

Barking Abbey, Essex (London Borough of Barking)
Site of a nunnery founded first in 666, refounded in the 10th century and rebuilt in the 12th century. Remains include the two-storey gatehouse on the eastern side of the precinct and parts of the excavated remains of the cruciform church and cloister to the north (figure 73).

Brewood White Ladies, Shrops (English Heritage)
Ruins of the 12th-century church of the Augustinian (or Cistercian) priory of nuns founded c1199 at Brewood, located 1.5 km south-west of Boscobel House. A number of grave-slabs survive, together with the walls of the cruciform, aisleless church built in red sandstone.

Bungay Priory, Suffolk
Site of a Benedictine nunnery founded by Gundreda and Roger Glanville in 1160. Fragments of the flint-built nuns' church and cloister survive to the east of the principal parish church of Bungay (figure 82).

Cambridge, St Radegund's Priory (Jesus College)
Jesus College incorporates buildings of the Benedictine nunnery founded in 1138 and suppressed in 1496. Extensive medieval remains are open to the public, including the attractive nuns' church and cloister to the north, predominantly of the 13th century. Private areas of the college include the rooms of the east, west and and north ranges, and the western part of the nave, now part of the master's residence.

Canterbury, Hospital of St John
Founded c1084 by Archbishop Lanfranc for 60 poor and infirm men and women, the hospital remains an almshouse today. Surviving fragments include those of the T-shaped medieval chapel and infirmary hall, the refectory and latrines (figures 5 and 6)

Carrow Priory, Norwich (Colman's of Norwich*)
Site of the Benedictine nunnery founded by King Stephen c1146, now

within Colman's works. Extensive remains include part of an aisled, cruciform Norman church, which survives east from the crossing, the south transept, and east and west ranges (figure 67).

Chichester, St Mary's Hospital
Still in use as a hospital, the late-13th-century infirmary consists of a four-bayed infirmary hall and chapel. The hall is divided into three aisles, and is separated from the chapel by an ornately carved screen (figure 3).

Clonmacnoise, Offaly, Eire
The nuns' church is located approximately 0.5km from the main monastic complex, approached by a causeway through the marsh. It was converted for the nuns in the 12th century, and retains a richly ornamented chancel arch (figure 66).

Coningsby Hospital, Hereford
Parts of the 17th-century hospital in Widemarsh Street date from the original 13th-century hospital of St John, which was held by the Hospitallers from the 14th century. Incorporated into later fabric of the north wing are parts of the 13th-century chapel and hall.

Coventry, Ford's Hospital
An almshouse founded by William Ford in 1529. Two jettied timber-framed ranges on either side of a court survive in Grey Friars Street, restored after bomb damage in the Second World War. The west range contained living accommodation on the ground floor and a chapel above (figure 30).

Craswell Priory, Herefords
Extensive remains of the Grandmontine priory founded *c*1225, one of only three established in Britain in the first half of the 13th century. The ruins consist of a church with chapels to the north and south of the choir, a *porticus* to the north of the aisleless nave, and claustral buildings to the south, including a vaulted chapter-house (figure 114).

Denny (or Denney) Abbey, Cambs (English Heritage)
Remains of the abbey church which began as a Benedictine monastery, was then transferred to the Templars, and was finally purchased in 1336 by Mary de St Pol, Countess of Pembroke, for her Franciscan nunnery (moved from Waterbeach, Cambs). The nuns' refectory survives as a barn, with indications of a former pentice on its south side. A complex and fascinating piece of buildings archaeology. The earthworks of the precinct survive and the site of the nunnery can be recognised as a slightly raised island in the fens (figures 38, 75 and 84).

Dinmore Preceptory, Herefords (privately owned and open to the public)
Site of the Hospitaller preceptory founded before 1189. The chapel survives in the grounds of a later house, itself an Arts and Crafts curiosity, including a grotto.

Dunwich Leper Hospital, Suffolk

Ruins of the 12th-century apsidal chapel of the *leprosarium* of St James survive in the churchyard of the rebuilt parish church of St James (figure 21).

Ellerton Priory, Swaledale, N Yorks (North Yorkshire Dales National Park)

Site of the Cistercian nunnery founded in the time of Henry II. Remains of the ruined church include a narrow, aisleless nave with a 15th-century west tower. Earthworks to the south of the church may represent the stone foundations of the monastic ranges.

Elstow Abbey, Bedfords

Site of the Benedictine nunnery founded *c*1075 and refounded by Judith, Countess of Huntingdon, *c*1178. Remains include the aisled nave of the parish church, a detached tower to the north and ruins of the claustral buildings to the south.

Ewelme, Oxfords

Almshouse for poor men founded by William de la Pole and his wife Alice, *c*1430. The almshouses are attached to the west end of the parish church, and a south aisle was added to the chancel for the use of the bedesmen. Remains consist of dwellings grouped around a brick-built court, each with a living room on the ground floor and dormitory above. Still in use as an almshouse.

Garway Preceptory, Herefords

The parish church was once the conventual church of a Templar preceptory founded *c*1185–8 on land given by Henry II. It contains an unusual 12th-century chancel arch. The church has a detached tower to the west, and an earlier round nave has been excavated on the site of the surviving 13th-century nave. The preceptory's dovecote, with its rare dated inscription, survives on the farm adjacent to the church (figures 40, 41, 57 and 60).

Glastonbury, Hospital of Mary Magdalene

To the west of the parish church are the remains of a 13th-century communal infirmary hall, partitioned into two-room houses in the 15th or 16th century (figure 20).

Godstow Abbey, Oxfords

Site of a Benedictine nunnery founded *c*1133 by Ediva, widow of Sir William Launcelene. The remains of this unorthodox layout consist of a rectangular enclosure with a chapel in its south-east corner. A conduit can be traced which ran across the site from east to west. Two halls or ranges flanked the conduit and a third abutted the outer court to the north, where a single buttress survives.

Killone Priory, Clare, Eire

Site of an Augustinian nunnery founded *c*1189 by Donal Mor O'Brian, King of Munster. Set in the side of a gently sloping valley, the extensive remains include a church raised over an eastern vault and including an eastern passage, and a trapezoidal cloister with ruined east and south ranges (figures 65, 70 and 85).

Knaresborough, St Robert's Cave Hermitage and Chapel (Harrogate Museums Service)

The late-12th- to early-13th-century cave hermitage is cut into the face of a cliff, located on Abbey Road in Knaresborough. Outside the cave is a domestic area with a grave and an altar platform. Foundations of the medieval chapel are still visible (figures 94 and 95).

Lacock Abbey, Wilts (National Trust)

A monastery of Augustinian nuns founded in 1232 by Ela, Countess of Salisbury. Following the Dissolution, the church was demolished and the cloister converted to a house by Sir William Sharington. The cloister and three ranges of monastic buildings survive in an excellent state of preservation, including the chapter-house, parlour and warming-room and *lavatorium* (figure 74).

Little Maplestead Preceptory, Essex

A Hospitaller preceptory was established on the site in 1225. An existing parish church was replaced by the present structure by 1245, which retains the round nave of the church of the Hospitaller Preceptory, built on the model of the Holy Sepulchre, Jerusalem (figure 56).

London Hospitallers, St John's Gate, Clerkenwell (The Order of St John of Jerusalem)

The priory gatehouse and parts of the 12th-century church survive at the headquarters of the order of St John of Jerusalem (Hospitallers). A museum of the Order contains artefacts and worked stone excavated from within the precinct, as well as material on their present-day activities as the St John Ambulance (figure 37).

London Temple

The church was consecrated in 1185, and today its round nave survives, containing effigies of Knights of the Temple. The church was heavily restored following bomb damage in the Second World War (figures 35 and 36).

Mount Grace Priory (Charterhouse), N Yorks (National Trust/English Heritage)

The best preserved of the Carthusian monasteries of Britain, with standing remains of cells, church, chapter-house, conduit houses and out-buildings. The layout of the great and little cloisters and courts is easily discerned and an excellent display and interpretation is provided in the former guest-house of the priory. One of the monks' cells has been reconstructed and furnished (figures 115 and 116).

Minster-in-Sheppey Abbey, Kent

Site of a Benedictine nunnery founded in the 12th century on the site of a Saxon female house founded by Sexburga *c*670. Remains include the parallel aisle church and the gatehouse to the west. The nuns' church was contained in the north aisle, where an eastern gallery is suggested by seven square recesses in the upper part of the east wall of the choir (figure 78).

Norwich, St Giles Hospital (The Great Hospital*)

A hospital remains on the site of Bishop Walter Suffield's foundation of *c*1249 for 30 infirm, seven poor scholars and 13 poor men who were to be fed at the gate. Impressive remains consist of a 15th-century cloister to the north of the largely 13th- and 14th-century parish church of St Helen. Attached to the west of the nave is the 15th-century infirmary hall. Ranges of the cloister accommodated the refectory to the west, staff lodgings to the north and the chapter-house to the east (figure 10).

Norwich, The Lazar House (Norfolk County Council)

Remains of a lepers' chapel outside Magdalen Gate consist of a two-storey building 30m in length, which retains 12th-century doorways and windows (figure 22).

Nun Monkton Priory, N Yorks

The parish church was part of the Benedictine nunnery founded by William and Juetta de Arches between 1147 to 1153. The church is an aisleless parallelogram with a fine west front, predominantly Early English in date. The village is a classic example of the medieval planned form, with the apex of the green at the gate of the nunnery precinct.

Polesworth Abbey, Warwicks

The parish church was part of the nunnery founded *c*1130 on the site of a 10th-century female house. The church contains the flat effigy of an abbess *c*1200. Fragments of the cloister survive near the south transept, and the two-storey gatehouse is to the north of the church.

Romsey Abbey, Hants

The abbey church of a nunnery founded *c*907 and reconstituted in 967 for Benedictine nuns. This important 12th-century church retains a square-ended choir with ambulatory carried round it, with chapels projecting east of the ambulatory. A painted reredos depicts the Benedictine nuns and the grave-slab of an abbess survives, depicting a crozier, her staff of office.

Shaftesbury Abbey, Dorset

A Benedictine nunnery founded *c*875 by King Alfred. Remains are principally that of the church of *c*1000, which originally terminated in five apses. Worked stone and ceramic tiles from the nunnery are exhibited in a museum on the site.

Stamford, Lincs, Browne's Hospital

Almshouse founded by William Browne for 12 poor people and two priests, completed *c*1490. Remains consist of a chapel and two-storey hospital.

Temple Balsall, Warwicks

The site of a Templar preceptory given by Roger de Mowbray c1146. The Templar church of the late 13th century survives, with unusual Geometric tracery, and a nearby hall dates from the 13th century (figures 42 and 43). A later addition to the site is the extant 18th-century almshouse for women.

Temple Bruer, Lincs (North Kesteven District Council)

The tower of c1200 survives at the site of a former round-nave Templar church.

Temple Cressing, Essex (Essex County Council)

The site of the Templar (and later Hospitaller) preceptory founded in 1136. Two 13th-century barns are extant. The Wheat Barn and Barley Barn are impressive for their size and the complexity of their timber-framing, and reflect the importance of agricultural storage facilities to a medieval preceptory (figure 62).

Temple Manor, Strood, Kent (English Heritage; local key holder)

Remains of a Templar preceptory founded on land given to the order by Henry II. The remains consist of a two-storey 13th-century structure of stone with 17th-century brick extensions, set incongruously in a themed industrial estate, 'The Knights' Park'. The extant Templar building consists of two chambers set over an undercroft. Excavations on the site revealed that a ground-floor hall was previously attached to the building (figures 50, 51 and 52).

Thetford Priory, Norfolk (British Trust for Ornithology*)

Site of a Benedictine nunnery founded c1160 by Abbot Hugh of Bury St Edmunds. Extensive remains include an aiseless church with south transept, portions of the chapter-house and a two-storey hall to the south of the cloister, possibly an infirmary hall and chapel.

Torphichen Preceptory, West Lothian

Chapel of the Hospitaller preceptory survives as a parish church, with fortified tower and fragments of buildings to the north.

Warkworth Hermitage, Warkworth Castle, Northumb (English Heritage)

Located in the park of Warkworth Castle is the Hermitage and Chapel of the Holy Trinity. Warkworth is the most elaborate of the surviving cave hermitages in Britain. The 14th-century hermitage consisted of three chambers hewn out of the cliff. In the later 15th or 16th century a substantial hall and kitchen were added to the site. The Hermitage is located on the River Coquet; access is by ferry across the river and by footpath up to the cliffs (figure 98).

Winchester, St Cross Hospital

The extensive remains include the original 12th- to 13th-century church of the hospital founded 1136 by Bishop Henry of Blois, intended for 13 poor men and daily alms for 100 men of good conduct, and later dwellings belonging to the almshouse of 1446, established by Cardinal Beaufort for 35 brethren and two priests. The hospital is entered through a three-storey gatehouse. The buildings are arranged around a quadrangle, with 13 dwellings on the west side, a refectory and master's house on the north side and a pentice on the east. The south side of the court was demolished in 1789 (figures 31, 32 and 33).

Witham Friary, Somerset

The village began as the community of lay-brothers (*correrie*) attached to the charterhouse at Witham, founded 1178–9. The 12th-century parish church was originally that of the lay-brothers.

Glossary

abbess: the spiritual and administrative head of an abbey of nuns, elected by the community or nominated by the founding family of the house.

alien priory: monastic cells owned by mother houses in France. In 1414 they were confiscated by the Crown, as enemy assets, pending a cessation of hostilities between England and France. After 1414 most were farmed out to individuals or to other monastic houses.

almshouse: hospitals of the 12th to 14th centuries founded in order to shelter the aged or infirm, or hospitals of the 15th to 16th centuries which acted as residential homes for the poor.

anchoress: the term commonly used to denote a female recluse who took vows of permanent enclosure and was walled up in a cell attached to a parish or monastic church.

anchorite: the term commonly used to denote a male recluse who took vows of permanent enclosure and was walled up in a cell attached to a parish or monastic church.

apse: the semicircular termination of the chancel, aisle or transept.

arcade: a series of arches supported on piers.

ascetic: the practice of self-denial as a way of religious life; from the Greek *asketikos*, meaning laborious.

assart: to form private farmland out of common land.

aumbries: recesses or cupboards used to hold sacred vessels.

bailiwick: the administrative unit of the English Province of the Templars, comprising a region, shire or group of villages.

bay: a unit of a building marked by vaulting or roof compartments.

bedesman/bedeswoman: the resident poor of almshouses.

beguinage: unenclosed communities of religious women common in the Low Countries from the 13th century. Originally, they supported themselves and their charitable activities by working or begging for alms.

camera: a term meaning either a subordinate chamber or suite within a medieval building, or, as it was used by the Military Orders, to refer to specialised farms or holdings without a resident preceptor.

canons regular: ordained canons living in community under a Rule, such as the Augustinian, Gilbertine or Premonstratensian.

cartulary: the collection of charters in which a monastic house recorded its properties and privileges.

cellarage: the ground-floor space of a two-storey structure, generally vaulted.

cenobitic: a monastic vocation in which religious lived as part of an organised community; from the Greek *koinobion*, meaning community.

chantry: a mass for the dead, believed to hasten the passage of the soul through Purgatory.

chemin de ronde: a corbelled-out and crenellated passage below the top of a round tower.

clerestory: the upper storey of the nave above the aisle roof, pierced with windows to light the central body of the church.

close: an open space enclosed on two or more sides by buildings and serving as a central area.

cob: clay mixed with sand, straw or gravel.

college: a community of secular clergy.

commandery: a monastery of the Military Orders; used particularly to refer to establishments of the Hospitallers.

convent: a monastic community of men or women.

corrodian: lay people who paid, or were sponsored, to lodge in private accommodation within a monastic precinct. Often this arrangement was permanent and served as a form of pension.

curtilage: a piece of ground within the limits or boundary of a property.

demesne: in the case of a monastic estate, land owned and administered directly by a monastery; in the case of a secular estate, the portion of land reserved for the lord's own use.

desert fathers: hermits of the 3rd and 4th century who withdrew to the deserts of Egypt, Palestine and Syria.

double house: a monastery which consisted of separate communities of religious men and women, generally presided over by the abbess.

eremitic: a monastic vocation in which individuals withdrew from the world to live as solitary religious; from the Greek *eremos*, meaning desert.

filiation: the act of belonging to a particular monastic order, such as the Cistercian.

Geometric tracery: dating to the second half of the 13th century, and consisting of simple symmetrical shapes such as circles and trefoils.

grange: farms or subsidiary residences of a monastery.

hermit: individuals following a religious vocation which involved isolation and the practice of asceticism.

hospice: a hospital established primarily in order to provide hospitality for travellers and pilgrims.

intercessory: prayers made on behalf of the soul of another.

keel moulding: a carved moulding with a sharp edge, resembling the keel of a ship.

king-post: the vertical member of an internal roof structure placed on the centre of a tie-beam to carry the ridge.

lavatorium, or laver: a washing place or basin in the cloister or infirmary supplied with piped water and distinguished architecturally due to its ritual significance.

manor: a unit of lordship in which land is divided between that of the lord (demesne) and that held by tenants, for which cash rents and labour services were owed to the lord.

misericorde: from the Latin *misericordia*, meaning pity or mercy. The term is used to refer either to the meat-kitchen of the monastic infirmary, where a special diet was prepared for the infirm, or for the hinged seats in the stalls of the monastic choir, which were provided in order to support the nuns or monks in their long religious offices.

monastery: a community or house of a religious order or congregation.

obedientaries: the officers of a monastic house who held special responsibility for a particular area or function, such as the cellarer, sacristan, infirmarer and hosteller.

obits: religious services conducted on the anniversary of a death.

patristic: a term referring to the church fathers or their writings.

penitential: the religious expression of poverty and self-denial as repentance for sin.

pentice: a passage way along the side of a building formed by a single-pitch roof supported on corbels.

phlebotomy: the letting or taking of blood, carried out in the belief that regular blood-letting was necessary to maintain good health.

piscina: a ritual basin set generally in the south wall of a church or chapel adjacent to an altar, in which communion vessels were washed and holy water was disposed.

pittance: a small amount of food or money given as a form of charity, or an extra to the main portions of food provided in the monastic refectory.

preceptor: the resident knight or sergeant in charge of a preceptory of the Military Orders.

preceptory: a monastery of the Military Orders; used particularly to refer to establishments of the Templars.

prioress: the spiritual and administrative head of a priory of nuns, elected by the community or nominated by the founding family of the monastery.

pulpitum: the stone or wooden screen that divided the west end of the monastic choir from the ritual nave.

reredorter: a name sometimes given to the latrines attached to monastic houses.

sacristy: a room attached to the church in which communion vessels, vestments, altar furnishings and other valuables were stored.

sedilia (sing. *sedile*): a series of seats for the clergy placed on the south side of the chancel.

titulus (tituli): the administrative unit of the English Province of the Hospitallers, based on a region with a preceptory at its centre.

toft: the site of a house and its outbuildings; from the Latin *tofta*.

triforium: a band of arcading sometimes incorporating a wall passage, above the main arcade and below the clerestory of a church.

vowess: a widow who took vows to live an unenclosed, celibate religious life.

Bibliography

Anderson, S. (1990, unpub.), 'The human skeletal remains from St Saviour's, Bury St Edmunds, Suffolk', Suffolk Archaeology Archive Report.

André, J.L. (1895), 'Compton Church', *Surrey Archaeological Collections*, 12: 1–19.

Andrews, D., Cook, A., Quant, V. and Veasey, E.A. (1981), 'The archaeology and topography of Nuneaton Priory', *Transactions of the Birmingham and Warwickshire Archaeological Society*, 91: 55–81.

Alcock, N.W. (1982), 'The hall of the Knights Templar at Temple Balsall, West Midlands', *Medieval Archaeology*, 26: 155–8.

Allen, H.E. (1931), *English Writings of Richard Rolle*, Oxford, Clarendon.

Armytage, G. (1908), 'Kirklees Priory', *Yorkshire Archaeological Journal*, 20: 24–32.

Aston, M. (1993), *Monasteries*, London, Batsford.

Aston, M. (1993b), 'The development of the Carthusian order in Europe and Britain: a preliminary survey', in M. Carver (ed.), *In Search of Cult. Archaeological Investigations in Honour of Philip Rahtz*, Woodbridge, Boydell: 139–51.

Aston, M. and Bettey, J. (1990), 'Hinton Charterhouse', *Avon Past*, 15, Autumn: 8–20.

Atkinson, M. and Malcolm, G. (1990), 'Recent excavations at St John's Priory in Cowcross Street EC1', *London Archaeologist*, 6: 171–8.

Baker, D. (1971), 'Excavations at Elstow Abbey, Bedfords, 1968–70', *Bedfordshire Archaeological Journal*, 6: 55–64.

Baker, D. and Baker, E. (1989), 'Research designs: timber phases and outbuildings with special reference to Elstow Abbey and Grove Priory', in R. Gilchrist and H. Mytum (eds), *The Archaeology of Rural Monasteries*, British Archaeological Report, 203, Oxford: 261–75.

Barley, M. (1964), 'The medieval borough of Torksey: excavations 1960–2', *Antiquaries Journal*, 44: 164–87.

Barley, M. (1986), *Houses and History*, London, Faber.

Barratt, M. and Thomas, C. (1991), 'The London Charterhouse', *London Archaeologist*, 6: 283–91.

Barrière, B, (1992), 'The Cistercian convent of Coyroux in the twelfth and thirteenth centuries', *Gesta*, 31.2: 76–82.

Bateson, M. (ed.) (1892), 'The register of Crabhouse Nunnery', *Norfolk Archaeology*, 11: 1–71.

Bishop, M.W. (1983), 'Burials from the cemetery of the Hospital of St Leonard, Newark, Nottinghamshire', *Transactions of the Thoroton Society of Nottinghamshire*, 87: 23–35.

Bitel, L.M. (1990), *Isle of the Saints, Monastic Settlements and Christian Community in Early Ireland*, London, Cornell University Press.

Blair, J. (1985), 'Saint Leonard's Chapel, Clanfield', *Oxoniensia*, 50: 209–14.

Blair, J. (1993), 'Hall and chamber: English domestic planning 1000–1250', in G. Meirion-Jones and M. Jones (eds), *Manorial Domestic Buildings in England and Northern France*, London, Society of Antiquaries: 1–21.

Blair, J. and Steane, J.M. (1982), 'Investigations at Cogges, Oxfords, 1978–81: the priory and parish church', *Oxoniensia*, 47: 37–125.

Bond, C.J. (1989), 'Water management in the rural monastery', in R. Gilchrist and H. Mytum (eds), *The Archaeology of Rural Monasteries*, British Archaeological Report, 203, Oxford: 83–112.

Bond, C.J. (1993), 'Water management in the urban monastery', in R. Gilchrist and H. Mytum (eds), *Advances in Monastic Archaeology*, British Archaeological Report, **227**, Oxford: 43–78.

Bond, J. and Aston, J. (1969), 'Earthworks at Washford Mill, Studley, Warwicks', *The Archaeology of Redditch New Town Progress Report*, **1**: 20.

Bottomley, F. (1993), *St Robert of Knaresborough*, Ruddington, Adlard Print.

Bourdillon, A.F.C. (1926; 1965), *The Order of Minoresses in England*, Manchester, Manchester University Press.

Brakspear, H. (1900), 'Lacock Abbey, Wilts', *Archaeologia*, **57**: 125–58.

Brakspear, H. (1903), 'Burnham Abbey', *Records of Buckinghamshire*, **8**: 517–40.

Brakspear, H. (1922–3), 'Excavations at some Wiltshire monasteries', *Archaeologia*, **73**: 225–52.

Brooke, C.N.L. (1974), *The Monastic World 1000–1300*, London, Elek.

Brown, P. (1982), 'The rise and function of the Holy Man in Late Antiquity', in P. Brown, *Society and the Holy in Late Antiquity*, London, Faber: 103–42; (1971), *Journal of Roman Studies*, **61**: 103–52.

Brown, W. (1886), 'Descriptions of the buildings of twelve small Yorkshire priories at the Reformation', *Yorkshire Archaeological Journal*, **9**: 197–215.

Burdon, E.R. (1925), 'St Saviour's Hospital, Bury St Edmunds', *Proceedings Suffolk Institute of Archaeology*, **19**: 255–85.

Burman, E. (1986), *The Templars. Knights of God*, London, Crucible.

Burrow, I. and Burrow, C. (1990), 'Witham Priory: the first English Carthusian Monastery', *Somerset Archaeology and Natural History*, **134**: 141–82.

Burton, J. (1991), 'The Knights Templar in Yorkshire in the twelfth century: a reassessment', *Northern History*, **27**: 26–40.

Butler, L.A.S. (1989), 'The archaeology of rural monasteries in England and Wales', in R. Gilchrist and H. Mytum (eds), *The Archaeology of Rural Monasteries*, British Archaeological Report, **203**, Oxford: 1–27.

Bynum, C.W. (1984), 'Women's stories, women's symbols: a critique of Victor Turner's theory of liminality', in R.L. Moore and F.E. Reynolds (eds), *Anthropology and the Study of Religion*, Chicago, Center for the Scientific Study of Religion: 105–25.

Cardwell, P. (1990), *Excavations at St Giles Hospital, Brough, North Yorkshire. Interim Report*, North Yorkshire Archaeology.

Carlin, M. (1989), 'Medieval English Hospitals', in L. Granshaw and R. Porter (eds), *The Hospital in History*, London, Routledge: 21–39.

Cattermole, P. (1990), *Norfolk Bells and Bell-ringing*, Woodbridge, Boydell.

Chitty, D.J. (1966), *The Desert a City: an Introduction to Study of the Egyptian and Palestinian Monasticism under the Christian Empire*, London, Mowbrays.

Christiansen, E. (1980), *The Northern Crusades. The Baltic and the Catholic Frontier 1100–1525*, London, Macmillan.

Christie, P.M. and Coad, J.G. (1980), 'Excavations at Denny Abbey', *Archaeological Journal*, **137**: 138–279.

Clapham, A.W. (1911–15), 'St John of Jerusalem, Clerkenwell', *Transactions of the St Paul Ecclesiastical Society*, **7**: 37–49.

Clapham, A.W. (1913), 'The Benedictine Abbey of Barking', *Essex Archaeological Transactions*, **12**: 69–89.

Clapham, A.W. (1926), 'The Priory and Manor House of Dartford', *Archaeological Journal*, **83**: 67–85.

Clarke, A. (1993), 'Royal care for medieval lepers', *British Archaeological News*, **9**: 5.

Clay, R.M. (1909), *The Medieval Hospitals of England*, London, Methuen.

Clay, R.M. (1914), *The Hermits and Anchorites of England*, London, Methuen.

Clay, R.M. (1953), 'Further studies on medieval recluses', *Journal of the British Archaeological Association*, **16**: 74–86.

Clay, R.M. (1955), 'Some northern anchorites, with a note on enclosed Dominicans', *Archaeologia Aeliana*, 33: 202–17.

Cloake, J. (1977), 'The Charterhouse of Sheen', *Surrey Archaeological Collections*, 71: 145–98.

Coldicott, D.K. (1989), *Hampshire Nunneries*, Chichester, Phillimore.

Coles, F.R. (1895–6), 'Notes on Saint Anthony's Chapel', *Proceedings of the Society of Antiquaries of Scotland*, 30: 225–47.

Colegrave, B. (ed. and trans.) (1940), *Two Lives of Cuthbert*, Cambridge, Cambridge University Press.

Colledge, E. and Walsh, J. (eds) (1978), *A Book of Showings to the Anchoress Julian of Norwich*, Toronto, Pontifical Institute of Mediaeval Studies, Studies and Texts, 35.

Colvin, H. (gen. ed.) (1975), *The History of the King's Works 3 (1486–1660). Part 1*, London, HMSO.

Cook, G.H. (1947/1963), *Medieval Chantries and Chantry Chapels*, London, Phoenix.

Cook, G.H. (1959), *English Collegiate Churches*, London, Phoenix.

Cook, G.H. (1961), *English Monasteries in the Middle Ages*, London, Phoenix.

Coppack, G. (1989), 'Thornholme Priory: the development of a monastic outer court landscape', in R. Gilchrist and H. Mytum (eds), *The Archaeology of Rural Monasteries*, British Archaeological Report, 203, Oxford: 185–222.

Coppack, G. (1990), *Abbeys and Priories*, London, Batsford/English Heritage.

Coppack, G. (1991), *Mount Grace Priory*, London, English Heritage.

Cowan, I.B. and Easson, D.E. (1976), *Medieval Religious Houses of Scotland*, London, Longman.

Cra'aster, M.D. (1966), 'Waterbeach Abbey', *Proceedings of the Cambridgeshire Antiquarian Society*, 59: 75–95.

Cramp, R. (1976), 'Monastic sites', in D.M. Wilson (ed.), *The Archaeology of Anglo-Saxon England*, Cambridge, Cambridge University Press: 201–52.

Cruden, S. (1986), *Scottish Medieval Churches*, Edinburgh, John Donald.

Cullum, P. (1993), 'St Leonard's Hospital, York: the spatial and social analysis of an Augustinian hospital', in R. Gilchrist and H. Mytum (eds), *Advances in Monastic Archaeology*, British Archaeological Report, 227, Oxford: 11–18.

Dashwood, G.H. (1859), 'Notes of deeds and survey of Crabhouse Priory, Norfolk', *Norfolk Archaeology*, 5: 257–62.

Dauphin, H. (1965), 'L'érémitisme en Angleterre aux XIe et XIIe siècles' in *L'Eremitismo in Occidente nei secoli XI e XII*, Milan, Miscellanea del Centro di Studi Medioevali, 4: 271–303.

Davis, P.R. and Lloyd-Fern, S. (1990), *Lost Churches of Wales and the Marches*, Stroud, Alan Sutton.

Davis, V. (1985), 'The Rule of Saint Paul, the First Hermit, in late medieval England', in D. Sheils (ed.), *Monks, Hermits and the Ascetic Tradition*, Studies in Church History, 22, London, Blackwell: 203–14.

Deschamps, P. (1973), *La Défense du Comte de Tripoli et de la Principalité d'Antioche*, Paris, Bibliothèque Archéologique et Historique et Institut Français d'Archéologie de Beyrouth.

Deswick, E.S. (1888), 'On the discovery of an ankerhold at the church of St Martin, Chipping Ongar, Essex', *Archaeological Journal*, 45: 284–8.

Dickinson, J.C. (1951), 'English regular canons and the continent in the 12th century', *Transactions of the Royal History Society*, Fifth Series, 1: 71–91.

Douglas, M. (1970), *Purity and Danger. An Analysis of Concepts of Pollution and Taboo*, Harmondsworth, Penguin.

Du Boulay Hill, A. and Gill, H. (1908), 'Beauvale Charterhouse', *Transactions of the Thoroton Society*, 12: 69–93.

Duffy, E. (1992), *The Stripping of the Altars. Traditional Religion in England 1400–1580*, London, Yale University Press.

Dugdale, W. (1655–73; 1846 edn), *Monasticon Anglicanum*, London, Bohn.

Dunning, G.C. (1969), 'The apothecary's mortar from Maison Dieu, Arundel', *Sussex Archaeological Collections*, 107: 77–8.

Dunning, R. (1991), 'The West Country Carthusians', in C. Harper-Bill (ed.), *Religious Beliefs and Ecclesiastical Careers in Late Medieval England*, Woodbridge, Boydell: 33–42.

Durham, B. (1991), 'The infirmary and hall of the medieval hospital of St John the Baptist at Oxford', *Oxoniensia*, 56: 17–75.

Dyer, C. (1989), *Standards of Living in the Later Middle Ages*, Cambridge, Cambridge University Press.

Dygo, M. (1989), 'The political role of the cult of the Virgin Mary in Teutonic Prussia in the 14th and 15th centuries', *Journal of Medieval History*, 15: 63–80.

Elkins, S.K. (1988), *Holy Women of Twelfth-century England*, Chapel Hill, NC, University of North Carolina Press.

Ellis, R.H. (1986), *Catalogue of Seals in the Public Record Office: Monastic Seals*, 1, London, HMSO.

Evans, K.J. (1969), 'The Maison Dieu, Arundel', *Sussex Archaeological Collections*, 107: 65–77.

Everson, P. (1989), 'Rural monasteries within the secular landscape', in R. Gilchrist and H. Mytum (eds), *The Archaeology of Rural Monasteries*, British Archaeological Report, 203, Oxford: 141–6.

Falkiner, C.L. (1907), 'The hospital of St John of Jerusalem in Ireland', *Proceedings of the Royal Irish Academy*, 26.12: 275–317.

Fanning, T. (1981), 'Excavation of an Early Christian cemetery and settlement at Reask, County Kerry, *Proceedings of the Royal Irish Academy*, 81: 67–172.

Farley, M. and Manchester, K. (1989), 'The cemetery of the leper hospital of St Margaret High Wycombe, Bucks', *Medieval Archaeology*, 33: 82–9.

Ferguson, J. (1909–12), 'The Carthusian Order in Scotland', *Transactions of the Scottish Ecclesiological Society*, 3: 179–92.

Finucane, R.C. (1977), *Miracles and Pilgrims. Popular Beliefs in Medieval England*, London, Dent.

Folda, J. (1982), 'Crusader frescoes at Crac des Chevaliers and Marqab Castle', *Dumbarton Oaks Papers*, 36: 177–210.

Forey, A. (1977), 'The military order of St Thomas of Acre', *English Historical Review*, 92: 481–503.

Forey, A. (1992), *The Military Orders from the Twelfth to the early Fourteenth Centuries*, London, Macmillan.

Gardam, C.M.L. (1990), 'Restorations of the Temple Church London', in L. Grant (ed.), *Medieval Art, Architecture and Archaeology in London*, London, British Archaeological Assocation: 101–17.

Gattie, G.B. (1892), 'The Minnis Rock Hermitage at Hastings', *Sussex Archaeological Collections*, 38: 129–36.

Gee, H. (1897), 'The Domus Inferior or Frary of our oldest Charterhouses', *Archaeologia*, 55.2: 525–30.

Gervers, M. (1982), *The Cartulary of the Knights of St John of Jerusalem in England. Secunda Camera. Essex*, British Academy Records of Social and Economic History New Series, 6.

Gibson, J. H. (1950), 'Compton Church: the oratory', *Surrey Archaeological Collections*, 51: 154–5.

Gilchrist, R. (1994), *Gender and Material Culture. The Archaeology of Religious Women*, London, Routledge.

Gilchrist, R. and Oliva, M. (1993), *Religious Women in Medieval East Anglia. History and Archaeology c1100–1540*, Studies in East Anglian History, **1**, Norwich, Centre of East Anglian Studies.

Gill, K. (1992), 'Open monasteries for women in late medieval and early modern Italy: two Roman examples', in C. A. Monson (ed.) *The Crannied Wall. Women, Religion and the Arts in Early Modern Europe*, Ann Arbor, University of Michigan Press: 15–47.

Gilyard-Beer, R., and Coppack, G. (1986), 'Excavations at Fountains Abbey, North Yorkshire, 1979–80: the early development of the monastery', *Archaeologia*, **108**: 147–88.

Godfrey, W.H. (1928), 'Church of St Anne's, Lewes: an anchorite's cell and other discoveries', *Sussex Archaeological Collections*, **69**: 159–69.

Godfrey, W.H. (1955), *The English Almshouse*, London, Faber.

Graham, R. (1927), 'The Order of St Antoine de Viennoise and its English commandery, St Anthony's Threadneedle Street', *Archaeological Journal*, **84**: 341–406.

Graham, R. and Clapham, A.W. (1924–5), 'The Order of Grandmont and its houses in England', *Archaeologia*, **75**: 159–210.

Gray, M. (1969), 'Interim Report, Washford', *The Archaeology of Redditch New Town Progress Report*, **1**: 12.

Gray, M. (1993), *The Trinitarian Order in England. Excavations at Thelsford Priory*, British Archaeological Report, **226**, Oxford.

Greene, J.P. (1992), *Medieval Monasteries*, Leicester, Leicester University Press.

Gwynn, A. and Hadcock, R.N. (1970), *Medieval Religious Houses of Ireland*, London, Longman.

Haigh, D. (1988), *The Religious Houses of Cambridgeshire*, Cambridge, County Council.

Hall, D.W. (undated interim report), 'Excavations at St Nicholas Farm, St Andrews, 1986–7', Scottish Urban Archaeological Trust Ltd.

Hammond, E.A. (1965), 'The Westminster Abbey Infirmarer's rolls as a source of medical history', *Bulletin of the History of Medicine*, **39**: 261–76.

Harris, H.A. (1919), 'The site of St Peter's Hospital Chapel', *Proceedings of the Suffolk Institute of Archaeology*, **17**: 199.

Harrison, A.C. (1980), 'Excavations at the site of St Mary's Hospital, Strood', *Archaeologia Cantiana*, **84**: 139–60.

Harrison, K. (1968), 'Vitruvius and acoustic jars in England during the Middle Ages', *Transactions of the Ancient Monuments Society*, **15**: 49–54.

Hart, J. (1989), 'Leprosy in Cornwall and Devon: problems and perspectives', in M. Bowden, D. Mackay and P. Topping (eds), *From Cornwall to Caithness*, British Archaeological Report, **209**, Oxford: 261–9.

Harvey, B. (1993), *Living and Dying in England 1100–1540. The Monastic Experience*, Oxford, Clarendon.

Haskins, S. (1994), *Mary Magdalen*, London, Harper Collins.

Hayum, A. (1989), *The Isenheim Altarpiece. God's Medicine and the Painter's Vision*, Princeton, Princeton University Press.

Heelis, A.J. (1914), 'The caves known as "Isis Parlis"', *Transactions of the Cumberland and Westmorland Archaeological Society*, **14**: 337–42.

Herbert, J. (1985), 'The transformation of hermitages into Augustinian priories in twelfth-century England', in D. Sheils (ed.), *Monks, Hermits and the Ascetic Tradition*, Studies in Church History, **22**, London, Blackwell: 131–45.

Herity, M. (1990), 'The hermitage on Ardoileán, co. Galway', *Journal of the Royal Society of Antiquaries of Ireland*, **120**: 65–101.

Hewitt, C.A. (1962), 'Structural carpentry in medieval Essex', *Medieval Archaeology*, **6–7**: 240–71.

Hills, P.J. (1961), *The Priory of the Wood*, Gainsborough, Belton Printers.

Hobson, J.M. (1926), *Some Early and Later Houses of Pity*, London, Routledge.

Hodson, M.O. (1940), 'Anker-hold at East Ham church', *Essex Archaeology*, 22: 245–6.

Hogg, J. (1975), 'The Architecture of Hinton Charterhouse', *Analecta Cartusiana*, 25.

Hogg, J. (ed.) (1981), 'An Illustrated Yorkshire Carthusian Religious Miscellany', *Analecta Cartusiana*, 95.

Holdsworth, C. (1990), 'Hermits and the powers of the frontier', *Reading Medieval Studies*, 16: 55–76.

Honeybourne, M.B. (1963), 'The leper hospitals of the London area', *Middlesex Archaeological Society*, 21.1: 3–61.

Honeyman, H.L. and Hunter Blair, H. (1954/1993), *Warkworth Castle and Hermitage*, London, English Heritage.

Hope, J.H. (1987), 'The Knights Templar and excavations at Cressing Temple', *Essex Journal*, 22: 67–71.

Hudson, E.W. (1902), 'The London home of the Knights Hospitaller, now the Order of St John of Jerusalem', *Home Counties Magazine*, 4.

Hughes, J., (1988), *Pastors and Visionaries. Religion and Secular Life in Late Medieval Yorkshire*, Woodbridge, Boydell.

Huish, M. (1941), 'The home of a hermit', *The Field*, February 1941: 141.

Hunt, T. (1990), *Popular Medicine in Thirteenth-Century England*, Woodbridge, Boydell.

Hurst, H. (1974), 'Excavations at Gloucester, 1971–3: second interim report', *Antiquaries Journal*, 54: 41–6.

Hutchings, J.B. (1969), 'Milton Ernest: a field survey', *Bedfordshire Archaeological Journal*, 4: 69–78.

Hutchison, C. (1989), *The Hermit Monks of Grandmont*, Kalamazoo, Cistercian Publications.

Johnson, P.D. (1991), *Equal in Monastic Profession. Religious Women in Medieval France*, Chicago, University of Chicago Press.

Johnston, P.M. (1899), 'The low side windows of Surrey churches', *Surrey Archaeological Collections*, 14: 83–133.

Johnston, P.M. (1908), 'An anchorite's cell at Letherhead Church', *Surrey Archaeological Collections*, 20: 223–8.

Keene, D. (1985), *Survey of Medieval Winchester: i and ii*, Winchester Studies, 2, Oxford, Clarendon.

King, I. (1932), *The Seals of the Order of St John of Jerusalem*, London, Methuen.

Knowles, D. and Grimes, W.F. (1954), *Charterhouse. The Medieval Foundation in Light of Recent Discoveries*, London, Longman.

Knowles, D. and Hadcock, R.N. (1971), *Medieval Religious Houses of England and Wales*, London, Longman.

Kollias, E. (1991), *The Knights of Rhodes*, Athens, Ekdotike Athenon.

Larking, L.B. (1857), *The Knights Hospitallers in England. The Report of Prior Philip de Thame, 1338*, Camden Society, 65.

Lawrence, C.H. (1984), *Medieval Monasticism*, London, Longman.

Lee, F. and Magilton, J. (1989), 'The cemetery of the Hospital of St James and Mary Magdalene, Chichester – a case study', *World Archaeology*, 21.1: 273–82.

Leech, R. and McWhirr, A.D. (1982), 'Excavations at St John's Hospital, Cirencester, 1971 and 1976', *Bristol & Gloucestershire Archaeology Society Transactions*, 100: 191–209.

Lees, B.A. (1935), *Records of the Templars in England in the Twelfth Century. The Inquest of 1185*, British Academy Records of Social and Economic History, 9.

Legg, J.W. (1899), *The Processional of the Nuns of Chester*, London, Henry Bradshaw Society, 18.

Leistikow, D. (1967), *Ten Centuries of European Hospital Architecture*, Ingelheim am Rhein, Boehringer.

Levitan, B. (1987), 'Medieval animal husbandry in south-west England: a selective review and suggested approach', in N.D. Balaam, B. Levitan and V. Straker (eds), *Studies in Palaeoeconomy and Environment*, British Archaeological Report, **181**, Oxford: 51–80.

Leyser, H. (1984), *Hermits and the new Monasticism*, London, Macmillan.

McGarvie, M. (1989), *Witham Friary*, Frome, Frome Society for Local Study, Church Histories, **1**.

McRoberts, D. (1966), 'Hermits in medieval Scotland', *The Innes Review*, **22.1**: 199–216.

Magilton, J.R. (1980), *The Church of St Helen-on-the-Walls, Aldwark*, The Archaeology of York, **10/1**, London, Council for British Archaeology.

Manchester, K. and Marcombe, D. (1990), 'The Melton Mowbray "leper head": an historical and medical investigation', *Medical History*, **34**: 86–91.

Manchester, K. and Roberts, C. (1989), 'The palaeopathology of leprosy in Britain: a review', *World Archaeology*, **21.2**: 265–72.

Manning, C. (1981–2), 'Excavations at Kilteel Church, Co. Kildare', *Journal of the Kildare Archaeological Society*, **16**: 173–229.

Mayes, P. (forthcoming), *The Templar Preceptory at South Witham, Lincolnshire*, English Heritage.

Mayr-Harting, H. (1975), 'Functions of a twelfth-century recluse', *History*, **60**: 337–52.

Micklethwaite, J.T. (1887), 'On the remains of an anker-hold at Bengeo Church, Hertford', *Archaeological Journal*, **44**: 26–9.

Moessner, V.J. (1987), 'The embroideries of convent Wienhausen', in M.P. Lillich (ed.), *Studies in Cistercian Art and Architecture*, **13**, Kalamazoo, Cistercian Publications: 161–77.

Moorhouse, S. (1989), 'Monastic estates: their composition and development', in R. Gilchrist and H. Mytum (eds), *The Archaeology of Rural Monasteries*, British Archaeological Report, **203**: 29–81.

Moorhouse, S. (1993), 'Pottery and glass in the medieval monastery', in R. Gilchrist and H. Mytum (eds), *Advances in Monastic Archaeology*, British Archaeological Report, **227**, Oxford: 127–48.

Morris, R. (1989), *Churches in the Landscape*, London, Dent.

Morris, R. (1991), 'Baptismal Places: 600–800', in I. Wood and N. Lund (eds), *People and Places in Northern Europe 500–1600. Essays in Honour of Peter Sawyer*, Woodbridge, Boydell: 15–24.

New, A. (1985), *A Guide to the Abbeys of England and Wales*, London, Constable.

Nicholson, H. (1993), *Templars, Hospitallers and Teutonic Knights. Images of the Military Orders 1128–1291*, Leicester, Leicester University Press.

O'Neil, H.E. (1964), 'Excavations of a celtic hermitage on St Helens, Isles of Scilly', *Archaeological Journal*, **121**: 40–69.

Orme, N. (1988), 'A medieval almshouse for the clergy: Clyst Gabriel Hospital near Exeter', *Journal of Ecclesiastical History*, **39.1**: 1–15.

Palliser, D. (1993), 'The topography of monastic houses in Yorkshire towns', in R. Gilchrist and H. Mytum (eds), *Advances in Monastic Archaeology*, British Archaeological Report, **227**, Oxford: 3–9.

Pantin, W.A. (1970), 'Minchery Farm, Littlemore', *Oxoniensia*, **35**: 19–26.

Park, K. and Henderson, J. (1991), '"The first hospital among Christians": the Ospedale di Santa Maria Nuova in early sixteenth-century Florence', *Medical History*, **35**: 164–88

Parker, G. (1981–2), 'The medieval hermitage at Grafton Regis', *Northamptonshire Past and Present*, **6.5**: 247–52.

Peers, C.R. (1902), 'The Benedictine nunnery of Little Marlow', *Archaeological Journal*, **59**: 307–25.

Pevsner, N. (1960), *The Buildings of England: Buckinghamshire*, Harmondsworth, Penguin.

Pevsner, N. and Harris, J. (1964), *The Buildings of England: Lincolnshire*, Harmondsworth, Penguin.

Platt, C. (1969), *The Monastic Grange in Medieval England. A Reassessment*, London, Macmillan.

Ponsford, M. and Price, R. (forthcoming), *Excavations at St Bartholomew's Hospital, Bristol 1977–78*, London, Council for British Archaeology.

Poster, J. and Sherlock, D. (1987), 'Denny Abbey: the nuns' refectory', *Proceedings of the Cambridgeshire Antiquarian Society*, **76**: 67–82.

Power, E. (1922), *Medieval English Nunneries*, Cambridge, Cambridge University Press.

Prawer, J. (1985), 'The Jerusalem the Crusaders captured: a contribution to the medieval topography of the City', in P.W. Edbury (ed.), *Crusade and Settlement*, Cardiff, University of Wales Press: 1–16.

Prescott, E. (1992), *The English Medieval Hospital 1050–1640*, London, Seaby.

Price, R. (1979), *Excavations at St Bartholomew's Hospital, Bristol*, Bristol Museums.

Pringle, D. (1986), 'The planning of some pilgrimage churches in Crusader Palestine', *World Archaeology*, **18.3**: 341–62.

Pritchard, J.E. (1911), 'Account of St John's Hermitage, Bristol', *Bristol & Gloucestershire Archaeological Society Transactions*, **34**: 1–2.

Pritchard, V. (1967), *English Medieval Graffiti*, Cambridge, Cambridge University Press.

Pugh, R.B. (1981), 'The Knights Hospitaller of England as Undertakers', *Speculum*, **56**: 566–74.

Qualman, K.G. (1986), 'Winchester Nunnaminster', *Current Archaeology*, **102**: 204–7.

Radford, C.A.R. (1967), 'Ickleton Church', *Archaeological Journal*, **124**: 228–29.

Rawcliffe, C. (1984), 'The hospitals of later medieval London', *Medical History*, **28**: 1–28.

Rawcliffe, C. (1995), *Medicine and Society in the Later Middle Ages*, Stroud, Alan Sutton.

Reddan, M. and Clapham, A.W. (1924), *The Parish of St Helen, Bishopsgate: Part 1*, Survey of London, vol. 9, London, London County Council.

Rees, W. (1947), *A History of the Order of St John of Jerusalem in Wales and the Welsh Border*, Cardiff, University of Wales Press.

Reid, A.G. and Lye, D.M. (1988), *Pitmiddle Village and Elcho Nunnery*, Perthshire Society of Natural History, Dundee, Stevenson.

Richards, J.D., Heighway, C. and Donaghey, S. (1989), *Union Terrace: excavations in the Horsefair*, The Archaeology of York, **11/1**, London, Council for British Archaeology.

Richardson, J.S. (1928), 'A thirteenth-century tile kiln at North Berwick, East Lothian, and Scottish medieval ornamental floor tiles', *Proceedings of the Society of Antiquaries of Scotland*, **63**: 281–310.

Rigold, S. (1964), 'Two Kentish hospitals re-examined: St Mary Ospringe, and SS Stephen and Thomas, New Romney', *Archaeologia Cantiana*, **79**: 31–69.

Rigold, S. (1962/1990), *Temple Manor*, London, English Heritage.

Rigold, S. (1965), 'Two Camerae of the Military Orders. Strood Temple, Kent and Harefield, Middlesex', *Archaeological Journal*, **122**: 86–132.

Rodwell, W.J. and Rodwell, K. (1982), 'St Peter's church, Barton-upon-Humber: excavation and structural study, 1978–81', *Antiquaries Journal*, **62**: 283–315.

Roebuck, J. and Coppack, G. with Hurst, J.G. (1987), 'A closely dated group of late medieval pottery from Mount Grace Priory', *Medieval Ceramics*, **11**: 15–24.

Roper, L. (1989), *The Holy Household: Women and Morals in Reformation Augsburg*, Oxford, Clarendon.

Rosser, G. (1989), *Medieval Westminster 1200–1540*, Oxford, Clarendon.

Rowe, J. (1958), 'The medieval hospitals of Bury St Edmunds', *Medical History*, 2: 253–63.

RCHM (1911), *Royal Commission on Historical Monuments in Wales and Monmouthshire: Montgomery*, London, HMSO.

RCHME (1931–4), *Royal Commission on Historical Monuments in England: Herefordshire*, Three volumes, London, HMSO.

RCHME (1972), *Royal Commission on Historical Monuments in England: Dorset 4*, London, HMSO.

RCHME (1987), *Churches of South-east Wiltshire*, London, HMSO.

Rubin, M. (1987), *Charity and Community in Medieval Cambridge*, Cambridge, Cambridge University Press.

Rubin, M. (1992), *Corpus Christi: the Eucharist in Late Medieval Culture*, Cambridge, Cambridge University Press.

Ryder, P.F. (1991), 'Low Chibburn. Archaeological Record and Structural Interpretation', unpublished report for Northumberland County Council.

Ryder, P.F. (1992), 'The Hermitage and Oratory, Southgate, Pontefract', unpublished report for West Yorkshire Archaeology Service.

St. John Hope, W.H. (1901), 'The ground plan of Watton in the East Riding of Yorkshire', *Yorkshire Archaeological Journal*, 58: 1–34.

St. John Hope, W.H. (1905), 'The architectural history of Mount Grace Charterhouse', *Yorkshire Archaeological Journal*, 18: 270–309.

St. John Hope, W.H. (1908), 'The round tower church of the Knights Templars at Temple Bruer, Lincolnshire', *Archaeologia*, 61: 177–98.

Salu, B. (1955/1990), *The Ancrene Riwle*, Notre Dame, University of Notre Dame Press.

Schulenburg, J.T. (1984), 'Strict active enclosure and its effect on the female monastic experience', in J.A. Nichols and L.T. Shank (eds), *Medieval Religious Women 1: Distant Echoes*, Kalamazoo, Cistercian Publications: 51–86.

SHARP (Soutra Hospital Archaeoethnopharmacological Research Project) (1989), *Sharp Practice 1. The third report on researches into the medieval hospital at Soutra, Lothian*, Edinburgh, privately printed.

Sherlock, D. (1970), 'Excavation at Campsea Ash Priory', *Transactions of the Suffolk Institute of Archaeology*, 32.2: 121–39.

Sherwood, J. and Pevsner, N. (1974), *The Buildings of England: Oxfordshire*, Harmondsworth, Penguin.

Simmons, L.N. (1992), 'The abbey church at Fontevraud in the later twelfth century: anxiety, authority and architecture in the female spiritual life', *Gesta*, 31.2: 99–107.

Sloane, B. (1992 unpub), 'St Mary's Clerkenwell: a Research Design', Museum of London Archaeology Service.

Sloane, B. (in preparation), *Excavations at the Priory of St Mary Clerkenwell*, London, English Heritage.

Sloane, B. and Malcolm, G. (in preparation), *Excavations at the Priory of St John of Jerusalem, Clerkenwell, London*, London, English Heritage.

Smallwood, J. (1978), 'A medieval tile kiln at Abbey Farm, Shouldham', *East Anglian Archaeology*, 8: 45–54.

Smith, G.H. (1980), 'The excavation of the Hospital of St Mary of Ospringe, commonly called Maison Dieu', *Archaeologia Cantiana*, 95: 81–184.

Smith, H. (1878), 'Bridgnorth Hermitage', *Transactions of the Shropshire Archaeology and Natural History Society*, 1: 159–72.

Soden, I. (1992), 'The Carthusians of Coventry: exploding myths', in *Medieval Europe 1992. Preprinted Papers Volume 6: Religion and Belief*, York: 77–82.

Talbot, C.H. (1959) (ed. and trans.), *The Life of Christina of Markyate*, Oxford, Oxford University Press.

Tanner, N.P. (1984), *The Church in Late Medieval Norwich 1370–1532*, Toronto, Pontifical Institute of Medieval Studies, Studies and Texts, 66.

Taylor, C.C. (1992), 'Medieval rural settlement: changing perceptions', *Landscape History*, 14: 5–17.

Tester, P.J. (1967), 'Excavations on the site of Higham Priory', *Archaeologia Cantiana*, 82: 143–61.

Tester, P.J. (1980), 'A plan and architectural description of the medieval remains of Davington Priory', *Archaeologia Cantiana*, 95: 205–12.

Thomas, Charles, (1971), *The Early Christian Archaeology of North Britain*, Oxford, Oxford University Press.

Thomas, C., Phillpotts, C. and Sloane, B. (1989), 'Excavations of the Priory and Hospital of St Mary Spital', *London Archaeologist*, 6.4: 87–93.

Thomas, C., Sloane, B. and Phillpotts, C. (forthcoming), *Excavations at the Priory and Hospital of St Mary Spital, London*, London, English Heritage.

Thompson, A.H. (1937), *The History of the Hospital and New College of the Annunciation of St Mary in the Newarke, Leicester*, Leicester, Leicester Archaeological Society.

Thompson, E.M. (1895), *A History of the Somerset Carthusians*, London, John Hodges.

Thompson, E.M. (1930), *The Carthusian Order in England*, London, Church Historical Society.

Thompson, S. (1984), 'Why English nunneries had no history: a study of English nunneries founded after the Conquest', in J.A. Nichols and L.T. Shank (eds), *Medieval Religious Women 1: Distant Echoes*, Kalamazoo, Cistercian Publications: 131–49.

Thompson, S. (1991), *Women Religious: the Founding of English Nunneries after the Conquest*, Oxford, Clarendon Press.

Tillotson, J.H. (1989), *Marrick Priory: a Nunnery in Late Medieval Yorkshire*, Borthwick Paper, 75, York, University of York.

Trabjerg, L. (1993), *Middelalderens Hospitaler I Danmark*, Arhus, Arhus Universitet.

Trotter, R. (1886), 'Notice of the excavations of St Medan's Cave and Chapel, Kirkmaiden, Wigtownshire' *Proceedings of the Society of Antiquaries of Scotland*, 20: 76–90.

Turner, V. (1969), *The Ritual Process: Structure and Anti-Structure*, Chicago, Center for the Scientific Study of Religion.

Twemlow, J.A. (1933), *Calendar of Papal Letters, Volume 12*, London, HMSO.

Underhill, E. (ed.) (1923), *The Scale of Perfection*, London, Watkins.

Upton-Ward, J. (1992), *The Rule of the Templars*, Woodbridge, Boydell.

VCH (1906), *The Victoria County History of the County of Norfolk*, 2, London, HMSO.

VCH (1907), *The Victoria County History of the County of Derbyshire*, 2, London, HMSO.

VCH (1907), *The Victoria County History of the County of Suffolk*, 2, London, HMSO.

VCH (1948), *The Victoria County History of the County of Cambridge*, 2, London, HMSO.

VCH (1962), *The Victoria County History of the County of Wiltshire*, 6, London, HMSO.

VCH (1969), *The Victoria County History of the County of Warwick*, 8, London, HMSO.

Walcott, M. E. C. (1868), 'Inventory of St Mary's Hospital or Maison Dieu, Dover', *Archaeologia Cantiana*, 7: 272–80.

Walcott, M.E.C. (1868), 'Inventory of Minster-in-Sheppey', *Archaeologia Cantiana*, 7: 287–306.

Walker, J. (1990), 'The motives for patrons of the order of St Lazarus in England in the twelfth and thirteenth centuries', in J. Loades (ed.), *Monastic Studies 1: the Continuity of Tradition*, Bangor: 171–81.

Wall, S.M. (1980), 'The animal bones from the excavations of the Hospital of St Mary of Ospringe', *Archaeologia Cantiana*, 96: 227–66.

Ward, B. (1987), *Harlots of the Desert*, London, Mowbray.

Ward, S.W. (1990), *Excavations at Chester. The Lesser Medieval Religious Houses: Sites Investigated 1964–1983*, Chester, Chester City Council.

Warren, A.K. (1984), 'The nun as anchoress: England 1100–1500', in J.A. Nichols and L.T. Shank (eds), *Medieval Religious Women 1: Distant Echoes*, Kalamazoo, Cistercian Publications: 197–211.

Warren, A.K. (1985), *Medieval English Anchorites and their Patrons*, Berkeley, University of California Press.

Wells, C. (1967), 'A leper cemetery at South Acre, Norfolk', *Medieval Archaeology*, 11: 242–8.

Whittingham, A. (1980), 'Thompson College', *Archaeological Journal*, 87: 80.

Williams, D.H. (1980), 'Usk Nunnery', *The Monmouthshire Antiquary*, 4: 44–45.

Wilson, H.A. (1910), *The Pontifical of Magdalen College*, London, Henry Bradshaw Society, 39.

Winnington, T.E. (1863–4), 'Southstone Rock and Hermitage, Worcestershire', *Associated Architectural Societies Reports*, 7: 133–6.

Wooldridge, K. (1990), '49–52 St John's Square, Clerkenwell, London EC1. Excavation and recording of the standing building', *Transactions of the London and Middlesex Archaeological Society*, 38: 131–50.

Index